SHAPING TERRAIN

City Building in Latin America

EDITED BY RENÉ DAVIDS

University Press of Florida
Gainesville · Tallahassee · Tampa · Boca Raton
Pensacola · Orlando · Miami · Jacksonville · Ft. Myers · Sarasota

Printed in the United States of America on acid-free paper

This book may be available in an electronic edition.

21 20 19 18 17 16 6 5 4 3 2 1

Library of Congress Cataloging-in-Publication Data
Names: Davids, René, 1949– editor.
Title: Shaping terrain : city building in Latin America / edited by René Davids.
Description: Gainesville : University Press of Florida, [2016] | Includes bibliographical references and index.
Identifiers: LCCN 2016015360 | ISBN 9780813062679 (cloth)
Subjects: LCSH: City planning—Latin America. | Cities and towns—Latin America—Growth. | Cities and towns—Latin America—History. | Latin America—Economic conditions. | Latin America—Social conditions.
Classification: LCC HT169.L3 S53 2016 | DDC 307.1/216098—dc23
LC record available at https://lccn.loc.gov/2016015360

The University Press of Florida is the scholarly publishing agency for the State University System of Florida, comprising Florida A&M University, Florida Atlantic University, Florida Gulf Coast University, Florida International University, Florida State University, New College of Florida, University of Central Florida, University of Florida, University of North Florida, University of South Florida, and University of West Florida.

University Press of Florida
15 Northwest 15th Street
Gainesville, FL 32611-2079
http://www.upf.com

Contents

Figures

Preface

Growing up in Chile, one develops an appreciation of many things found nowhere else on earth, including its extraordinary and often violent topography. Isolated by the still-forming Andean cordillera to the east, the transverse and coastal hills bordering the Pacific Ocean to the west, and the Atacama Desert in the north, Chile is an island on the continental landmass of South America, with some of the world's most geologically dynamic landscapes. There are frequent major earthquakes, tsunamis, landslides, debris flows, and volcanic eruptions; many short rivers plummet down the slopes of the Andes to the Pacific in cascades, rapids, and waterfalls, some through deep gorges; glaciers erode mountains and themselves break up as they reach the sea. Moving from my hometown of Santiago, where the massive backdrop of the Andes is visible from most places, for postgraduate studies in London, a featureless sprawl spreading out in all directions with no hills higher than several hundred feet, made clear the extent to which the mountains had been a compass and spiritual anchor.

My interest in the human settlements and built forms of the often dramatic topography, mostly mild climates, and greatly varying ecologies of Latin America has its origins in a continuing fascination with the reciprocity between the raw elemental landscapes of the New World and European culture, beginning with the enormous city-building project imposed by Spanish and Portuguese colonizers on their conquered territories from the sixteenth through the early decades of the nineteenth centuries. Like many European cities, Greater London was assembled organically as small towns grew together over many centuries, a very different process from the mix of classical Roman and Italian Renaissance town planning theories which inspired the template for Santiago and most other cities in Spain's New World empire: a rectilinear grid of straight streets centered on a *plaza mayor* intended for ground presumed to be more or less level but in actuality surrounded terrain that would make their development a challenge. The confrontation between the complex social and topographical realities of Latin America and the Europeans' mistaken preconceptions about what they would find there set the stage for centuries of conflict but also, as these cities adapted to their diverse physical and cultural contexts and began to shape their own destinies after independence, a common urban heritage.

As the editor of this book, I am most grateful to its contributing authors for their essays, some of them originally written in Spanish; for the assistance with translation, graphics, and bibliography provided by architecture students Adriana Valencia, Daniel Backman, Lucy Fang, Mia Ritzenberg, David Gregory, Lan Lee, and Nina Hormazábal, as well as the many other students who joined lively seminar discussions and explorations of urban Mexico and South America; for the Fellowship awarded by the John Simon Guggenheim Memorial Foundation, which initiated the book's formal research phase; for opportunities to participate in the Fulbright Specialist Program; for travel grants received from the Center for Latin American Studies at the University of California, Berkeley; for funds received from the Department of Architecture subsidizing travel with my graduate students in conjunction with a series of design studios focused on water in Latin American cities; for the support and encouragement from University Press of Florida director Meredith Morris-Babb, acquisitions editor Erika Stevens, and acquisitions assistant Stephanye Hunter; for the patient copyediting of Joyce Elaine Otto; for advice generously given over the years from colleagues at the College of Environmental Design, Marc Treib in particular, and for the dedicated staff at the CED Library including Elizabeth Byrne, Jason Miller, and David Eifler, whose passion for their work has made it an indispensable resource; for my many friends and colleagues in Chile and elsewhere; and for the support and encouragement of my wife, Christine Killory: she is my best critic, and I dedicate this book to her and to the memory of my parents.

Introduction

RENÉ DAVIDS

Shaping Terrain: City Building in Latin America supports the proposition that cities and their surroundings—suburbs, exurbs, rural or agricultural lands, and wilderness—are best understood as interdependent areas of a continuously transforming spatial continuum whose every modification has an impact on the totality of the constructed environment. Transcending preoccupations with nature intended to define national or regional identity, the essays contained in this book provide lenses focused on the diversity of approaches to the Latin American landscapes and ecosystems which have informed a centuries-long history of settlement.[1]

Humanized Landscape

Among Latin America's indigenous cultures, decisions about the location of settlements were informed by a combination of ecological, agricultural, and religious imperatives, and permanent communities were established around the continental perimeter, where conditions were most favorable for human habitation: the highlands and valleys irrigated by streams carrying runoff from the Andes, the arid lowlands of northern Chile and the southern Peru deserts, as well as the extensive Brazilian highlands were all preferred to the hot, humid continental interior (figures I.1 and I.2).[2]

Although Latin America is mostly located in South America, there is also a significant presence in the Northern Hemisphere, including Mexico, Central America, Venezuela, and parts of Colombia, Ecuador, and Brazil, and the region's most extensive areas occupy a wide strip around the equator. Located on the continent of North America, Mexico is a plateau laced by mountain ranges and rimmed by narrow coastal shelves with the Valley of Mexico midway between them, while Central America

Figure I.1. Contours of Latin America. Image based on a similar figure in F. Carson, *The Geography of Latin America* (Englewood Cliffs, N.J.: Prentice-Hall, 1957).

Figure I.2. Geography of North and South America, superimposed. Image based on a similar figure in F. Carson, *The Geography of Latin America* (Englewood Cliffs, N.J.: Prentice-Hall, 1957).

is divided into three sections, the Pacific highlands of Chiapas, Guatemala, and El Salvador, the Maya region north of the highlands, and eastern Central America.[3] The largest landmass in Latin America, continental South America, is often compared to a huge bowl because its relatively flat interior is ringed by high mountains, the Andes ranges along the west coast, the large landmass of the Guiana shield, and extensive Brazilian highlands along the east coast. Interspersed between the Western Andes and a second, third, and fourth range to the east are vast plateaus of which the Bolivian *altiplano* is the best known example. Although most of Latin America is located in tropical and subtropical latitudes, the South American perimeter with the Andean highlands to the west and the Brazilian highlands along the Atlantic has a cooling effect, dividing the region into two contrasting but interdependent geosystems that influence the region's climatic and hydrological patterns. Rich soils from the erosion of the Andes formed the basis for the continent's most advanced pre-Columbian civilizations: those of the Inca Empire and its predecessors.

The first European explorers were stunned by the lush fertility and dense populations of the newly discovered lands.[4] Columbus himself described the islands of Hispaniola and Tortuga as "a humanized paradise . . . densely populated and completely cultivated, like the countryside around Cordoba . . . not so thickly wooded as to be impassable," indicating that open space may have been created by clearing or burning.[5] The urban centers, which the Spanish discovered on their arrival, acted as support nodes for reaching new territories that would subsequently be added to the empire.

Despite early reports to the contrary, the notion that the New World was barely occupied took firm hold of the European imagination. As geographer William Denevan has written, the commonly accepted notion that human civilization was sparse at the time of the Conquest was largely attributable to the decimation of native populations by contact with European pathogens during the sixteenth century, to such an extent that even during the nineteenth century they remained depleted, but recent discoveries of the remains of many pre-Hispanic settlements have established that human populations were much larger and more widespread than previously assumed.[6] The misrepresentation of a primeval wilderness was attributable in part to the desire for uncontested extraction of gold and silver, followed by the cultivation of wheat, rice, cotton, coffee, tobacco, indigo, quinine, and sugar cane for export, activities that appeared less greedy when the continent was presented as empty and its resources available for the taking.[7] The concept of the new world as virgin territory was reinforced by the belief that nature was separate from humanity and that man-made artifacts were separate from the natural world, distinctions not recognized by the indigenous peoples. In ancient Peru, a *huaca* or *wak'a*, a Quechua word meaning "sacred," was derived from another Quechua word meaning "to wail," a term used to describe a place for worship, such as hand-built mud pyramids, but by extension also referred to objects perceived to be sacred, such as massive rocks, or feared and admired because they were imbued with supernatural powers. For the indigenous peoples of the Americas, the transformation of nature was a process in which the human, natural, and divine worlds were inseparable.[8]

A mixture of economic self-interest, the tragic consequences of the European invasion, and differing worldviews combined to promulgate the notion of the New World as a virgin territory, but while the idea that the Americas were sparsely populated at the time of the conquest has been discredited, the actual number of inhabitants continues to be hotly debated. To suggest how densely populated the Americas may have been, according to some estimates, the central Mexican plateau alone contained more than twice the population of Spain and Portugal combined. To sustain such numbers, the native people of the Andean highland regions, the Mexican plateau, and the Yucatán peninsula would have had to transform all available land into environments suitable for agriculture through earth-moving on a grand scale, which was practiced throughout much of the New World long before the arrival of the Europeans.[9] Large quantities of earth and stone were transferred to create various raised and sunken features, transforming terrain otherwise too steep, dry, or wet, including widespread modification for agricultural terraces. Slopes were leveled, or their angle of inclination reduced with fill; embankments, ponds, sunken fields, irrigation canals, underground conduits, ridges, platforms, and raised fields were dug; crop mounds, boundary walls, fences, and markers were built (figures I.3–I.9). Religious beliefs determined the construction of pyramids representing mountains, and in some regions plazas were built to stand in for the primordial sea and funerary stone steles for trees.[10]

As the size and economic potential of the conquered lands became gradually more apparent, the Spanish devised a strategy to guide the process of the founding settlements that would consolidate control of the conquered territories and allow their resources to be more efficiently exploited. To guide and regularize the establishment of military posts, missions, and towns, King Phillip II of Spain developed the first version of the Laws of the Indies, a comprehensive guide composed of 148 ordinances to aid colonists in locating, building, and populating settlements. They codified the city planning process and represented some of the first attempts at a general plan. Signed in 1573, the Laws of the Indies were wide-ranging guidelines pertaining to the design and development of communities.[11] This model had to adapt itself to the geographical characteristics of the

Figure I.3. Incan *acequia* channeling water down from the hills into the valley to increase arable land and availability of drinking water. Tipón, Sacred Valley of the Incas, Moray, Peru. Photo by René Davids, 2014.

Figure I.4. Sacred city of Caral-Supe, Peru, the oldest known built complex in the Americas. Photo by René Davids, 2014.

Figure I.5. Machu Pichu, Peru, built in the fifteenth century. Photo by René Davids, 2014.

Figure I.6. Incan *moray*, terraced circular depressions, Sacred Valley of the Incas. Photo by René Davids, 2014.

Figure I.7. Incan farming terraces at Pisac, Sacred Valley of the Incas, Peru. Photo by René Davids, 2014.

Figure I.8. Salt works consisting of small pools filled with saltwater flowing from a natural spring from which the water gradually evaporates. Maras, Sacred Valley of the Incas. Photo by René Davids, 2014.

Figure I.9. Pyramid of the Sun, the largest structure in the ancient city of Teotihuacán, Mexico. Photo by René Davids, 2000.

newly conquered territories which posed a number of restrictions in the application of the royal ordinances for the settlement of the New World. The enormous distances and challenging terrain of the territory led to a dispersed occupation in diverse geographic locations, but managed to produce a relative uniformity in the newly founded settlements through a development process that went on for more than three hundred years. Although the Spanish built new ports and *presidios* (military towns), population density and distribution at the turn of the nineteenth century did not vary significantly from that of the indigenous settlements at the time of their arrival three centuries earlier. The growth of the planned cities was based on a layout in which the exact form of the settlement, the alignment of the roads, the arrangement of the blocks, and the protocols for allocation of land parcels among the founding members were defined. These cities were subject to modifications in their form, at all stages of their development, due to topographical modifications or the territorial inclinations of the inhabitants.

The new Spanish settlements were built according to the precisely ordered layouts proscribed by the Laws of the Indies but on or near dramatically irregular topography; most contemporary capitals and urban centers of Latin American countries are also situated in close proximity to rugged terrain. Santiago de Chile faces some of the highest peaks of the Cordillera de los Andes, Bogotá is settled on a savannah at the edge of the Eastern Cordillera, and Caracas is situated in a dramatic valley surrounded by hills, highest among them the Cerro Avila, which separates it from the Caribbean. The national capitals Quito and La Paz and major cities Arequipa or Cuzco, Peru, Medellín, Colombia, and Sucre, Bolivia are located on high plateaus amid the towering peaks of the Andes. Even cities with less obvious spectacular topography include dramatic landforms: São Paulo is cut by a deep canyon on the Serra do Mar, or "Sea Range" plateau, Lima's mostly flat terrain slopes gently from the Pacific Ocean into valleys of the Andes as high as 1,600 feet above sea level interrupted only by some isolated hills (figures I.10 and I.11).[12] Latin America is not unique in featuring cities located at high elevations or adjacent to unusual topography: Cape Town, South Africa, Lisbon, Portugal, and Hong Kong, among other cities, have dramatic and spectacular sites, but they are exceptional whereas in Latin America such locations are relatively common. Historic agricultural infrastructure, religious structures, and settlements created an enduring legacy in Latin America to which

Figure I.10. View of Cuzco, Peru. Photo by René Davids, 2014.

Figure I.11. View of La Paz, Bolivia. Photo by René Davids, 2011.

successive generations would contribute by altering the existing terrain, developing architecture and urban planning concepts in accordance with their own evolving values and technologies. The resulting landscapes were manipulated by humans but closely followed natural forms. By contrast the Spanish imposed geometric patterns of settlement on flat land, intended to rectify what they perceived as disorderly indigenous practices, but as colonial cities were expanded, many eventually encountered the same challenging terrain originally chosen by the indigenous people for their settlements. The impact of topography on the still-evolving cities of Latin America constitutes a rich source for understanding the region's constructed environments and is the focus of this book.

Natural landscapes untouched by humans have become increasingly rare. Edward Relph[13] writes that the twentieth century may be the first period in history when it became possible for most people to survive without firsthand knowledge of their natural surroundings. Demarcations of territory that are not dependent on strict boundaries have become more common due to recent recognition and definition of interdependent economic and ecological systems extending over whole regions, such that previous definitions of city forms dependent on the rural/urban and natural/human dichotomies are now regarded as obsolete.

Perhaps the most powerful demonstration of how a fluid definition of territory can alter perception of the landscape is to be found in the work of Brazilian architect Vilanova Artigas, who conceived of architecture as a series of incidents on a spatial continuum. Ramps were a feature of Vilanova Artigas's architecture, used less to connect different levels of a building than to replace the concept of levels with continuous movement in a fluid landscape. His School of Architecture in São Paulo has no doors to separate the interior from the surrounding environment, so that once liberated from similarly restrictive physical boundaries, the city can be perceived not as a bounded physical object with areas outside it but as part of an unlimited field of multiple configurations.

Introduction to the Essays

A shared geography, topographical features, extended periods of colonial occupation and economic dependence on powers outside the region, marginal involvement in major world historical events, and pronounced disparities among social classes have been used to define general or local Latin American identities, but the essays featured in *Shaping Terrain* avoid prescriptive approaches and a general definition of Latin America. Rather than searching for universal truths, the book highlights distinct cultural attitudes toward the environment and landscapes, their relationships, and how they have changed over time.[14]

The individual chapters engage various issues pertaining to Latin American topography and ecology: the infrastructure developed to overcome physical obstacles to expansion and prosperity which then became, as in Valparaíso, Bogotá, or Medellin, central to their vision of themselves. Landscapes were changed, razed, or reconstructed as in Rio de Janeiro, Mendoza, and Santiago de Chile; productive landscapes were demolished and preserved in Bogotá and Mexico City. Similar topographies were used to establish racial and class distinctions in Rio, Caracas, and Lima. The same landscapes were perceived as environmentally irrelevant or sensitive at different times; a confluence of social, political, and economic circumstances such as occurred in Bogotá; landscapes configured to provide a sense of national or regional identity in Mexico City, Rio, and Santiago de Chile and Mendoza, Argentina. *Shaping Terrain* is organized into three sections, the first dealing primarily with buildings and landscapes, the second with cities and water, and the third with cities and topography, but the definitions are broad. The essays on cities also focus on architecture, and the section on architects places their work in the context of the city as a whole.

Buildings, Terrain, and Form

The essays in this section demonstrate different ways in which landforms and ecology have affected Latin American architecture and urbanism. "Mythical Terrain and the Building of Mexico's UNAM" examines El Pedregal, a site where archaeological evidence indicates that pyramids had been constructed as early as 1000 BC, and demonstrated the symbolic importance of the ground itself, a desolate wilderness associated with myths, superstitions, and rituals of the indigenous people. By the time of UNAM's inauguration in 1952, the site's lava-encrusted surface that had submerged its pre-Columbian settlements was replaced by the new campus, and much of the lava reused for pavements, reinforcing the notion that the university and Mexico's future were physically linked to and had emerged from the ruins of its glorious past. A similar ambition to express the state's vision of a new society was shared by the architects of the Universidad de Panamá, in which the formal language of architecture was linked conceptually with that of the country itself. In "Universidad de Panamá: Designing on the Outside Edge of the Periphery," the editor examines the construction of the Universidad de Panamá within the context of local history, exploring the paradox by which Panamanian national identity came to be expressed through forms deliberately purged of regional cultural references. Like Panama itself, a narrow isthmus connecting two much larger land masses, the university aimed to establish a bridge between cultures, ethnicities, and continents by avoiding architectural idioms associated with specific elements of society.

"Topography and Ideology: The Museum of Modern Art and the Helicoide de la Roca de Tarpeya" by Iván Gonzáles, José Rosas, and René Davids, compares the Museum of Modern Art (MAM) in Caracas, designed by Brazilian architect Oscar Niemeyer, with the Helicoide de La Roca de Tarpeya, Caracas's first commercial shopping center, whose form is adapted to the contours of the hill on which it is situated. Both are monumental constructions as well as visionary feats of technical daring which sought to replace the landscapes of poverty on the *barrio*-covered hills with a modern, socially progressive society, and used the expressive power of topographic forms to communicate architectural ideas. A progressive vision also informs "São Paulo's Topography and the Utopian Democracy" by Angelo Bucci in collaboration with the editor. The essay explores the architectural and political movement of São Paulo Brutalism, a regional variant of European modernism inspired by the landscape of deep ravines and vast plateaus, as well as the belief of its leading figure, Vilanova Artigas, that if Brazilian social, cultural, and economic circumstances could be visualized as a continuum without physical barriers, social inequities between races and classes would also be removed. Even though the ideals of São Paulo Brutalism proved to be unattainable, its emphasis on the integration of topography and urban space symbolized the desire to create civic architecture that encouraged human interaction and fostered community spirit.

The difference in interpretation and meaning of European movements as they crossed the Atlantic has generally been accompanied by a lack of interest in researching any reciprocal influence that might have been exerted by Latin America and its natural, material, and cultural context on European architecture, either before or after World War II. "Le Corbusier, Rio de Janeiro, Topography, and Housing: A Cross-Cultural Exchange," written by the editor, describes how the Swiss architect's design proposals for various South American cities demonstrated that modern architecture could be site-specific, and infrastructure, landscape, and architecture could be synthesized into a unified whole, an approach which influenced not only Brazilian architects but the next generation of European masters as well. The essay also challenges the prevailing critical consensus which holds that from 1929 through the 1960s, modern architecture exported from the centers of high culture in Europe was adapted to the lush tropical landscapes of the New World where it flourished as an exotic regional variant. By examining some of the complex ways in which architectural ideas develop, this essay investigates the impact on Le Corbusier of his encounter with the dramatic landscapes of the New World, as well as the influence that his unbuilt schemes for Rio de Janeiro had on a new generation of Brazilian architects some twenty years later.

Cities and Water

The essays in this section examine the creative challenges presented to the foundation and development of selected Latin American cities by their natural environments. An abundance of water was perceived to be both an asset and a hindrance to Mexico City's development, thus the lakes in the middle of the site on which the city was founded were gradually drained to make way for what has become an immense polluted urban sprawl. In "Mexico City as Reinvented Geography, Its Looming Environmental Crisis, and Recent Proposals for Regenerative Landscapes," Edward R. Burian identifies Mexico City's zones of wealth and poverty as well as the underlying causes of the environmental apocalypse it may one day face as residents contend with rising levels of pollution, noise, traffic congestion, and crime. As in Mexico City, many of the wetlands that once surrounded Bogotá were encroached upon, drained, or contaminated, but in his essay "Mountains, Wetlands, and Public Space in Bogotá," Julián Alejandro Osorio and the editor describe the systematic process of reclaiming Bogotá's polluted rivers, the restoration of its wetlands, natural corridors, and construction of civic spaces that have become models for urban renewal throughout Latin America and the world.

A city located in the arid foothills of the leeward side of the Andes, the identity of Mendoza, like that of Bogotá, was linked to water resources, but unlike its northern counterpart, Mendoza's networks of canals were expanded, dug to allow urbanization to take place. In "Topography, Hydrology and the Irrigated Landscapes of Mendoza, Argentina," Jorge Ricardo Ponte and the editor describe how Mendoza's pre-Columbian irrigation system was appropriated and enlarged by the Spanish to continue land cultivation more extensively. Rather than apply the rigid rules set forth in Laws of the Indies, the Spanish settlers continued the *acequia* (canal) system established by the indigenous Huarpe people and adapted it to the alluvial streams running down from the Andes. When a devastating earthquake forced the city to rebuild in the nineteenth century, the *acequia* network was expanded, trees were planted along the sides, and Mendoza became a green metropolis with a dense cover of poplars and acacias that refreshes its downtown streets and plazas and confers its enduring urban character. Over the course of the twentieth century, mismanagement of water resources and unregulated discharge of dangerous agricultural and industrial pollutants now threaten to overwhelm the entire *acequia* network. Contrary to common understandings, in Mendoza therefore it wasn't the sixteenth-century *conquistadores* but their nineteenth- and twentieth-century descendants who placed their urban and environmental heritage in serious jeopardy.

Hills, Infrastructure, and Social Order

The essays in this section are focused on the phenomenon of urban hills and their influence over time on the growth of the cities that surround them. "Demolishing Urban Hills: Establishing New Identities" analyzes hills that were regarded as impediments to city building, notwithstanding the fact that despite advances in engineering technology, the process of erasing them remained difficult and controversial throughout the late nineteenth and early twentieth centuries. This essay explores the destruction of historic fabric and existing topography that removed the physical vestiges of Rio de Janeiro's urban past. Santiago de Chile opted for transformation rather than erasure of the hill adjacent to the original colonial city. In "Santiago de Chile and the Changing Meaning of Its Hills," Rodrigo Perez de Arce considers two isolated hills surrounded by the city of Santiago, the Cerro Santa Lucía and the Cerro San Cristóbal, each transformed into an urban park at the end of the nineteenth and the beginning of the twentieth centuries. Despite overall layouts modeled on European, mainly Parisian examples, the hillside parks featured some original creative design solutions and became showcases of invention, with viewing platforms from which to savor the surrounding landscapes and Santiago's ongoing urban development.

While Santiago is situated in a large bowl-shaped valley surrounded by mountains, the nearby port city of Valparaíso is wedged onto a narrow sliver of coastal land with a backdrop of steep hills overlooking the Pacific Ocean. "Valparaíso, a Future in the Balance," written by the editor, studies the transformation of Valparaíso from a colonial outpost into a thriving cosmopolitan center of global commerce that lost much of its international trade after the opening of the Panama Canal in 1914 eliminated the need for a voyage around Cape Horn to travel between the Atlantic and Pacific Oceans. When Valparaíso received a UNESCO World Heritage designation in 2003, it was widely perceived as an opportunity to recover former prosperity without sacrificing cultural identity, but conflicts have arisen between business leaders and politicians intent on developing the tourist industry and longtime residents protective of their unique urban and architectural heritage. "Topography and Social Order in Latin America," also by the editor, examines how the topographical factors that have contributed to the social, economic, and racial divisions present in Latin America since before the Spanish conquest have impacted the growth of the colonial grid and plaza towns to the sprawling mega-cities they have now become, many with informal neighborhoods located in close proximity to natural and human-created hazards and inhabited by the most vulnerable populations.

I

BUILDINGS, TERRAIN, AND FORM

1

Mythical Terrain and the Building of Mexico's UNAM

RENÉ DAVIDS

Recent trends in global capitalism have transformed the university into a corporation interested in the production of "excellence" rather than a representation of the national state.[1] In the late 1940s, however, Latin American states were heavily invested in the building of new universities that would help to promote their image as socially progressive and technologically forward-looking societies. Mexico had lived through a dramatic revolution at the beginning of the twentieth century, and the postrevolutionary regimes were particularly committed to providing universal education. The symbolism attached to the university was so strong that the new campus for the Universidad Nacional Autonóma de Mexico (UNAM), the oldest public university in the country, was inaugurated on November 20, 1952, the day that commemorates the beginning of the Mexican Revolution. The new university constituted a visible emblem of the revolution's ambition to achieve a fair distribution of the country's assets and free universal education for all.[2] Internal migration to urban centers, a growing middle class, and a surge in the number of women seeking professional training led to the expansion of the universities during the 1950s.

The UNAM, with its scattered buildings in downtown Mexico City, could no longer cope with the increasing number of students, leading officials to search for a replacement site. Inspired by the American campus model, their goal was to gather all the dispersed facilities in one place, which meant looking for a site on the capital's periphery. This had the added appeal of moving politically radical students away from the centers of power. The Revolution of 1910 had succeeded, and authorities sought to celebrate and mythologize its legacy while pushing any possibility of continued debate and dissent to the margins.[3] The site eventually chosen was in El Pedregal, an outlying district situated south of San Angel that enjoyed the dual benefits of clean air and immunity from the seasonal flooding that plagued Mexico City.

Believed to have been formed about 2,500 years ago by the eruption of the volcano Xitle, El Pedregal was a 30-square-mile area covered in basalt. Sparsely inhabited before 1945, it was a volcanic landscape in a country where volcanoes have long held profound mythical connotations providing the building of Mexico's UNAM cosmological and cultural significance.[4] It was also the home of several rare animal species, lichens, and grasses, flowering plants such as the Palo Loco, agaves, and various species of pines and oaks that took advantage of the scarce water and the dust that accumulated in the cracks and crevices of the lava. Native Mexicans had sought refuge from their Spanish colonizers in the area, and in the early part of the twentieth century revolutionaries hid there from the forces they finally overthrew. Untouched by European imperialism, El Pedregal was often referred to as a new Eden and equated with the ancient heart of Mexico. Infused with ideas of death and regeneration as well as resistance to persecution, El Pedregal seemed ideally suited to house the new campus that carried the mandate to fulfill the democratic educational goals of the revolution.

Within these ambitious and lofty goals, Mario Pani and Enrique del Moral, the architects charged with designing the university's master plan, explained their objectives as easing "the relationship between departments and creating physical and pedagogical unity for the convenience of students, professors, and researchers."[5] Many complex ambitions and symbolic decisions belied that humble explanation, however. For example, the UNAM's distribution of building commissions to 140 architects was an expression of the Mexican Revolution's aim to redistribute the country's resources that stood in sharp contrast to the construction of the contemporary Universidad Central de Venezuela, which was charged to just one architect, Carlos Raúl Villanueva.

The layout of the different schools on the UNAM campus was indebted to the superblock concept. Initially introduced at the end of the nineteenth century in Britain by the Garden City movement and adopted by the modern movement in the early twentieth century, superblocks were larger than traditional urban blocks and featured pedestrian-only public

Figure 1.1. Aerial view of UNAM. Master plan by Mario Pani and Enrique del Moral, 1953. Courtesy of ICA Fondo Acervo Oblicuas, Negó 01_009678, Ciudad Universitaria, Volado, Mexico.

grounds in the center. Le Corbusier, who disseminated the idea through his writings, designed his superblocks with strict, rational, orthogonal street layouts. The street system at the UNAM, however, was configured organically around the lava formations. The scholastic area of Ciudad Universitaria (CU), UNAM's main campus and the most interesting of its zones, was situated along an east–west axis, bounded by lava deposits and the north–south running Avenida de Los Insurgentes at its western end, and the School of Medicine at the east. A large public space flanked on the south by the humanities buildings and on the north by the sciences wing unified the different departments and structures, their placement organized symbolically around it (figure 1.1). The School of Medicine, designed by Roberto Alvarez Espinoza, Ramón Torres, and Pedro Ramírez, was sited to link the north and south areas, signifying medicine's reliance on both the sciences and the humanities, while the placement of the School of Science at the center of the university suggested that scientific knowledge was the key to Mexico's future.[6]

Ultimately it was the adherence of the building designs to some of the principles of the modern movement around a large plaza (campus) rather than the content-laden symbolic relationships that held the university together compositionally. By using a style that had been imported from Europe, the campus forms provided an advanced and technologically progressive image and gave a sense of departure from the Spanish colonial past. Iconic features of the modern movement such as horizontal windows, flat roofs, covered walks, and pilotis were incorporated into most buildings, while a Mexican flavor was imparted through controversial deviations from the modern orthodoxy, such as the inclusion of figurative murals with stirring nationalist narratives (figure 1.2). Adding to the nationalist overtones of the design were the lava stone steps, extracted from the site itself, which recalled pre-Hispanic Mexican monuments and the use of *tecali*, a delicate green onyx-marble, or alabaster, from Puebla (figure 1.3).

The murals—depicting populist messages and historical narratives—were among the most controversial elements of the university's design. The Rectory Tower designed by Mario Pani, Enrique del Moral, and Salvador Ortega Flores, for example, featured a mural by David Alfaro

Figure 1.2. UNAM School of Medicine. Architects Roberto Alvarez Espinosa, Pedro Ramírez Vásquez, and Ramón Torres, 1952–58. Photo by René Davids, 2000.

Figure 1.3. Lava steps at UNAM. Photo by René Davids, 2000.

Siqueiros that presented the extended arms of a large figure representing Mexico's thrust toward the future while the small individuals in the background stood for the people's battle against capitalism.

The university's main library, situated close to Avenida de los Insurgentes at the head of the CU's main public space, featured an even more prominent mural. Designed by Juan O'Gorman, it complemented the message of the Rectory Tower by featuring on each of its four facades a narrative of different stages of Mexican history, stories that reverberated with the political and social mission of the public university and the government that sponsored it. In this regard, the CU's architecture became associated with the nationalistic trend that, particularly after the Revolution of 1910, was prevalent in the Mexican arts. Architects who wished to adhere to the principles of the modern movement resisted this trend, but ultimately joined the project when Miguel Alemán rose to the presidency. Alemán presided over a technocratic administration that emphasized industrialization over agrarian reform as the solution to Mexico's problems and encouraged the construction of public works.[7]

The attempt to "Mexicanize" the architecture through the murals was not universally accepted; some rejected it as an "architecture of the state, of propaganda and of national exaltation."[8] Others hailed the use of murals as an example of the integration of the arts. In any case, the murals were a far cry from the subtle way in which the architect Luis Barragán managed to seamlessly integrate the Mexican vernacular Hispanic colonial tradition with the plain and simple forms of modernism as seen in his own house, built in 1947 in Tacubaya, Mexico. For despite O'Gorman's contention that the criticism leveled against his murals was made by snobs unwilling to express their vulgar sentiments, the painterly works failed to integrate smoothly into the architecture, but given the absence of signature buildings on campus, they gave the rather humble modernist buildings an iconic presence that became recognizable around the world.[9]

The Olympic Stadium was the most dramatic example of this seemingly paradoxical combination of the modest and the monumental. Located just across the Avenida de los Insurgentes from the Rectoría and connected by a large underpass to the lower Plaza de la Rectoría, the Olympic Stadium was at the head of the west–east axis. Designed by Augusto Pérez Palacios and his collaborators, Raul Salinas Moro and Jorge Bravo Jiménez, the stadium emerged as a reincarnated volcano, a building that recalled the numerous pre-Columbian pyramids, an imposing artificial topography: part landscape, part built monument. Thrown up from the center of the "crater," the lava was deposited in high embankments. Rows of seats were designed inside, while the outer ring was faced with lava rock also extracted from the site. The level of the fields and tracks was 4–6 meters below the surrounding sidewalk (figure 1.4).

By simultaneously making reference to pre-Columbian myths associated with volcanoes and creating a technologically sophisticated building for the masses, the stadium expressed the national ambition of providing a progressive future through education rooted in tradition.[10] The success of the Olympic Stadium can also be seen as the reconstruction of José Villagrán García's Greek-style National Stadium built in 1924 as a venue for large-scale performances and political rallies but demolished after only twenty years because of structural flaws. The new Olympic Stadium succeeded where the National Stadium had failed, expressing both a timeless and a modern Mexican identity. However, the stadium's success was in part attributable to the small number of urban sports arenas, which limited its influence on other buildings.[11]

While the stadium recalled the pre-Columbian pyramids and the volcanoes of the Mexican landscape, the CU was in some ways reminiscent

Figure 1.4. Olympic Stadium, UNAM, 1953. Architects Augusto Pérez Palacios with Jorge Bravo Jiménez and Raúl Salinas Moro. Courtesy of ICA, Fondo Acervo Oblicuas, Negó 01_009678, Ciudad Universitaria, Volado.

of Le Corbusier's 1936 plan for the University of Brazil. Although he had generated inspired but unrealistic propositions for some of the continent's cities, when confronted with a real commission Le Corbusier developed a project that, while never realized, became highly influential. The first designs for the UNAM seemed uncannily similar to the Swiss architect's design. Not only did the plans for both universities share similar layouts, but they were also sited in valleys set against a backdrop of not-too-distant mountains.[12] In both schemes, the Department of Medicine was at the head of the axial composition, and a prominent vertical library building was set in the center. Both projects also featured pedestrian-friendly public spaces and a major circulation network that crossed the campus, linking the university to the city.

Orthogonally placed in relation to its long northern side, the first design for the UNAM, completed in March 1947 (figure 1.5), featured three identical, parallel slab blocks running north–south to the northern edge. Their placement appeared to open windows into the surrounding landscape. A central plaza was defined mainly by covered walkways. Two slab blocks were positioned to the south of the plaza with only minor buildings running parallel to the walkways. The buildings changed orientation

Figure 1.5. Preliminary project design for UNAM. Originally published in *Arquitectura México*, 1947.

as the project developed; the final 1952 version featured a large, leveled public space that was strongly bound by buildings. The progressive iterations of the plan show its gradual transformation from a design that featured figures in space to a composition where the space becomes the figure.[13]

For the most part, critics have overlooked this important evolution and its link back to the Hispanic tradition of space making, which privileged enclosure over movement. In this respect, the design was actually at odds with the UNAM's professed ambition to create a central public space in the pre-Columbian tradition. Space making for the indigenous peoples of the Americas always connected the user to the surrounding landscape even when, as in the case of Teotihuacán, the buildings were aligned along a monumental street, La calzada de los muertos (figure 1.6). The main public "campus" at the UNAM, by contrast, was an enclosed space that linked the university to the Hispanic rather than the indigenous tradition.

The UNAM's buildings, while modern in style, were similarly not in sync with Le Corbusier's idea of placing magnificent pure volumes bathed in light on an open and continuous field. Compared with other famous modernist compositions of the period, such as the capitol complex at Chandigarh, the UNAM's central space (*el campus*) seemed conventional. Not so the architecture of both complexes that wished equally strongly to signify, through modernist architecture, a new beginning for their people. The modern style was associated with ridding societies of traditional constraints by bearing little resemblance to the traditional architecture of their respective countries. Le Corbusier was commissioned to design Chandigarh in 1951 as a result of the partition of India following independence from British imperial rule. The Punjab region had been split in two, and Lahore, the old capital, fell on the Pakistani side. As a result, a new seat of government was needed on the Indian side of the border. Chandigarh was not conceived merely as the capital of an Indian state, but according to William J. R. Curtis as "a visible and persuasive instrument of national economic and social development, consonant with Nehru's idea that the country must industrialize or perish."[14]

The vast new urban spaces in both India and Mexico had precedents in the pre-Columbian and Mughal traditions. Le Corbusier's earliest sketches of India depict the eighteenth-century Mughal garden at Pinjore, close to Chandigarh. The garden design used clever effects to compress terraces of water within the confines of the rugged landscape, which had

Figure 1.6. Calzada de los Muertos, Teotihuacán. Photo by René Davids, 2000.

a noticeable influence on Le Corbusier. Perhaps even more striking was the relationship between the sunken garden, pools, stairs, bridges, and ramps that Le Corbusier conceived as a forecourt to the Governor's Palace at Chandigarh and the Diwan-i-Khas at Fatehpur Sikri, a site he had also seen and admired.

By carving into the earth, regarded with reverence in traditional societies, the modern spaces suggested a method by which both Mexico and India could connect to their pasts. As at Fatehpur Sikri, in Chandigarh the excavations in front of the Assembly and High Court (1951–55) are filled with water to reflect the buildings' presence. The most striking excavation is the sunken garden in front of the never-finished Governor's Palace, a place that, because it is below grade, does not interrupt the vast sweep of the capital plaza. Division of the garden's walkways into four quadrants is also typical of Mughal gardens. Rather than accommodating activities, these precincts were intended as places for contemplation, sensory delight, and sedentary relief from the intense heat.[15]

By sinking the quadrants but not the paths, Le Corbusier allowed them to become elevated walkways, vantage points with unobstructed views of the garden's totemic column, artificial mountain, and monumental stairs. More of an inverted podium for sculptural objects than a sunken public retreat, the Governor's Palace garden, like the rest of the capital's public spaces, privileged views and contemplation over inhabitation. Not surprisingly, all of Le Corbusier's sketches of the garden are bird's-eye perspectives (figure 1.7). Unlike the sunken garden at Chandigarh, the excavated plaza at UNAM was intended to allow people to gather, meet, or play, a large rectangular public space more indebted to Spanish colonial precedents than the pre-Hispanic tradition. The European influence in Mexico had produced a hybrid practice that fused some of the pre-Hispanic traditions, such as the large scale of public spaces, with Spanish practices. Maria Azevedo Saomao argues that the monumental scale of pre-Hispanic public spaces directly influenced the size of Spanish colonial plazas, a difference that becomes clear when comparing the dimensions of plazas designed after the conquest in both the old world and the new. Mexico City's Zócalo, built on Aztec ruins, is substantially larger than the roughly contemporary plaza of Valladolid, Spain. Another feature that was often incorporated into Mexican plazas after the conquest was the steps found in pre-Hispanic public spaces leading from one space to

Figure 1.7. Sketch of the Governor's Palace in Chandighar, India. Le Corbusier, 1952. Courtesy of F.L.C. / ADAGP, Paris / Artists Rights Society (ARS), New York.

another, clear examples of which can be found in Michoacán, such as the Plaza de Charapán or Terecuato.[16]

Pre-Hispanic plazas included monumental, free-standing buildings situated in dynamic spatial relationships with each other while maintaining a strong relationship with the larger landscape. The neo-Hispanic plaza, by contrast, featured modest buildings, with the exception of the church, arranged so as to achieve a sense of static enclosure. While architects and scholars have argued that the Mexican character of the UNAM was provided by its direct connections to the pre-Hispanic past, the hybridized plaza which emerged after the conquest was also an important precedent. El Campus, the main public space at UNAM, is a large-scale stepped and enclosed space not unlike those created by the Spaniards after they had become familiar with indigenous traditions. Determined to prove the pre-Hispanic purity of UNAM's cultural antecedents, researchers have diminished or even ignored colonial influences, inflicting a form of aesthetic cleansing on the architectural history of Mexico.

The "Mexicanness" of the Ciudad Universitaria

When discussing the "Mexican-ness" of UNAM's architecture, scholars have typically focused on its modern movement influences and connections to the pre-Hispanic past.[17] However, the spatial configuration of UNAM is significant for more than its symbolic references. According to Alberto Kalach, "The gardens of El Pedregal, a suburban development designed by architect Luis Barragán, were a direct source of inspiration for the open spaces of the Ciudad Universitaria.[18] Barragán believed that public gardens could be built where individuals still felt themselves to be in their own gardens.[19] For Barragán, the Generalife in Granada—a public garden with partially enclosed areas and outdoor rooms—constituted a suitable precedent. While the individual intimacy Barragán sought to achieve is arguably missing at the CU, the concept of a large communal space subdivided into smaller areas with physical boundaries is undeniably present.

Not surprisingly perhaps, the design of UNAM has similarities with Barragán's proposal for la Plaza de la Constitución, better known as El Zócalo. One of the largest public plazas in the world and the heart of Mexico City, it occupies the site of the old ceremonial center of Mexico: Tenochtitlán, the capital of the Aztec Empire and the locus of political events, public festivities, celebrations, informal gatherings, commerce, and performances. Regarded as an undistinguished proposal by architectural historian Marc Treib, the project's main characteristic was its dramatic simplicity and unified stone texture that eliminated the existing green square to restore a space more closely resembling the eighteenth-century Zócalo (figure 1.8).[20]

To contrast with the lofty spires of the cathedral, Barragán proposed a grotto-like subterranean passage and a striking water fountain suggestive of the opposition between divine power and the darker forces of the world. A perspective sketch by Barragán shows an eerie space in which the people are made to look insignificant by the sheer power and scale of their surroundings. As at UNAM, most of the traffic was relegated to the periphery, and a new, smaller square placed on the east side of the cathedral. The plaza's surrounding colonnades provide containment, recalling the *pilotis* at the front of the university's campus which read more like a cloister than an example of the orthodox modern movement precept to lift a building as a means of freeing the ground. Barragán conceived of the

Figure 1.8. Ciudad Universitaria campus, Mexico City. Photo by René Davids, 2000.

Zócalo as a shallow concavity that would create the illusion of a perfectly level surface.[21]

Conclusion

UNAM's modest architecture and sense of enclosure connects it more strongly to the traditions of the American campus and Mexican colonial plazas and monasteries than to Teotihuacán or Monte Alban. For Mario Pani, UNAM's enclosed spaces are both a symbol and a physical expression of convergence and community, but also repose and containment.[22] Critics obsessed with the continuity of its pre-Hispanic precedents have consistently underplayed what is arguably UNAM's most significant contribution, the renewal of a hybrid Mexican tradition of urban space-making in the New World.[23]

2

Universidad de Panamá

Designing on the Outside Edge of the Periphery

RENÉ DAVIDS

The Universidad de Panamá presents the interesting paradox of an architecture created to affirm national identity that was deliberately purged of regional and cultural references. With its pure geometries, long strip windows, flat roofs, *pilotis*, and white walls, when it was officially inaugurated in 1953, the campus of the Universidad de Panamá was considered an outstanding example of modern or "International Style" architecture, the term coined by Philip Johnson and Henry-Russell Hitchcock as the title of an exhibition and its eponymous catalog at New York's Museum of Modern Art (MOMA) in 1932. Modernism was "international," they wrote, because it relied on basic design principles.[1] Designed by Panamanian architects Ricardo J. Bermúdez, Guillermo De Roux, and Octavio Méndez Guardia, the Universidad de Panamá was included in a subsequent MOMA exhibition, "Latin American Architecture since 1945" (1955) and its catalogue, also curated by Hitchcock and Johnson, as well as in many other international publications, but it has been mostly overlooked in more recent histories of modern architecture.[2]

Despite the declaration by Hitchcock and Johnson that "this new style is not international in the sense that the production of one country is just like that of another," the perception that international modernism ignored the particulars of location, site, vernacular traditions, and national identity eventually achieved consensus. From the 1950s onward, modern architecture without obvious references to local architectural traditions began to be perceived as unresponsive to its vernacular context, and regional modernism, or modernism produced outside the cultural centers of Europe and the United States, became valued for its idiosyncratic variations of its original tenets.[3] By 1954, eminent architectural historian Sigfried Giedion was discerning relationships between the polders in the Dutch landscape and de Stijl's compositions of lines and rectangles, arguing that regionalism as a variant of modernism was both rooted in and dynamically connected to local cultural traditions, and comparing the impact of the International Style on the history of art with that of a "bulldozer upon a flower garden."[4] Although Giedion's powerful image implied that buildings communicate exclusively through their architectural idioms, they are also shaped by the aspirations of those who create and inhabit them. In the middle of the twentieth century, the modern movement's rational approach to design problems, ambitious reform agenda including mass housing, and determination to discard the past perfectly matched Panama's desire to move beyond the Spanish and American architecture of the colonial period while solving its social and economic problems. As was the case elsewhere in Latin America with institutions of higher education built at midcentury, Panamanians were hopeful that a new national university would earn their country a place among the world's progressive nations.

The particular role the university was expected to play in establishing Panama's national identity was based on its history and geographical situation. Four million years ago, the Isthmus of Panama was most likely a peninsula of southern Central America before movement of the underlying tectonic plates merged it with the continent of South America, a major geological event that separated the Atlantic and Pacific Oceans, established a land bridge between North and South America, and later linked the indigenous Maya of Central America and the Chibcha, or Muisca, who occupied the high valleys in what is now Colombia; although they shared commonalities with both groups, the indigenous people of Panama belonged to neither of them.[5] Eventually the Isthmus of Panama connected the colonial powers of the Iberian Peninsula with their South America territories, particularly the Viceroyalty of Lima (figures 2.1 and 2.2).

Panama remained an eastern province of Colombia well after Colombian independence from Spain in 1819, but with the encouragement and assistance of the United States, which had developed economic and military interests in its strategic location, Panama achieved its independence

Figure 2.1. View of Panama from Ancon Hill. Photo by René Davids, 2006.

in 1903. The following year, the United States was offered concession rights to develop and control a stretch of Panamanian territory they referred to as the Canal Zone, and ten years later, the Panama Canal opened, a major technological, engineering, and geopolitical achievement that signaled both the ascendancy of the United States and its overwhelming influence on the newly independent country.[6] The U.S. presence in Panama City was even more conspicuous after the establishment of Balboa, an adjacent American enclave at the Pacific entrance to the Canal, which also included Balboa Harbor, the city's main port, and the Canal Administration Building (1913), a monumental structure situated on an artificial hill at the

Figure 2.2. Satellite view of Panama. Courtesy of NASA's Earth Observatory, 2000.

Figure 2.3. Panama Canal Administration Building, Balboa. Photo by René Davids, 2006.

end of an axial route lined with four rows of palm trees and symmetrical buildings on either side. Designed by American architect Austin Lord, the Canal Administration Building featured a simplified variant of classicism well suited to the tropics, with huge overhanging eaves affording protection from the rain and spacious open galleries for cross-ventilation (figures 2.3 and 2.4).[7] Unlike Daniel Burnham's largely unrealized proposals for Manila (1905), which were layered over the national capital, the Canal Administration Building occupied a site in a commanding position over the American colonial complex, but with an unmistakable appearance of disengagement from Panama City and the local culture.

Low-density garden towns such as Paraíso, Pedro Miguel, La Boca, Las Cruces, and Silver City (later changed to Rainbow City) were also part of the American enclave. Simple, open, with wide eaves and often raised above the ground allowing breezes to cool the entire envelope, the buildings in these settlements were better suited to Panama's humid tropical climate than the narrow party-wall structures built in the old town according to colonial Spanish practices. Panama City and nearby Colón, a seaport near the Atlantic entrance to the Canal, also began to impose segregation and other racially restrictive American planning practices,

Figure 2.4. Canal Administration Building, Balboa. Photo by René Davids, 2006.

which reinforced existing prejudices among the local population and most adversely affected Caribbean immigrants seeking work opportunities related to the construction of the Canal.[8]

The pervasive influence of the United States on all aspects of Panamanian life and control of the Canal Zone convinced other Latin American countries that Panama was in actuality not an independent country but an American colony, derided by its critics as a sham, an invention of sordid interests and brazen U.S. aggression: "Panama is now a Yankee protectorate," wrote the Venezuelan Rufino y Blanco Fombona in 1908, and Vargas Vila claimed, "The Panamanians have been snatched by the 'barbarians' from the Spanish race."[9]

To counter these perceptions, Panamanian intellectuals put forward the proposition that Panama was essentially a *mestizo* nation of European and indigenous people who had come together during Spanish colonization, creating the basis for an autonomous Hispanic country, a narrative which necessarily excluded all non-Hispanics, particularly Caribbean immigrants of African descent. According to this narrative, Panama was the first stable settlement on the South American continent, established when Spanish *conquistador* and explorer Vasco Núñez de Balboa first sighted the Pacific Ocean in 1513. The desire that Panama be perceived as possessing an exclusively Hispanic heritage inspired the introduction of Spanish colonial architecture, a style imported from California and popular in countries intent on emphasizing their assumed Spanish heritage such as Mexico and Peru. New middle- and upper-class suburbs of Panama City such as La Exposición, Bella Vista, Campo Alegre, La Cresta, and Altos del Golf were all built in the Spanish colonial style.[10]

Another significant influence on the effort to establish Panama's Hispanic provenance was the legacy of Simón Bolívar, "El Libertador" and the leader of the struggle for independence of Colombia, Ecuador, Peru, and Bolivia in the early nineteenth century. The revival of Bolívar's plan to create a federation of independent South American states with Panama at the center had the potential to finally settle arguments about its origins and status as an independent country: at the center of the Western Hemisphere with Asia to one side and Africa and Europe to the other, the capital of the world would be located on the Isthmus of Panama.[11] When representatives of Latin American governments met in Panama in 1926 to celebrate the centenary of Bolívar's call to plan a unified path to independence, it provided prominent Panamanian intellectual and future rector of the Universidad de Panamá Octavio Méndez Pereira with an opportunity to infuse new life into the old dream by proposing the creation of a Pan-American Bolivarian university: "As the entry of the Canal cut through the heart of an altruistic nation, the Bolivarian university shall become the mastermind of two races, a colossal lighthouse for the continent. The peoples of the new world shall feel brotherhood beneath its beams of light and peoples from everywhere will understand the virtues of love, peace, work, and solidarity. Bolívar's vision of its future role in regional affairs was also the most convincing justification for Panama's independence in 1903."[12] Given the competing national aspirations and rivalries among the Latin countries, there was little chance that Méndez Pereira's concept of the Bolivarian university would succeed, but for Panamanians the university had the potential to provide an intellectual hub that reflected Panama's position as the link between oceans and continents and crossroads of the world.

Because it had been a backwater province at the time of Colombian independence, Panama possessed no institutions of higher learning. The

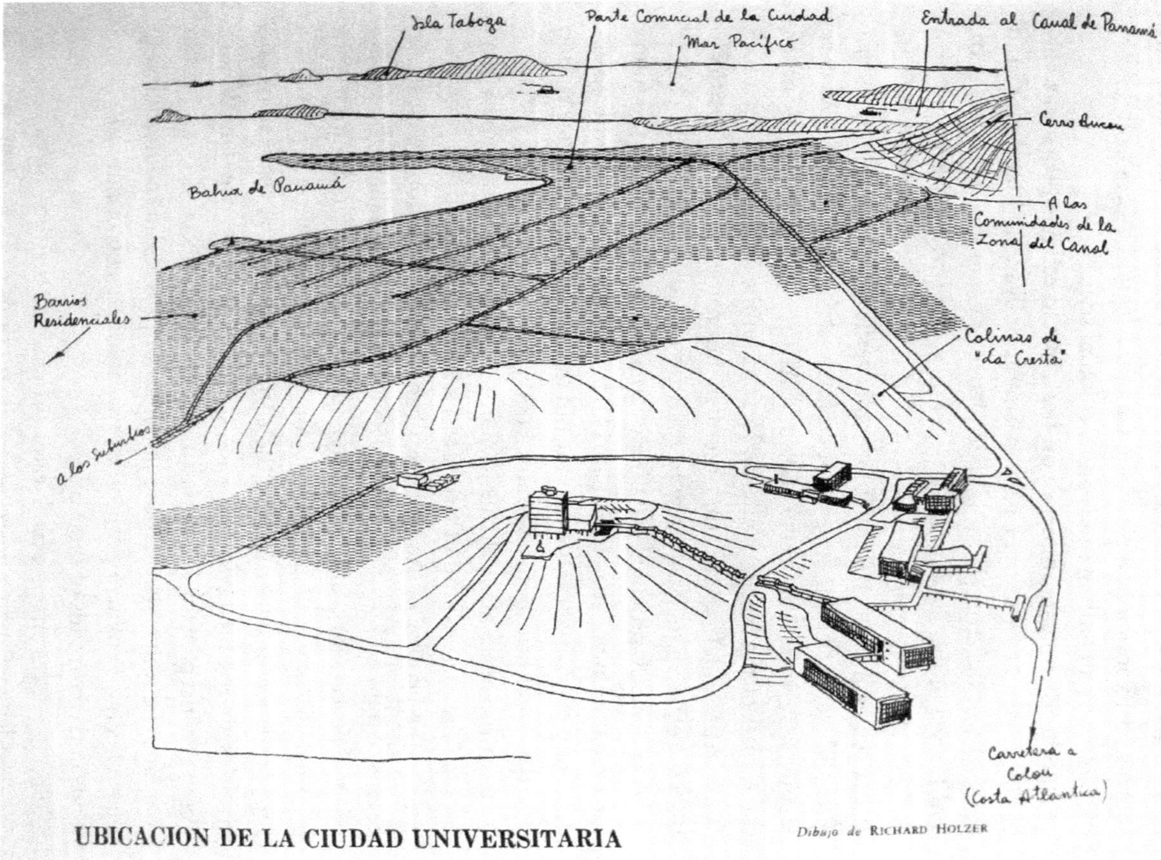

Figure 2.5. University of Panama location sketch. Architects Ricardo J. Bermúdez, Octavio Méndez Guardia, and Guillermo De Roux. Image from *Modulo 7*, 1951.

Figure 2.6. University of Panama Engineering, Architecture, and Science faculties. Architects Ricardo J. Bermúdez, Octavio Méndez Guardia, and Guillermo De Roux, 1950. Photo courtesy of the William Brockaway Fellowship, Tulane School of Architecture.

Universidad de Panamá, created in 1935 to fill the vacuum, initially operated only in the evenings at the Instituto Nacional, a local secondary school. A law passed in 1946 authorizing the government to purchase 40 hectares for the construction of a new campus set the stage for the university to become a significant force in Panama's education system. In 1948, architect Octavio Méndez Guardia, the son of university president Octavio Méndez Pereira, together with Guillermo De Roux and Ricardo J. Bermúdez, all of whom were educated abroad, received the commission

Figure 2.7. University of Panama Architecture and Engineering Building. Architects Ricardo J. Bermúdez, Octavio Méndez Guardia, and Guillermo De Roux, Panama, 1950. Photo by René Davids, 2006.

to study and eventually design the new university (figures 2.5–2.7). Buildings for the humanities, sciences, engineering and architecture, university administration, research library, and the Faculty of Medicine were built in 1952, and the campus was officially inaugurated on November 1, 1953, the fiftieth anniversary of Panama's independence.

The university commission provided the idealistic young architects with a unique opportunity to implement their radical concepts of an urban future unconstrained by social injustice, disease, and civic disorder. Advocating intervention in the existing city, which he compared to an ulcer treated with ineffective ointments, Guillermo De Roux passionately believed that adoption of the modern movement's urban principles, application of new technologies and materials, and fluid spatial organization could change Panama and the world for the better. All three architects despised the eclectic stylistic revivals, traditional street layouts, and stolid housing blocks built mainly as profit-making real estate for developers.[13]

The site chosen for the new university was El Cangrejo, an undeveloped area in Panama City only a few miles from the Canal Zone and separated from it by the Curundú River, part of a hilly spine extending from the volcanic Cerro Ancón to the northeast, also including the La Cresta and Bella Vista hills, which drained into the Curundú Valley to the west and Panama Bay to the east.[14] The site's elevated topography was significant because it would allow the university to become a highly visible urban presence, advertising Panama's status as an intellectual and cultural center to the Canal Zone and the world. Preeminent among the university buildings, sitting like a cultural acropolis on the summit of El Cangrejo, was the university library, modest when compared with the majestic Canal Administration Building but an imposing presence because of its setting and lighthouse on top announcing university events to Panama City and the international traffic of the canal, a symbol of the university's mission as a beacon illuminating the path to cultural renewal.[15]

The university's progressive image was further reinforced by the modern urban design principles intended to remediate the dark, congested, disease-ridden cities of preceding centuries. Its streamlined functional buildings sited to take advantage of the prevailing winds and most favorable solar orientations, white, well-lit, airy, and spaced widely apart in a lush green setting, the new university campus buildings provided a dramatic contrast not only with the neoclassical idiom of the Canal Zone but also the neocolonial Spanish vernacular of the middle-class suburban

Figure 2.8. University of Panama, School of Administration and Business, Panama. Architects Ricardo J. Bermúdez, Octavio Méndez Guardia, and Guillermo De Roux, 1950. Photo by René Davids, 2006.

neighborhoods, the housing informally built by the poor, and the colonial-era buildings still standing in older areas of Panama City. The university's circulation plan clearly separated vehicles from the ribbon-like network of covered walkways for pedestrians that provided shelter from sun and rain and was linked to superblock high-rise buildings separated by ample space for recreation. Le Corbusier had previously employed the superblock concept in his project for the Universidade do Brazil (1936), the first modern proposal for a campus in a tropical climate, which included a circulation concourse to direct rail and motor traffic through the site. The individual buildings of the Universidad de Panamá vehicular traffic were mostly restricted to streets around the periphery and terminated by the architectural school at one end and the Faculty of Medicine at the other. The layout produced by Le Corbusier for the Universidade do Brazil was more formal, with a stronger emphasis on structured public space, but plans for both campuses included vehicle-free pedestrian zones, covered linear walkways, and the library as the most prominent building in their respective complexes.

Superblocks were also installed at the Universidad Nacional Autónoma de Mexico (UNAM), designed at approximately the same time as the Universidad de Panamá in 1954 by architects Mario Pani and Enrique del Moral to consolidate the functions of isolated buildings scattered around

Figure 2.9. University of Panama Library. Architects Ricardo J. Bermúdez, Octavio Méndez Guardia, and Guillermo De Roux, 1950. Image from *Modulo* 7, 1951.

Mexico City. With its buildings arranged around a sequence of large, plaza-like spaces on an ancient solidified lava bed, UNAM differed markedly from the Universidad de Panamá in the various ways its modern architecture adopted an overtly nationalistic expression, including the installation of murals on buildings, the use of local lava stone, and the inclusion of Pre-Columbian motifs. By contrast, the character of aesthetic expression at the Universidad de Panamá was intentionally abstract, nonfigurative, and devoid of references to local culture beyond responses to what Bermúdez, De Roux, and Méndez considered the essential factors affecting architecture: topography, climate, and local construction materials; only when these factors were balanced in equilibrium would good architecture result. The library featured a *brise-soleil* on the east facade and series of egg-crate sun blinds for windows set between long stretches of blank wall on the south side.[16] The west facade, a challenging exposure in the tropics, was completely blank, and large windows were located on the wall facing north, but the architects' responses to other climatic challenges were less successful (figure 2.8). Axial corridors in the engineering and architecture, humanities, and Faculty of Medicine buildings made no provisions for cross-ventilation, and the large volume of runoff from frequent tropical downpours was diverted into catch basins, because the network of water channels that structure the landscaping and could have accommodated the overflows was installed well after the completion. Unlike some other regional work that featured successful collaborations between architects and landscape designers, notably that of Brazilian architect Oscar Niemeyer and landscape designer Roberto Burle Marx, whose dance club at Pampulha, Brazil, is an integrated synthesis of buildings and landscape, the Universidad de Panamá lacked a coordinated design strategy for the extensive open spaces surrounding each building, perhaps its most significant shortcoming.

Because of similarities of climate, multicultural and Latin roots, and widely circulated international publications featuring the work of its celebrated practitioners, Brazilian modernism exerted an exceptionally strong influence on midcentury architecture in many Latin American countries, including Panama. Modern architecture had taken root in Brazil in the 1930s as the government of Getulio Vargas offered state patronage in a concerted effort to modernize the country. The building for the Ministry of Education and Public Health in Rio de Janeiro (1936) designed by young Brazilian architects Lucio Costa, Alfonso Reidy, Jorge Moreira, Carlos Leao, and Ernani Vasconscelos, with Oscar Niemeyer playing a significant role, also included Le Corbusier as a consultant and was the first building to incorporate his ideas for hot-climate sun shading. A generation of brilliant architects influenced by Le Corbusier and led by Niemeyer went on to develop a fluid, sensuous style of modernism inspired by Brazil's exotic landscapes, vegetation, and multiethnic people. Celebrated in the exhibition "Brazil Builds" at MOMA (1943) and its accompanying catalog, Brazilian modernism became admired and influential throughout the world. Bermúdez regarded the practice of finding inspiration in foreign work as legitimate as long as it responded to universal human needs. "Vista desde el campus" (View from the campus), an illustrated article published in *Modulo 7*, showed that buildings designed for the law and public administration and commerce faculties designed by De Roux, Bermúdez, and Méndez bore remarkable similarities to the vaulted profiles and inclined roofs of the gymnasium and school at Alfonso Reidy's Pedrogulho housing scheme in Rio (1946), both influenced by Oscar Niemeyer's Yacht Club and Church of Saint Francis of Assisi in Pampulha (1943).[17] The honey-combed screen that shaded the Science Faculty's south facade appears to have been copied directly from the Brazilian pavilion at the New York World's Fair (1939) designed by Lucio Costa and Oscar Niemeyer. These and similar borrowings were acknowledged early on: the catalog of the exhibition "Latin American Architecture since 1945" (1955) praised the sun and rain protection and rest opportunities between buildings at the Universidad de Panamá's School of Public Administration and Business, but complained about its lack of assertiveness when compared with the work of the Mexican architect and muralist Juan O'Gorman at UNAM or Venezuelan architect Carlos Raúl Villanueva's designs for the Universidad Central de Caracas.[18]

What distinguished the architecture at the Universidad de Panamá was not its Brazilian-style exuberance but its straightforward expression of international modernism. Unlike the architecture at UNAM that was adorned with murals whose themes illustrated Mexican history and alluded to Pre-Columbian construction practices, the Universidad de Panamá made no overt references to an indigenous past or Spanish colonial traditions. For a country with difficulties finding recognition of its independence, the so-called International Style fulfilled the Panamanian longing to join the community of independent, progressive nations, and the immediate worldwide attention bestowed on the university buildings—publications in *L'Architecture d'Aujourd'Hui* and *Building* (later *Architectural Forum*), a design award at the 7th Panamerican Congress of Architects in Cuba, and inclusion in MOMA's second survey of Latin American architecture—was regarded as an acknowledgment that these intentions had been recognized and well received.[19]

Octavio Méndez Pereira's utopian ambition to fulfill Simón Bolívar's dream of Pan-American unity by creating a university on the Isthmus of Panama never materialized, but the vision of a model campus that would forge the national character remained: "The university (Ciudad Universitaria) shall be what it already is: the place where the uncontaminated strength of our destiny is forged; the culture that is going to transform each Panamanian citizen into a free and noble human being, able to live without inhibitions in peace and harmony with other men on earth. What we have done and will continue to achieve is to place barriers against the anti-democratic, regressive, materialist, anti-social forces that open their jaws to the test of fire in our cosmopolitan streets, bridges of passage to all sorts of commerce."[20] The new Universidad de Panamá affirmed the Panamanian government's commitment to progressive values and reflected its national ambitions with an architectural style whose themes were universal, devoid of local influences. Panamanian identity was based on a sense of national destiny determined by its geography as the path between the seas. The absence of overt local or regional expression in the International Style architecture at the Universidad de Panamá was perfectly suited to the motivation of a country longing to transcend its ambiguous identity and become the world's most important international crossroads. Rejecting what they regarded as the compromises of the neo-Spanish colonial and American neoclassical idioms, the architects of the new Universidad de Panamá embraced international modernism to free their country from a future defined by its colonial past.

3

Topography and Ideology

The Museum of Modern Art and the Helicoide de la Roca de Tarpeya

IVÁN GONZÁLES, JOSÉ ROSAS, AND RENÉ DAVIDS

During the twentieth century the demolition and reconstruction of blighted urban areas in developed and developing countries alike was motivated by visions of social transformation. Two buildings designed in the 1950s for Caracas, Venezuela—the Museo de Arte Moderno de Caracas and the Helicoide de la Roca de Tarpeya—exemplify the notion that these objectives could also be achieved through the construction of new buildings on empty land with designs informed by progressive ideals of international modernism.

The process of urban renewal as practiced in Caracas was exemplified by the destruction of the impoverished neighborhood of El Silencio in 1944 to make way for a new development consisting of seven megastructure housing blocks designed by Carlos Raúl Villanueva, a Venezuelan architect born and trained in Europe.[1] Replacing plans for a costly, impractical ceremonial space conceived in 1939 by the French urban planner Maurice Rotival during the dictatorship of Eleazar López Contreras, the housing development was a symbolic gesture of commitment to social welfare and constitutional reform by the government of General Isaías Medina Angarita after it won a national election in 1941.[2] Following a coup in 1952, the government of General Marcos Pérez Jiménez came to power and initiated a series of massive public infrastructure projects not merely to improve the quality of urban life but to act as a potent civilizing force that would transform Venezuela's topography as well as its social fabric with progressive ideals.[3] The coup was touted by the regime as the beginning of a new era, and the inauguration of grandiose projects became an annual ritual through which General Pérez Jiménez sought to validate the legitimacy of his regime with a presentation of its tangible achievements as the fulfillment of the national interest. During the five years before the regime was toppled in January 1958 by a popular uprising, Venezuela became the most modernized nation in Latin America.

The rapid transformation of Venezuelan society and the urban landscape of Caracas was made possible by the discovery of vast offshore petroleum reserves in the early twentieth century, after which its economic base quickly shifted from subsistence farming to petroleum extraction. Throughout the 1950s, Venezuela had the highest growth rate based on annual GDP in all of South America and one of the highest in the world.[4] Between 1950 and 1957, ordinary oil revenue and government income grew steadily. The accelerating pace of internal migration from the countryside and immigration from abroad expanded the boundaries of Caracas until it fully occupied the valley and spread into the surrounding foothills, transforming an agricultural landscape into a rapidly urbanizing metropolis, a materialization of the Pérez Jiménez government's vision of the city's role as a mediator between the agrarian society surrounding it and the developed cultures of the modern world (figure 3.1).

The new infrastructure of Caracas built in the 1940s and 1950s would elicit high praise in the popular press and international architecture publications: "With its admirable mountain-backed site and spectacular cloudscapes Caracas already provided a more advanced sketch of the modern city than even São Paulo," wrote Henry-Russell Hitchcock in 1955.[5] In 1957, the following comparison appeared in *Time* magazine: "Manhattan has its skyscrapers, Paris its Eiffel tower, but the hilltops of Caracas in Venezuela will soon be capped with a pair of architectural shapes that are calculated to match any man-made wonders anywhere."[6] The two buildings referenced in the quote, Oscar Niemeyer's unbuilt project for the Museo de Arte Moderno and the Helicoide de la Roca de Tarpeya shopping center, advanced the reputation of Caracas as the capital of Latin American modernism. A new architecture responsive to the local topography helped to establish its progressive urban identity.

Figure 3.1. Current view of the Caracas Valley from Cerro de Avila, Caracas, Venezuela. Photo by René Davids, 2006.

Museo de Arte Moderno (MAM)

Designed in 1954, Oscar Niemeyer's Museo de Arte Moderno (MAM) was to be built in southeast Caracas on land belonging to the old hacienda of Colinas de Bello Monte, a spectacular site in what was considered to be among the most privileged locations in the city, a "hanging suburb," like a theater balcony, from which to observe and to be observed.[7] The cultural acropolis intended to crown the summit of this exclusive hillside enclave of single-family homes would include an open-air amphitheater built into the slope, a sculpture garden, and the MAM. Developer Inocente Palacios, the owner of an important art collection, and Gustavo Ferrero Tamayo, the planning director of the Ministry of Public Works, first offered the commission to Mies van der Rohe. He declined to accept it because of his workload; it was subsequently offered to Niemeyer. The involvement of celebrated architects reflected the existence of a marketing strategy intended to establish both the Colinas de Bello Monte and Caracas as international cultural landmarks.[8] Gio Ponti, then the editor of the influential Italian magazine *Domus* who had also been considered for the museum commission, regarded the metropolis as an international event and a universal feat.[9]

Niemeyer's early sketches for the MAM revealed his unwillingness to build into the hill, as well as his awareness of both the poetic possibilities and practical limitations of the site. His proposal for an inverted pyramid was intended to minimize the museum's impact on the surface of the land

and maximize its visual impact when viewed from the city below. Niemeyer admired the formal simplicity of the pyramids, standing against the vast horizontal plane of the Sahara Desert.[10] And he believed that the Caracas Valley and the surrounding mountains deserved an equally imposing form: the museum had to generate "maximum impact even when seen from long distances, something that would in daring purity stand out against the landscape."[11] Even had its form been unremarkable, Niemeyer's choice of reinforced concrete construction, a new technology at the time, would have ensured iconic status for the museum. A 90-meter-long bridge at the third level supported by inverted catenary cables would provide access, reinforcing the impression that the building was only lightly anchored to the slope. Upon entering the museum, the contrast between its massive, seemingly solid volume and cavernous interior was intended to inspire a sense of awe; visitors would then either ascend to its upper levels, including the central gallery, or descend to a 25-meter-square auditorium and other services, the only areas of the building that would actually make contact with the ground (figures 3.2 and 3.3).

Figure 3.2. Modern Art Museum (MAM), Caracas. Architect Oscar Niemeyer, 1955. Photo courtesy of the Artists Rights Society (ARS), New York / AUTVIS, São Paulo.

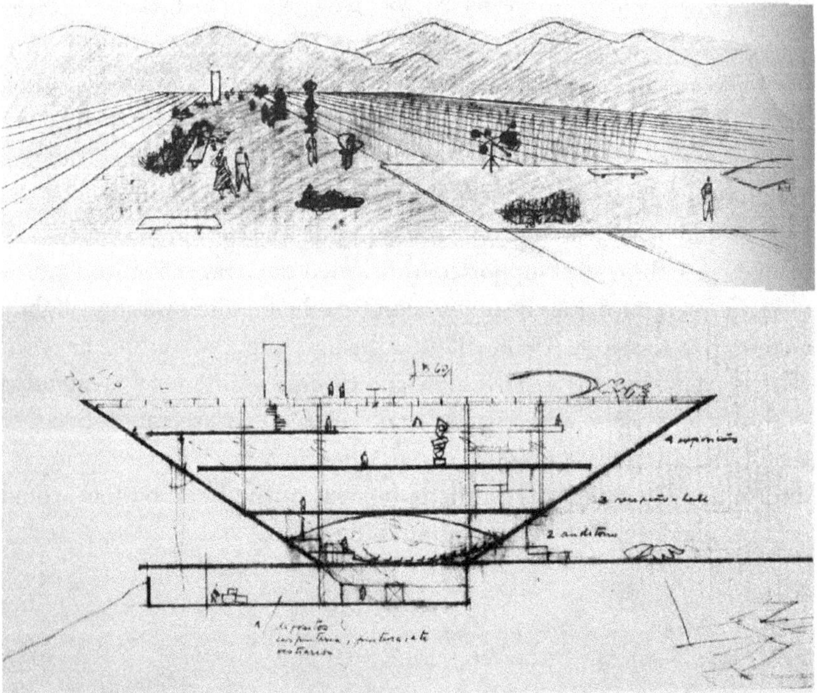

Figure 3.3. MAM sketch view from the top and cross section. Photo courtesy of the Artists Rights Society (ARS), New York / AUTVIS, São Paulo.

The 30-meter-high museum culminated in a 100-meter-square roof with a grid of mechanically controlled louvers that filtered the light, interrupted only by a 10 × 100 meter sculpture terrace. The free-form main exhibition gallery mezzanine was suspended from the steel beams of the roof structure. Its exceptional inverted form and intended visibility linked the MAM to Frank Lloyd Wright's Guggenheim Museum in New York, conceived in 1943 and finished after Wright's death in 1959.[12] As soon as they walk through the front doors of the Guggenheim, visitors are confronted with a huge interior space that swirls upward to a high domed ceiling, but its introverted facade deliberately conceals the soaring drama of the interior.[13] The Guggenheim's spiraling ramp embodied the evolutionary concept first used by Le Corbusier in his design for the Musée Mondial in Paris (1929), based on the idea that the art of the past had meaning only if explained in evolutionary terms.[14] The inverted conical volume of the Guggenheim exemplified Wright's lifelong interest in archetypes such as the ziggurat, first expressed in his project for the Gordon Strong Automobile Objective (1924–25), a building intended to complete the mountain on which it sat (figure 3.4).

By inverting both the ziggurat and the pyramid, Wright and Niemeyer designed interior museum spaces that expanded upward and outward, producing a feeling of spatial and formal lightness, simultaneously achieving continuity with the past and a break from it.[15] While Niemeyer's inverted pyramid did not contain a spiraling movement, its form was intended to suggest growth ascending toward the light, and the inversion

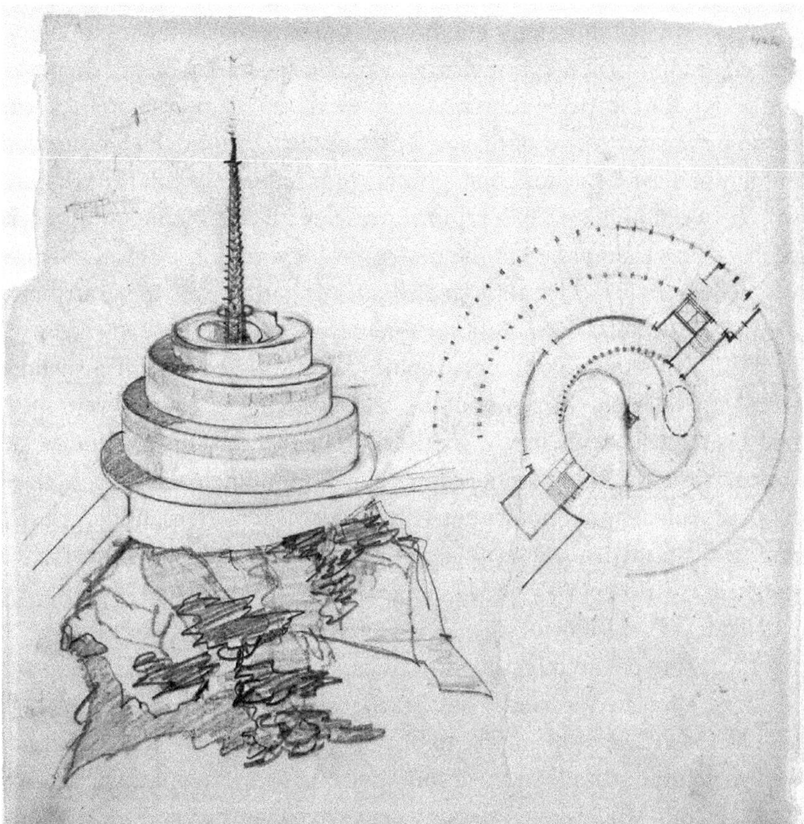

Figure 3.4. Gordon Strong Automobile Objective project for Sugarloaf Mountain, MD. Architect Frank Lloyd Wright, 1925. Reproduced with permission from the Frank Lloyd Wright Foundation, Archives MAM / Avery Architectural and Fine Arts Library, Columbia University. All rights reserved.

of a formal archetype also signified a break from the social and economic disparities prevalent throughout Latin America.[16] A similar although more understated strategy to express a sense of progressive upward movement while maintaining continuity with tradition was employed by Le Corbusier in his only proposal for the city of Caracas, the 1951 funerary monument for General Carlos Delgado-Chalbaud, which used asymmetry and unconventional copper cladding to counter the massive appearance traditionally associated with pyramidal funerary monuments.[17]

Both Wright and Niemeyer devised a potent formal strategy for engaging in the debates about monumentality that took place in the 1940s, each claiming that modernism's charge in the postwar years would be the reorganization of community life through the planning and design of civic centers, monumental ensembles, and public spectacles.[18] For Niemeyer, the design for the MAM represented a new direction away from the more complex organic forms of his earlier years, such as those he had used in Pampulha near Belo Horizonte. But his preoccupation with the relationship between built and natural form was a recurring theme in his work, perhaps best exemplified in the design for his own house at Canoa, near Rio de Janeiro, in which topography and vegetation were integrated into a fluid architectural composition.[19] Niemeyer's architecture evolved by responding directly to local topographic conditions, yielding forms whose simplicity reflected the power of the landscapes on which they were sited, and his formal vocabulary was directly influenced by his mentor, Lucio Costa. Costa believed that the expression of monumentality was induced by nature and should not "ignore the part played by trees, undergrowth, and fields in the natural setting," and that modern urbanism was distinguished "by incorporating the bucolic into the monumental."[20]

Niemeyer's design for the MAM prefigured his work several years later as principal architect for the Brazilian national capital of Brasilia, a commission he received from Brazil's president Juscelino Kubitchek. The MAM reflected his desire to challenge the established architectural and structural orthodoxies with buildings that appeared to be tenuously balanced but which simultaneously conveyed a sense of permanence and stability, a recurring paradox in his work that he would perfect in the designs for Brasilia. Although he did not regard his architecture as directly expressive of his political views, Niemeyer's challenging formal explorations went hand in hand with his lifelong commitment to social justice and opposition to the inequities present in many Latin American societies: "What bothers me is not life's rough edges, but the tremendous suffering of the destitute confronted with the indifferent smiles of the well-to-do." In *The Curves of Time*, Niemeyer wrote: "I was always something of a rebel. Having left behind all the old prejudices of my Catholic family, I saw the world as unjust and unacceptable. Poverty was spreading as if it was only natural and inescapable. I joined the Communist Party and embraced the thinking of Marx, as I still do today. But life brings both joy and sorrow, and as unprotected citizens all we can do is move ahead, laughing and crying in this harsh world. . . . I do not know why I have always designed large public buildings, but because these buildings do not always serve the functions of social justice, I try to make them beautiful and spectacular so that the poor can stop to look at them and be touched and enthused. As an architect that is all I can do."

Comparisons of the design for the MAM with other midcentury architecture in Caracas reveal that Niemeyer's interest in the relationship of buildings with site topography and his subtle and sensitive treatment of the ground plane were unusual. The housing project 23 de Enero, forty 15-story superblocks designed between 1955 and 57 by the architects Carlos Raúl Villanueva, José Manuel Mijares, Carlos Brando, and José Hoffman of the Taller de Arquitectura del Banco Obrero (TABO), was built on level building pads cut into the hillsides, and the housing blocks had no connection with the landscape other than their foundations. The architects' failure to exploit design opportunities presented by the sloping terrain with circulation elements such as entrances at various levels or access to roof terraces from outside locations resulted in buildings indistinguishable from those built on flat land in many places around the world. The 23 de Enero housing blocks were intended to replace the *ranchos* or local shantytowns, which despite their substandard living conditions were adapted organically to the topography and often fostered a strong sense of community among the residents.[21] Locally the superblocks of 23 de Enero were regarded as symbols of economic progress rather than successful living environments, and they were deserving of the criticism delivered by planner Francis Violich that monuments designed in a modern idiom were often accorded more attention in the design press than those responsive to the needs of the public such as social housing (figure 3.5).[22]

Figure 3.5. Contemporary view of 23 de Enero superblocks, Caracas. Architect Carlos Raúl Villanueva and Taller de Arquitectura del Banco Obrero, 1955–58. Photo by René Davids, 2006.

Helicoide de la Roca de Tarpeya

The explosive growth of middle-class suburbs in outlying areas of Caracas during the 1950s and the rising popularity of the automobile stimulated a demand for consumer goods in locations well beyond the traditional shopping precincts of its urban core.[23] Because of its proximity to a new expressway, the Autopista del Valle, which linked modern suburban developments and older central city neighborhoods with the interior of the country, the Helicoide de la Roca de Tarpeya was ideally situated to serve the rapidly expanding population of Caracas. When planners and shopping mall developers envisioned this new kind of consumption-oriented community center in the United States, they set out to perfect the concept of downtown, not to obliterate it. It is easy to overlook this visionary dimension and focus only on the commercial motivation of developers and investors, but they also believed that they were participating in a rationalization of consumption and in creating a community no less significant than the way highway engineers were improving transportation.[24]

Designed by three young Venezuelan architects—Dirk Bornhorst, Jorge Romero Gutierrez, and Pedro Neuberger—in its original version the Helicoide contained 360 shops, exhibition areas for industrial products, offices, an owners club, a television studio, a childcare center, and a large exhibition hall, a combination of programs that seemed to fulfill the vision of a shopping mall as a center for community life (figures 3.6–3.9).

Above: Figure 3.6. Proyecto Helicoide under construction. Architects Jorge Romero Gutierrez, Pedro Neuberger, and Dirk Bornhorst, 1958–61. Photo courtesy of Proyecto Helicoide / Archivo Bornhorst.

Left: Figure 3.7. Proyecto Helicoide under construction. Photo courtesy of Proyecto Helicoide / Archivo Bornhorst.

Figure 3.8. Proyecto Helicoide under construction. Photo courtesy of Proyecto Helicoide / Archivo Bornhorst.

Figure 3.9. Proyecto Helicoide. Photo courtesy of Nelson Garrido.

The building was carved into the hill in the form of a double spiral so that the roofs of one shopping level served as the parking areas for the next level up. Six ramps 4 kilometers long, for vehicular circulation, and the equivalent of 3 linear kilometers of exhibition space were built. Pedestrian circulation followed the same upward spiraling route through the building's interior as the automobiles. The outermost ramp contained approximately sixty shops at a 2.5 percent gradient, and the other five ramps each contained fewer.

The Helicoide was constructed through a series of massive excavations of the rocky hillside and divided into four zones separated by vertical circulation nodes and service areas containing elevators, escalators, information desks, television screens, and public service facilities.[25] The articulation of the ascending and descending spirals was resolved at the building's summit with an *S* curve that allowed traffic to flow in one direction with no intersections. The grand cupola on top, designed by Buckminster Fuller, was similar to Wright's design for the Guggenheim, as was its spiraling movement up and around the hill. Like the MAM, the Helicoide also resembles Wright's Gordon Strong Automobile Objective project, his first spiral building to fully integrate a roadway within a continuous ramp of space[26] and another Wright project that explored this concept, the Point Park Civic Center (1947), designed for the site in Pittsburgh where the confluence of the Monongahela and Allegheny Rivers becomes the Ohio River. Like the Helicoide, these buildings celebrated the synthesis of formal archetypes and automobile technology.

In his introduction to the catalog of the *Visionary Architecture* exhibition held at New York's Museum of Modern Art in 1961, which included both the Point Park Civic Center project as well as the Helicoide, Arthur Drexler wrote: "Visionary architecture is an architecture unhampered by technical details and un-compromised by the whims of patrons or the exigencies of finance, politics, and customs."[27] For Drexler this architecture could be classified in three categories: buildings in which technological virtuosity was exploited for its own sake, buildings in some way related to the road, and buildings associated with the symbol of the mountain. Among the latter was the "Ideal City" project by Jean Claude Mazet, which took the form of a truncated cone; the Helicoide fit all three of Drexler's categories.

After the fall of the Pérez Jiménez dictatorship in 1958, political support for both the MAM and the Helicoide declined. The MAM was never built, and work on the Helicoide ceased in 1961. It was abandoned and taken over by squatters before being transformed into a police station and later a detention camp for political prisoners of the Hugo Chávez regime. The locus of Latin American modernism shifted to Brasilia, where Niemeyer was soon to develop the ideas he had begun to explore a decade earlier in Caracas.

Conclusion

In 1954, renowned architect Gio Ponti wrote in the magazine *Domus* that Caracas was in an excellent position to become the world capital of modern architecture because as a new metropolis, it wasn't dependent on the legacy of cultural capital accumulated over time. Ponti believed that new architecture and building technologies made it possible for great modern cities to be created from scratch, but he failed to recognize that cities comprise not only buildings but also the ground on which they stand and the history and memories of the civilizations that produce them.[28] Soon afterwards the new capital of Brasilia, built mainly between 1960 and 1964, inherited Caracas's position of preeminence as the "most modern city in South America." Brasilia was designed and built on a nearly flat, mostly uninhabited savanna on the assumption that a modern, economically self-sufficient, and socially progressive city could be created instantaneously where there had been only empty land. The surrounding emptiness provided a stark contrast with the setting of Rio de Janeiro, the previous national capital, whose history of settlement extended back over four centuries to the early sixteenth century. While the prospect of starting from scratch has retained its almost universal appeal, sites believed to be empty are still subject to cultural imperatives, and buildings, even great ones, are not sufficient in themselves to create successful cities.

The architecture of the past is often identified with oppressive, disreputable social structures, and it provides an easily accessible target for those opposed to their injustices. During the twentieth century in many Latin American cities, it was the hope and belief of many politicians, planners, and architects that modern architecture when preceded by large-scale urban demolitions could replace the physical traces of a discredited political regime with new structures that would usher in an era of improved and healthy living environments, equality, and freedom. The Helicoide and the Museo de Arte Moderno embodied a variant of this progressive narrative by inverting existing formal archetypes and infusing built form with dynamic movement. "Oil is magic and induces fantasies," wrote Venezuelan playwright José Ignacio Cabruja,[29] and in mid-twentieth century Caracas, the magic-induced dreams of social and economic progress materialized as monumental works of architecture.

Although both projects were privately financed, the MAM and Helicoide bolstered the "New National Ideal," the ideology of a dictatorship that put a higher premium on national unity and material and technological progress than on personal and political freedom or improved social and economic conditions.[30] Propped up by a booming economy based on revenue from oil extraction, Pérez Jiménez declared his ideal image of the nation to be the house he had built as a monumental construction, a pronouncement that was in itself emblematic of a patriarchal notion of politics and a self-serving view of social and economic progress. Pérez Jiménez sought to improve the lot of the Venezuelan population by redefining politics as the process of transforming the nation into a physical construct and using emblems of modernity as instruments of political control, confining them within the imposing walls of a nation to be built like a dictator's castle writ large.[31] "The public good and therefore the nation's interest is the sum total of the work we have built."[32] Not for the last time was the progressive image of modernism used for propaganda by a regime that brutally persecuted its political opponents and denied basic personal freedoms to Venezuela's citizens.[33]

4

São Paulo's Topography and the Utopian Democracy

ANGELO BUCCI AND RENÉ DAVIDS

Brazil's two major cities provide a study of historical and geographical contrasts. Rio de Janeiro is the national epicenter of social life as well as a city of spectacular topography. Its rival, São Paulo, the commercial and financial hub of the country, has grown from a small village 800 meters above sea level into a dynamic, modern metropolis steeply dissected by the river Tietê and its tributaries. Travel brochures place an emphasis on São Paulo's rich diversity rather than its topographical qualities, while Rio is widely known for the sensuality of its natural landscape.[1] But as is the case with Rio, São Paulo's topography, with its deep, quiet ravines, plateaus, bridges, and stunning coastal hillsides, has served as a major source of inspiration for architects.

The architectural styles within these cities also set them apart. Rio was the birthplace of what has been identified as the Brazilian style, a regional variation of the international modern movement. Oscar Niemeyer, whose work consists largely of undulating, exuberant forms that mimic the contours of the city's hillsides, most prominently represents this style. In the early 1940s, at Pampulha, an outpost of Belo Horizonte, Niemeyer had already contradicted the modernist dogmas of form and function with the plasticity made possible with reinforced concrete. "I was attracted to the curve," said Niemeyer of the fluid, sensuous contours enabled by the emerging technologies. "I deliberately disregarded the right angle and rational architecture that is designed using rulers and squares, to boldly enter the world of curves and straight lines offered by reinforced concrete."

These new forms that became the emblematic signatures of his work reflect not only the technological advances of his time but also the inspirational source of his homeland. "This deliberate protest arose from the environment in which I lived, with its white beaches, its huge mountains, its old baroque churches, and its beautiful suntanned women."[2] Some scholars have questioned the source of inspiration for the curves in Niemeyer's buildings, as he did not use those associations at the beginning of his career.[3] But whether he understood the origins of his inspiration after an extended period of reflection or eventually came to believe his own narrative, it became the official explanation for the sensuality of his work.[4]

Rejecting Niemeyer's modernist formal experimentation, a movement known as New Brutalism influenced São Paulo's leading architectural practitioners during the 1950s. These architects designed with a predilection for simple forms, raw, unfinished materials, and exposed service pipes, expressions of moderation they regarded as appropriate for a developing country. This reductive aesthetic promoted the belief that by not establishing a "Brazilian identity" through architecture, designers could preserve the virtuosity of the existing Brazilian cultural identity. Vilanova Artigas, the most prominent São Paulo architect of his generation, openly excluded European and American influences from his own work. He claimed that the "Brazilian style" was an imperialist expression, created and promoted by the Americans and Le Corbusier to serve their own interests.[5] Although traces of western influences are evident throughout his work, Vilanova Artigas continued his contradictory condemnations of Euro-American styles, claiming that the formal restraint characteristic of New Brutalism was a politically motivated socio-architectural technique. Artigas's intention was to prevent the establishment of a Brazilian style that would inevitably be subjected to the degradation of the western value system, which he believed would benefit Brazilian citizens of all classes. However, Artigas's architectural commissions mostly benefited Brazilian elites, rather than the many dispossessed, impoverished citizens of São Paulo.

The native population of São Paulo originally settled in the plateau region, alongside the Anhangabaú or "the devil's hideout," a branch of the Tietê River that cut through the gorge. In 1554, the Jesuits founded a village and religious mission on the borders of this gorge. The Anhangabaú defined the western edge of the village of São Paulo, and the Tamanduateí River, another Tietê tributary, determined its eastern boundary. Extensive

Figure 4.1. Anhangabaú Park and the Viaduto do Chá (Tea). Image from Francisco Prestes Maia, *Estudo de um Plano de Avenidas para a Cidade de São Paulo*, 1930.

panoramic views could be enjoyed from the edge of the plateau, as it did not rise back up on the opposite bank.

The village of São Paulo remained within the boundaries of this naturally isolated and protected plateau until the end of the eighteenth century. Transportation of goods and people by mule across the 20-meter deep, 150-meter wide Anhangabaú was slow and extremely inefficient. Once the need for protection had vanished, the gorge became a major development obstacle to efficient transportation infrastructure. In 1892, Jules Martin, a French printmaker, would assemble the first industrial steel bridge over the river and through the gorge. With a clear sight-path, the viaduct contrasted São Paulo's narrow canyon streets. This marked the beginning of São Paulo's expansion, which transformed a small town into the megalopolis that it is today.

The construction of the viaduct, called the "Tea" (*Viaduto do Chá*) after the tea plantations in the river valley, stimulated new development on the eastern side of the Anhangabaú. Easily colonized because it was perceived to have a good climate by virtue of the high altitude, this newly developed area provided a place for the elites to seek refuge from the dense and insalubrious former town center. The nearby municipal theater became the center of the city's social life, but the most important new amenity was the Anhangabaú Park, designed by French landscape architect Joseph Bouvard in 1911 (figure 4.1). Devised to integrate the valley gorge into the overall urban structure of the metropolis, the park (inaugurated in 1917) was a new spatial setting in which São Paulo's elites could display their European sophistication. It also provided a new center associated with a progressive, dynamic, and technologically advanced republican era, and its residents distanced themselves from the old colonial town center associated with the Brazilian monarchy whose reign had ended in 1889. Despite its smaller size, the new park was often compared to New York's Central Park, an indication of the civic pride it inspired among the citizens.[6]

With the transfer of capital from the coffee industry to the industrial manufacturing sector, already growing during the first decades of the twentieth century, the park provided a much-needed set of green lungs to refresh an increasingly densifying city. Between 1905 and 1930, São Paulo's population tripled.[7] Claude Lévi-Strauss reported that in 1935, "the people of São Paulo liked to boast that their city was expanding at the rate of one house every hour."[8] Planning debates centered on the rapid pace and unregulated nature of growth attracted reputable experts such as Le Corbusier, who sketched planning proposals during his short visit to São Paulo in 1929. Architect Francisco Prestes Maia published the *Estudo de um plano de avenidas para a cidade de São Paulo* (Study for a plan for the avenues of São Paulo) in association with João Florence de Ulhôa Cintra, around the same time as Le Corbusier's visit.[9]

Influenced by Joseph Stuebben, George Herrold, Harland Bartholomew, Daniel Burnham, and French traffic specialist Eugène Hénard, Prestes Maia produced a study aimed at rationalizing traffic, enlarging the central business district, and developing an identity appropriate for the city's growing commercial importance. The plan consisted of a radial scheme intersected by concentric circular rings located at the center of São Paulo between the São Francisco and Santa Ifigenia viaducts. The proposal modified Joseph Bouvard's picturesque winding park at the Anhangabaú with a formal layout in which monumental neoclassical buildings that simultaneously operated as viaducts and majestic palaces marked the termination of each axis.

The focal point of the newly proposed master plan was a space that Prestes Maia identified as São Paulo's main visitors hall (la sala de visitas),

Figure 4.2. Viaduto do Chá. Image from Francisco Prestes Maia, *Estudo de um Plano de Avenidas para a Cidade de São Paulo*, 1930.

a closed-off area that formed an urban room within the city. However, Maia's proposal failed to acknowledge the inherent grandeur of the Anhangabaú as a vital part of the region's character (figure 4.2). To materialize this room, the original steel Viaduto do Chá would have to be demolished and replaced with a bridge that Prestes Maia argued "had to be rebuilt with a grand, slim, monumental, reinforced concrete arch that unlike the current structure of crossed bars would not obstruct the view."[10] Made up of clean, simple lines, the original viaduct was hardly the obstruction Prestes Maia claimed that it was. Maia's influence nevertheless led to the replacement of the original bridge with a design by Elisario Bahiana, the winner of a national competition of 1938. Prestes Maia's neoclassical approach was so de-contextual and universal in character that it would have been a better fit at Daniel Burnham's 1893 Chicago World's Columbian Exposition than its location in São Paulo. Maia's indifference to São Paulo's landscape was most clearly exemplified through his attempt to force a traffic network into the circular loop of his idealistic diagram, blatantly disregarding the original triangular form of the plateau (figure 4.3).

Taking inspiration from the undulating São Paulo plateau divided by rivers and canyons, Le Corbusier demonstrated that a deferential

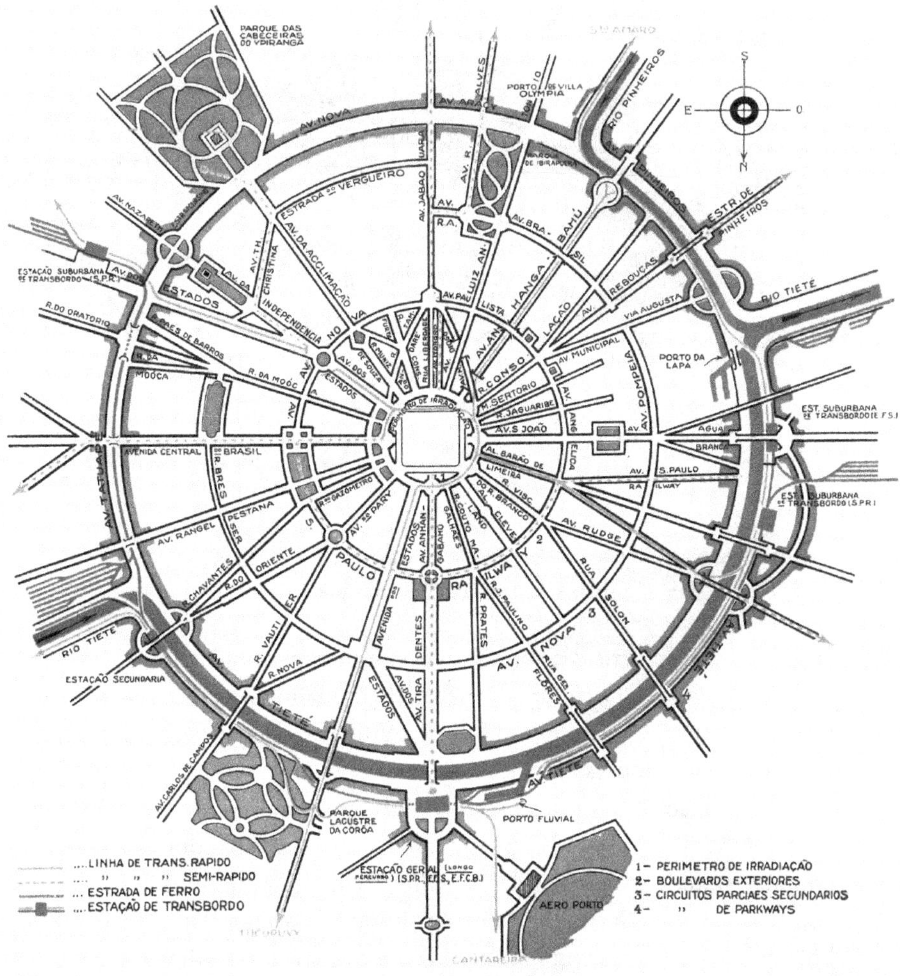

Fig. 37 — Schema theorico de São Paulo

De conformidade com o presente estudo. É caracteristicamente um schema radial-perimetral.

Figure 4.3. Organizational diagram for São Paulo. Image from Francisco Prestes Maia, *Estudo de um plano de avenidas para a cidade de São Paulo*, 1930.

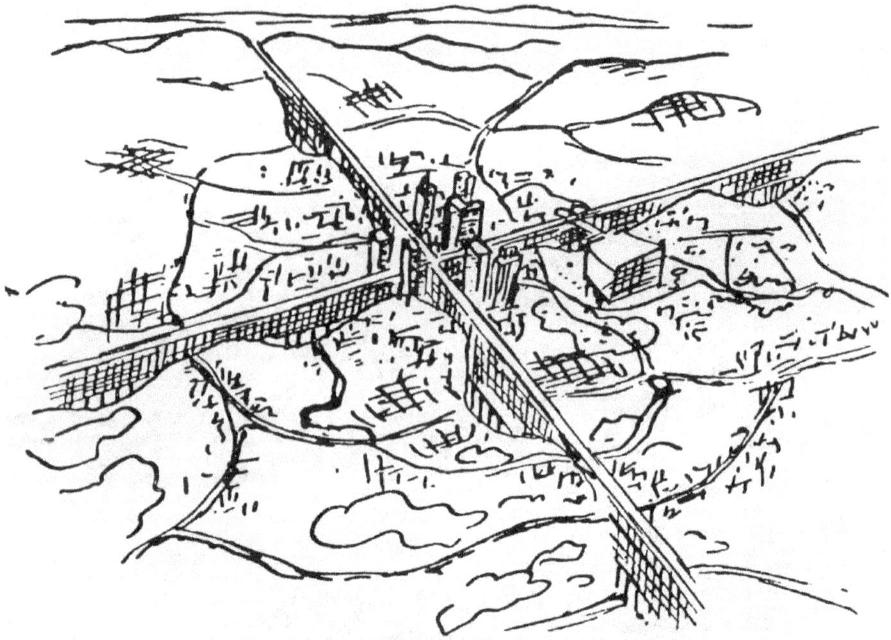

Figure 4.4. Sketch proposal for São Paulo. Le Corbusier, 1929. Courtesy of F.L.C. / ADAGP, Paris / Artists Rights Society (ARS), New York.

approach to an existing landscape was not incompatible with bold design and simple geometry (figure 4.4). Sketched during his short visit in 1929, Le Corbusier's design proposal for São Paulo was structured by two 45-kilometer long viaducts intersecting at a right angle that connected two hills from summit to summit. The straight horizontal lines of his sketches represent vast expressways coming into the city, a major component of his plan. He stated: "You won't fly over the city in your automobiles, but you will drive over it. Do not build expensive arches to hold up your bridges, but carry your bridges on reinforced concrete structures that will contain offices in the center of the city and homes in the outskirts." Le Corbusier's plan left the bottoms of the valleys unbuilt and available for public spaces such as recreational areas and parking. "You will plant palm trees in them, sheltered from the wind. Besides, you have already created the beginning of parks for the trees and spaces for automobiles in the center of town."[11] Unlike Prestes Maia's proposal, Le Corbusier's was a vision for São Paulo based on an imaginative leap which acknowledged the existing conditions.

Le Corbusier's proposal revealed traces of other planning ideas, such as the "linear city" proposed by Arturo Soria (1892). Soria believed that the development of efficient mass transit systems capable of transporting passengers across vast distances and monumental structures, such as the Roman aqueduct, was crucial to the success of building large cities. But while the aqueduct was built using structural masonry arches that allowed for visual permeability, Le Corbusier's sketches display two monolithic buildings that intersect at different levels. Although the boldness and scale of Le Corbusier's vision condemned it to remain an idea on paper, the influence of his proposal was arguably more widespread than Prestes Maia's. Though the latter was able to fully realize his plans for the city while serving as mayor from 1938 through 1945 and again in 1961 for another four years, Le Corbusier's unrealized proposals continued to exist as seminal influences.

One of the buildings most heavily influenced by Le Corbusier was the São Paulo Art Museum (MASP). The museum was commissioned by Pietro Maria Bardi in 1957 and designed by his wife, Lina Bo Bardi, an architect who emigrated from Italy to Brazil in 1945. Completed in 1968, the museum was located on Avenida Paulista, which had become São Paulo's primary city street. The building consisted of an immense glass box that rested between two thin slabs of concrete and housed a collection of paintings by prominent artists from around the world. The glass box, inspired by Mies van der Rohe's Crown Hall, appeared to hang weightlessly from two bright, orthogonal concrete arches, hovering 70 meters above the ground. The museum framed the Trianon Park and Avenida Nove de Julho, a multi-lane thoroughfare in the Anhangabaú valley that ran 100 feet below the museum across the Avenida Paulista. The exhibitions, contemporary art, and the auditorium were located in the subterranean portion of the museum. Between the airborne crystalline box and the half-buried subterranean portion was a void that served as a public square.[12] This space maintained a constant tension between the two areas it connected: the floating box and the subterranean galleries.

While Mies van der Rohe's influence was most apparent, Le Corbusier's was perhaps most profound. Bardi inaugurated his directorial debut in 1950 with an exhibition of Le Corbusier's work, coordinated by Lina Bo Bardi. In fact, the Bardis' first built work, "The Glass House" (1951), contained many elements in common with Le Corbusier's Villa Savoye at Poissy (1929), including the arrival entrance below pilotis, the floating volume above the ground, the view of the surrounding landscape, and a white stucco finish. Rather than simply incorporating the forms of Le Corbusier's structures, Bo Bardi's later design for the MASP denotes Le Corbusier's influence on a more conceptual level. Both Le Corbusier and Bo Bardi proposed that their buildings be recognized as landscape registers, and the latter's achievement was apparent as one traversed the canyon when moving in section from the top to the bottom of the museum. More significantly, both projects featured intersections as prominent design elements. Bo Bardi's was implied by the flow of the Nove de Julho to the Parque Trianon in one direction, and the intersection of the museum in the other, while Le Corbusier's plan centered on the physical interpenetration of the two intersecting buildings. The most striking element in Bo Bardi's work was the powerful idea of a building that extended over the plaza possessing the metaphorical significance of a bridge that was a threshold as well as a pause on a larger continuum.

The idea of a bridge as an interval in a field became a recurring theme in Paulista architecture. While the landscape of the plateau intersected by river gorges must be considered part of the inspiration, other factors contributed. Architects were being trained at the University of São Paulo (USP), an institution that continued the engineering tradition of the Polytechnic School that preceded it with an emphasis on structural form and engineering that was infused into the architecture curriculum. The availability of reinforced concrete, a common and relatively cheap construction material, further inspired the bourgeoning penchant for strong structural expression.

These elements were certainly present in the work of João Batista Vilanova Artigas, considered the most influential Paulista architect of his generation. Educated at the Polytechnic School before the founding of the University of São Paulo, Vilanova Artigas received formal training as an engineer from a cadre of instructors that included important conservative personalities such as Prestes Maia. Initially influenced by Frank Lloyd Wright and later by Le Corbusier, Vilanova Artigas's formal vocabulary became geometrically simpler as his career progressed. Artigas firmly believed that architecture could be used as an instrument of political and social transformation. By maintaining a formally restrained language and by staying true to his materials, he thought he was advancing a new construction ethic appropriate for Brazil's stage of development.

For Artigas, buildings were not objects but rather like pauses in the landscape. Many of his projects reflect his exploration of the potential for continuity of the built and natural environments. His works often included level changes, double- and triple-height voids, and the use of mezzanines linked by ramps in order to instill a sense of accessibility throughout the space. Artigas's built works incorporated their topographical context through a substitution of columns for load-bearing walls below large free-standing roofs that established fluid connections between the inside and outside.

Artigas added a territorial dimension to his architectural proposals when he claimed that the opposite bank of the river could become habitable space by constructing a bridge. He added that the train station and the airport were not discrete buildings but "instruments," or bridges that enabled space to become universal. For Artigas, the bridge illustrated the idea that architecture could exist simply as a subtly distinct episode on a spatial continuum: "From his dwelling, primitive man would have crossed his no less primitive threshold to take possession of a larger space."[13]

Artigas would repeatedly use the idea of the bridge in his built work. In his boathouse project for the Santa Paula Yacht Club (figure 4.5) he

Figure 4.5. Santa Paula Yacht Club, São Paulo. Architect Vilanova Artigas, 1961. Photo by René Davids, 2008.

created a boat shelter whose roof could be used as a bridge structure supported by two pylons. The Faculty of Architecture and Urbanism at the University of São Paulo, which he designed in 1961 and finished in 1969, is the clearest example of the bridge concept employed to maintain spatial continuity in the environment. The project used ramps that functioned as bridges and spanned the two wings of the building, and a floating roof covered the entire structure. In order to streamline this space, Artigas omitted any doors from his design to allow for an uninterrupted spatial flow between the campus, the atrium, and even studio spaces (figure 4.6).

The opportunity to explore the idea of spatial continuity at the urban scale emerged for Vilanova Artigas in 1974 when the EMURB, a municipal urban planning corporation, asked him to remodel the Anhangabaú, which was seriously afflicted by incessant traffic-related accidents. The EMURB requested that the 500-meter stretch between the bridges of the Tea and the Santa Ifigenia be the site of the remodeling. Artigas chose instead to design a 13-kilometer-long area stretching from the River Tietê in the north to the Pinheiros River in the south. He selected this area because he believed that the Anhangabaú required a sense of enclosure to assume the intimacy of an established urban space. It is apparent in this proposal that Artigas valued the regional dimension represented by

Figure 4.6. University of São Paulo School of Architecture. Architect Vilanova Artigas, 1968. Photo courtesy of Nelson Kon.

Figure 4.7. Proposal for Anhangabaú Valley, São Paulo. Architect Vilanova Artigas, 1974. Image courtesy of Rosa Artigas.

the transitional character of the old riverbed. He intended to recapture the sense of monumentality of arriving in the city by adding two wide sidewalks connected by footbridges along the valley's edges. In addition to providing the city with a grand entrance, the wide pathways provided a space for local activities and leisure (figure 4.7).

Vilanova Artigas's plans for the Anhangabaú were shelved by the military dictatorship that governed Brazil from 1964 to 1984. However, the increasing traffic congestion and pedestrian accidents, partly caused by an unrelenting population increase, created pressure to resolve the enduring problems. In 1981, the EMURB and the IAB (Institute of Brazilian Architects) called for an open national competition to remodel the gorge. A team headed by Jorge Wilhelm proposed the winning design. Their scheme covered the motorway with a new concrete deck that reduced the depth of the Anhangabaú and made it twice as shallow, reducing São Paulo's most powerful topographic feature into merely a shadow of its former self. The construction of the motorway below 8 hectares of a lifeless "plaza" resolved some urban problems affecting the area by seperating traffic and pedestrians; however, it also removed the sense of enclosure and the regional pride that made the Anhangabaú the heart of São Paulo (figure 4.8).

Paulo Mendes da Rocha, a follower of Artigas, also used the landscape as his primary source of inspiration. His work pursued what he called *forca geografica* (geographic force), an ephemeral quality contained in the land. He admired Brazil's Santos Dumont Airport and compared it to the city of Venice because its elusive, indeterminate character transcended the boundaries of architecture, infrastructure, and landscape. For Mendes da Rocha, buildings in this ambiguous category can be understood not as fortified shelters but as spaces that establish subtle differentiations on a continuous path. He considered his buildings analogous to bridges or houses that "one enters through one door and exits through another."[14] Mendes da Rocha's buildings are temporary demarcations of space within a larger territory, and this quality is always present in his work.

The pavilion at the underground exit of the Praza do Patriarca is a strong example of this architectural philosophy, with a striking roof canopy hung from a steel arch that provides protection from rain and creates a pause, or interval, for travelers entering or exiting the underground station. This "pause" is conceptually a bridge, a zone differentiated within a continuous stream. Mendes da Rocha illustrates this idea most clearly in

Figure 4.8. Aerial view of Anhangabaú Valley, São Paulo. Photo courtesy of Nelson Kon.

Figure 4.9. Brazilian Museum of Sculpture, São Paulo. Architect Paulo Mendes da Rocha, 1995. Photo by René Davids, 2008.

the Brazilian Museum of Sculpture. Designed as a 12 by 60 meter orthogonal arch spanning a concrete plane that shelters the gallery, the entire museum acts as a massive public shade structure (figure 4.9). The concrete arch is placed against the main street, suggesting a fragment of Le Corbusier's sketch for São Paulo and a commentary on Bo Bardi's MASP. It is also Mendes da Rocha's own reinterpretation of Artigas's idea of the interval as an establishment of differences within the continuous space of the landscape. Mendes da Rocha believed that this notion was particularly poignant in the Americas, where land was still being settled: "Our eyes turn toward the notion of building cities in nature, establishing new rationales about the state of the waters, plains, and mountains, the spatiality of a continent, and in new horizons for our imagination in the shape and ingenuity of the things we are destined to build."[15]

Conclusion

In a financial and cultural capital where the elites avoid sharing space with the impoverished masses, the notion of an open, fluid city was at best a fragment of a utopian ideal and at worst an unrealistic form of escapism. Socially stratified and segregated, São Paulo is typified by an extreme contrast between the rich and the poor and the spaces that they inhabit. For Paulista architects, the idea of a spatial continuum represented a denunciation of the status quo and an expression of Brazil's utopian longing for an interracial dialogue and social equality. For Mendes da Rocha, "The flower of all knowledge is the city, and the architect's obligation is to imagine it for everyone so that it may bloom." Even if the idea was an illusion or an unattainable dream, the geographically conscious approach to architecture captured both the vastness of Brazil's landscape and a sincere desire to create a better world. Summarizing the spirit behind the Paulista school, Mendes da Rocha has stated: "I think it is very important that we never lose our belief in the metaphor that America is a 'New World,' where dreams and desires may one day come true. If this is lost, we have nothing left."[16] In their idealistic pursuit, Paulista architects availed themselves of the landscape in which they lived as inspiration for designing the fragments of their utopian dreams.

5

Le Corbusier, Rio de Janeiro, Topography, and Housing

A Cross-Cultural Exchange

RENÉ DAVIDS

The prevailing critical consensus on Brazilian modernism holds that from 1929 through the 1960s, an exotic regional variant of modernism flowered as the theory emanating from centers of high culture in Europe was adapted to lush tropical landscapes. Leonardo Benévolo cites the Brazilian context as representing a new area of opportunity for development of modern movement principles.[1] Implicit in Benévolo's statement is the assumption, commonly shared among critics, that culture originates in the Old World and flows to the New, an oversimplification of the complex ways in which architectural ideas, concepts, and forms develop. This chapter delves into the encounter between two worlds: the influence of dramatic New World topography and infrastructure on the work of Le Corbusier, arguably the modern movement's most influential architect, whose purist formal vocabulary of white machine-like forms was infused with a more organic, lyrical expression after a tour of South America in the late 1920s, and the delayed impact of unbuilt urban proposals Le Corbusier developed during his first visit to Rio de Janeiro on a new generation of Brazilian architects twenty some years later.

Unlike the Spanish conquistadores who controlled the rest of South America, the Portuguese colonizers of Brazil were more interested in establishing trading outposts than in imposing a new political, social, and religious order. In contrast to the abstract geometrical forms and rigid hierarchical organization of the grid and plaza towns imposed by their

Spanish counterparts, the Portuguese settlements were characterized by functional relationships and adaptation to local topography (figure 5.1). By 1891 the colonial city of Rio de Janeiro had become a destination for both internal and foreign immigration; with a population of around 500,000 and growing, it ranked among the world's largest cities. The surrounding hills left only a narrow sliver of flat swampy land for development, and the relentless pressure to expand required a series of major public works projects. During the late nineteenth and early twentieth centuries, tunnels were dug, hills demolished, and land reclaimed from Guanabara Bay. The desire to project a progressive image abroad triggered another series of urban revisions inspired by Haussmann's Paris, including construction of broad avenues, straightening and widening of existing streets, and the demolition of slums that interfered with the desired civic atmosphere. An extensive urban renewal program launched in 1922 resulted in the destruction of Morro do Castelo (Castle Hill), Rio's decaying birthplace, and the site of its oldest urban fabric. The spoils were used to build Avenida Beira Mar, an elegant coastal boulevard, and to provide enough flat land for the Centennial Exposition of 1922, celebrating a century of Brazilian independence from Portugal. The exposition featured specially designed buildings in a neocolonial style to present a new and authentically Brazilian architectural face to the world. Significantly, it was the reclamation areas around Guanabara Bay that became the face of Rio de Janeiro and the whole of Brazil because these were the first parts of the city seen from arriving ships.

In 1930, at the invitation of the mayor, the French urban planner Alfred Agache devised a master plan that would have imposed a European neoclassical order thought to be more suited to an aspiring national capital than the looser, more organic morphology of previous undertakings. In the manner of Baron Haussmann, Agache's plan would have removed economically, socially, and racially undesirable elements from Rio's most visible neighborhoods.[2] After a change of political power, Agache's plan was abandoned, and with the new government an opportunity was created to impose a socially progressive, technologically innovative architecture. Unlike the abstract monumentality that had been proposed by Agache, the new architecture would be more responsive to the existing topography and consistent with the traditions of Portuguese colonial urbanism. Modernism would achieve dominance as the new political administration's public building program was implemented, including the design

Figure 5.1. Rio de Janeiro. Photo by René Davids, 2001.

and construction of housing for the underprivileged. The new generation of urban planners and architects in Rio de Janeiro managed to shift the discourse away from the aesthetics of design to the ethics of building.[3] The new approach to planning was evident in the urban renewal scheme for Rio proposed by Le Corbusier in 1929 (figure 5.2) and given credibility later that year when the first significant modernist building in Latin America, the Ministry of Education and Health, was completed.

During Le Corbusier's first visit to South America from September through December 1929, his airplane trips over the continent prompted the creation of large urban proposals for Buenos Aires, Montevideo, São Paulo, and Rio de Janeiro. In their responsiveness to the local topography, these schemes marked a significant departure from the machine-like forms and clear distinctions between landscape and built form that had characterized his previous work. But it was his proposal for Rio inspired by the landscape of spectacular hills and the exuberant topography—Sugar Loaf Mountain, the Corcovado, Gavea, and the Gigante Tendido—that marked the strongest departure from his previous designs. "From out at sea, I saw in my mind the ample and magnificent line of buildings, crowned horizontally by the highway striking from hill to hill

Figure 5.2. Sketch for Rio de Janeiro. Le Corbusier, 1929. Courtesy of F.L.C. / ADAGP, Paris / Artists Rights Society (ARS), New York.

and stretching hands from one bay to the next."[4] The most famous of his sketches from 1932 shows a viaduct-like structure with offices and apartments underneath winding through the hills surrounding Rio in which the grid-like infrastructure of the existing city was relegated to an abstract background texture. Le Corbusier's monumental vision eliminated such traditional features of urban design as the division of land into smaller individually owned parcels in favor of a unified composition that combined buildings, landscape, and infrastructure into a synthetic whole.

When compared with the long-domesticated landscapes of most parts of Europe, the hilly terrain of eastern South America had a primitive, sensuous character that appealed to Le Corbusier; he referred to these landscapes as "violent and sublime," "something to inspire the work of man . . . to exalt his courage to provoke creative acts."[5] Their wildness exuded an explosive power he interpreted as a metaphor for the creation of the whole of the New World. Le Corbusier perceived the hills as both a backdrop against which a new order could be established and landforms that were themselves an expression of joy, at once outbursts of pleasure and foundations for the establishment of a new civilization. "You in South America are in a country both old and young; you are young nations and your race is old. Your destiny is to act now. Will you act under the despotic dark sign of hard labor? No, I hope you will act as Latins who know how to order, to regulate, to rule, to estimate, to measure, to judge, and to smile."[6]

Le Corbusier's sketch scheme proposal for Rio de Janeiro, a serpentine viaduct supported by housing on *pilotis* spanning the coastal hills, exemplifies the transformation in his work that was taking place in the late 1920s and early 1930s. By his own account, Rio's mesmerizing landscape of undulating hills and curving shorelines inspired a new urban formal aesthetic. Spanning between the hills of Santa Teresa and Santo Antonio, the monumental Aqueduto da Carioca (1723), also called the Arcos da Lapa, is one of the few surviving landmarks from the colonial era, converted to serve as a bridge for the new electric streetcars (*bonde*) in 1896. The striking 800-foot Aqueduto, among the most conspicuous built forms in Rio (figure 5.3), appears nowhere in the many powerful sketches Le Corbusier made of its topography and people, although he had flown over it. Le Corbusier's sketch scheme proposal for Rio de Janeiro in the form of a viaduct crossing Rio's hills bears an unmistakable resemblance to the

Figure 5.3. Arcos da Lapa, Rio de Janeiro. Photo by Marc Ferrez. Image courtesy of Thiele / Coleção Gilberto Ferrez / Instituto Moreira Salles Collection.

Aqueduto, but he was notorious for concealing his sources of inspiration and selectively editing his publications.

By showing both an inclination to adapt built form to the contours of the terrain and a desire to celebrate the landscape, Le Corbusier's urban sketch plan for Rio stood in marked contrast to his earlier Cartesian proposals intended for universal application such as Une Ville Contemporaine (1922) or the Plan Voisin for Paris (1925), anticipating the development of the Obus Plan (1930), a proposal for Algiers whose forms it closely resembled. Influenced by contemporary intellectual fashions such as syndicalism, which promoted the attainment of that which was natural or organic to man, the Obus Plan put forward the concept of adaptability not only as applied to the landscape but extended to include the notion of the individual building as a framework within which people could define their own identities.[7]

The first sign of the impact of his South American visit on Le Corbusier's built work can be seen in his student housing project at Cité Universitaire (later the Université Paris), the Pavillon Suisse (1932), which can also be understood as an exploration and demonstration of the principles of urbanism. Although built in a very different context to the one he had encountered in Rio, the residential slab on *pilotis* can be perceived as a fragment of a viaduct. The communal areas are located on the ground floor, and the student rooms contained in a glazed slab lifted above the ground on *pilotis*. To ensure a healthy living environment, the rectilinear residential slab was oriented toward the sun, contrasting with the curving entry and communal areas on the ground floor. Whereas the curves present in his previous buildings were geometrically precise, the walls and stairs of the lobby at the Pavillon Suisse have a fluid, sensuous quality. As if attempting to reinforce the fusion of topography and architecture, the communal area also features a photographic mural with a collage of abstract landforms. While Le Corbusier had previously used curvilinear forms in the League of Nations project (1927) and the Palais du Centrosoyus in Moscow (1929), those of the Pavillon Suisse have a biomorphic quality also present in the paintings and murals of the ground floor reception areas. The curving wall is made of rubble stone, a reflection of Le Corbusier's increasing preoccupation with nature and vernacular building materials. In the Pavillon Suisse, Le Corbusier abandoned the finish coat of white plaster applied in his earlier work and for the first time left the bare reinforced concrete with impressions from the formwork clearly exposed; stone panels, another natural material, were used on the end walls. The top floor features a solarium that provides yet another link to the natural environment and the sky. The changes in his architectural production emerged at the same time that the female figure and other natural forms appeared in his painting as *objets à réaction poetique* (objects of poetic reaction) to be distinguished from the *objets-types* (object types) of his earlier compositions.

Rio de Janeiro as imagined by Le Corbusier was never built, but his plans materialized, at least in part, in the work of Brazilian architect Affonso Eduardo Reidy. Born in 1909 to an Irish father and a Brazilian mother, Reidy was a student at the National School for Fine Arts in Rio when Le Corbusier came to visit in 1929, and like many other young Brazilian architects, he was deeply inspired by the European master's visions for Rio's future. He graduated just as the new government came to power in 1930, initiating a wave of political, social, and industrial change. In 1932, Reidy became an employee of the Federal District Government (Distrito Federal) where he would remain until shortly before his death in 1964 at the age of 55. An invitation to join the team responsible for the design of the Ministry of Education building in Rio, headed by Lucio Costa with Le Corbusier as a consultant (figure 5.4) was a life-changing experience for the young Reidy, transforming his ideas about urban space and the potential of architectural form to shape human experience.[8] As a public employee, Reidy had the opportunity to work on important civic commissions, but it was the Pedregulho housing development, built on the outskirts of Rio between 1949 and 1951, that brought him to international prominence. His wife, engineer Carmen Portinho, the director of the Department of Popular Housing in Rio, initiated the Pedregulho development, a model residential development for municipal workers who could afford the direct deduction of rent from their wages. Portinho then appointed her husband as the chief architect for the project, effectively enabling him to design it (figure 5.5).

Located near an industrial area of Rio, the Pedregulho housing development covers nearly 13 acres and consists of four apartment blocks, an elementary school, a gymnasium, a swimming pool with dressing rooms, a health center, playgrounds, a laundry, and a daycare center. The program was distributed among several building types, the most prominent of which is a roughly 850-foot long serpentine block with 272 apartments sited on a hill overlooking the rest of the complex with distant views of

Figure 5.4. Ministry of Education and Health, Rio de Janeiro. Architects Lucio Costa and Oscar Niemeyer with Le Corbusier, 1943. Photo by René Davids, 2001.

Guanabara Bay. Two other apartment buildings, both 262 feet long, are located below the serpentine form; a fourth slab was never built. Reidy chose to use rectangular sections for the residential buildings, trapezoidal sections for the service buildings, and arches for the gymnasium and swimming pool. The complex housed 478 families in apartments of various sizes, from efficiencies to duplexes with four bedrooms. The streets connecting the various buildings were reserved for pedestrians, and the Pedregulho gardens were designed by Roberto Burle-Marx, the renowned Brazilian landscape architect.[9] The main serpentine block, a seven-story

Figure 5.5. Pedrogulho housing complex, Rio de Janeiro. Architect Affonso Reidy, 1950–52. Photo by René Davids, 2001.

building without elevators, was structured so that the third floor became a sort of interior street with four floors of residential units above and two below, making the installation of expensive elevators unnecessary. By locating the main entrance on that floor, Reidy combined an interesting formal device with an effective strategy to reduce the cost of the building. The decision also enhanced the building's formal appeal by avoiding the visual monotony which would have resulted had six stories of apartments been stacked one on top of the other. The third floor was designed as a mainly open space so that it could be used as a covered playground, but it also contained the administrative offices, social services, a nursery, kindergarten, and an acoustic shell at the very end which functioned as a children's theater. Three main staircase systems connected the open floor to the other floors. Another design decision that had both an ideological and economic inspiration was the use of *pilotis* on the ground floor, one of Le Corbusier's "Five Points" of architecture that in this case also eliminated the necessity for expensive retaining walls.

Reidy designed another housing scheme in the Gavea neighborhood of Rio de Janeiro, the Conjunto Residential Marques de São Vincente (1952), which followed a similar formal strategy but included such compositional and structural flourishes as a distinctive rooftop canopy, V-shaped columns that added a decorative motif on the third floor, and a greater variety of window shapes.[10] One of the most important differences between the Conjunto Residential Marques de São Vincente and the Pedregulho was the way in which each project framed the surrounding landscape. The scheme in Gavea was built above a small lagoon, the Lagoa da Freitas, and established a datum line that framed the hill behind it. The Pedregulho scheme offered views of Guanabara Bay and embraced its own hill as an integral part of the composition. Reidy designed a third serpentine housing scheme in 1951, the Catacumbas Housing Development, also located on the shore of the Lagoa da Freitas, to house shantytown dwellers who had previously lived on the land where the Conjunto Residential Marques de São Vincente was built, but the project was never executed. Transcending their functions as housing developments, the Pedregulho, Gavea, and Catacumbas projects all resemble aqueducts and retain characteristics typical of Portuguese colonial urbanism. Elsewhere in South America, the uniformity mandated by the Spanish Laws of the Indies imposed a rigid urban grid that was intended to be inflexible and unrelated to the immediate context. The designs of Portuguese colonial settlements tended to be both pragmatic and responsive to their surroundings, and these qualities are also characteristic of Reidy's housing projects.

Despite Reidy's claims that his schemes were indebted to John Wood the Elder's design for the Royal Crescent in Bath (1767–74) and Alvar Aalto's Baker House student residence at MIT (1947–49), they most closely resemble Le Corbusier's urban proposals for Rio de Janeiro.[11] Both of Reidy's projects bear a strong sectional resemblance to the Unité d'Habitation at Marseille, developed practically simultaneously with the Conjunto Residencial Prefeito Mendes de Moraes (the official name of Pedregulho), itself a development of earlier ideas by Le Corbusier for the Ville Radiuse (Radiant City), an unrealized urban masterplan first presented in 1924 and published in a book of the same name in 1933. Both Pedregulho and the Unité were built on *pilotis* and featured a public space located roughly in the center of the section. To a lesser extent, some aspects of these schemes appear to be derived from Oscar Niemeyer's free-form modernist projects in Pampulha, Minas Gerais, such as the dressing rooms resembling Niemeyer's Church of St. Francis of Assisi (1943) and the primary school that recalls the Yacht Club (1942). Even before the Pedregulho complex was completed, it was greeted with enthusiastic approval. Max Bill, the Swiss artist and architect known in Brazil as the founder of the concrete movement, claimed that he wished to live in a Pedregulho apartment. Walter Gropius, according to his wife's notes, was "in love" with the building, stating that it was "a model not only for Brazil but for the world." Sigfried Giedion judged Pedregulho the winner of the First International Biennial of São Paulo in 1953, writing that it was a simple example of how every city should be built.

Like some European proposals for postwar reconstruction, the Pedregulho was intended as a social experiment, as well as a model for the world of Brazilian social reform. Otherwise eligible families were thoroughly checked for communicable diseases before they were allowed to occupy their units. An additional requirement compelled the tenants to declare their willingness to preserve the pure white appearance of the building. To ensure their compliance, residents had to allow periodic inspections by Municipal Workers Housing Department officials to confirm that they were abiding by the regulations; they could be evicted if the information provided by the inspectors proved otherwise. Residents were also expected to practice personal cleanliness and to keep the premises sparkling, particularly the communal laundry room and washing machines. To encourage its use, each family was given two kilos of laundry detergent annually as a gift from the city and allowed to wash four pounds of laundry per person per week. The laundry room and some apartments of selected residents were part of a regular tour conducted for VIPs, such as Aloisio de Paula, then director of the Museum of Modern Art in Rio. Thus both the architecture and residents of Pedregulho served as a demonstration project, living proof that Brazil was becoming a modern, technologically advanced society.[12]

According to Lauro Cavalcanti, "The desire to improve the poor by placing them in sophisticated residential spaces clashed with the architects' ignorance of the taste and social skills of the inhabitants, and the social experiment failed. In attempting to give women more free time and prevent them from hanging clothes from the windows, the architects eliminated washtubs from the apartments and provided only a room with washing machines. For women of humble means, washing clothes provided a social occasion." Lacking a substitute for this opportunity to socialize, the women washed their clothes together in the almost Olympic-size swimming pool, instead of using the machines.[13] But even if the social engineering was misguided, the architecture of Pedregulho achieved an

Figure 5.6. Église Saint-Pierre, Firminy, France. Designed by Le Corbusier in 1963, begun in 1971 six years after his death in 1965, and completed in 2006. Photo courtesy of Keith Plymale, 2006.

inspiring synthesis of landscape, infrastructure, and dwellings that became, at least in part, a realization of the visionary unbuilt scheme for Rio de Janeiro first imagined by Le Corbusier twenty-five years earlier.

The Pedregulho and Gavea projects were both conceived at a time when Le Corbusier's own hillside housing schemes were becoming less imposing and he was adopting a landscape strategy closer to the more organic urban forms he had encountered in Rio de Janeiro. Both the Le Sainte-Baume (1948) and "Roq et Rob" at Cap Martin (1949) projects embrace their hillside sites, establishing identities as independent objects while following the contours of the topography as had the buildings included in his urban proposals for Rio. The hillside proposals from the late 1940s were dense aggregations of individual units grouped together to avoid spoiling the landscape and to maintain good views of the ocean.[14] In adopting a more traditional approach to building on hillsides, Le Corbusier abandoned the monumentality of his earlier urban visions but continued to draw inspiration from his encounter with the South American landscape.

The Église Saint-Pierre (1960) (figure 5.6), designed for Firminy-Vert, a mining, steel, and textile town located at the bottom of a valley 50 miles southeast of Lyon, contains the figure of an isolated mountain in the landscape, a form that Le Corbusier found particularly compelling and one he sketched repeatedly during the late 1920s and early 1930s as an *objet à réaction poetique,* like shells found on the seashore or a beef bone recovered from the butcher's meat room. Sugar Loaf Mountain retained its totemic status, taking on human qualities and superhuman attributes in dozens of sketches as it had in every sketch for Rio de Janeiro for which Le Corbusier could find a pretext to include it (figure 5.7). Described by Le Corbusier as a "hyperbolic-paraboloid shell and a third new type of church," after the pilgrimage chapel at Ronchamp and the monastery La Tourette, the design of Saint-Pierre simultaneously evokes a cooling tower and Sugarloaf, as does his design for the roof of the Assembly Palace at Chandighar, designed in 1952 and completed in 1962.[15]

Both buildings are likely to have influenced the design of Rio's Metropolitan Cathedral of Saint Sebastian (1976) by Brazilian architect Edgar Oliveira da Fonseca, who would have seen Le Corbusier's work in European architecture magazines widely read by South America's elites (figure 5.8). Ironically, the cathedral was built on land where the demolished Morro de Santo Antonio and one of Rio's earliest colonial settlements once stood, metaphorically restoring Le Corbusier's magic mountain to the site. The cathedral's design referenced both Sugarloaf as transformed

Figure 5.7. Sugar Loaf Mountain sketch. Le Corbusier, 1929. Courtesy of F.L.C. / ADAGP, Paris / Artists Rights Society.

Figure 5.8. Metropolitan Cathedral of Saint Sebastian, Rio de Janeiro. Architect Edgardo Fonseca, 1964–79. Photo by René Davids, 2004.

by Le Corbusier and expressed in his architecture, and the cathedral as the reincarnation of a previously demolished hill, reborn on the same site.

Conclusion

The sensuous forms of Rio's hills curving along the Atlantic coast made a powerful impression on Le Corbusier, inspiring him to develop a new urban aesthetic. Among his additional likely sources of inspiration were the female figure, natural objects such as sea shells, and the massive 800-foot long Aqueduto da Carioca, a monumental construction transformed into a viaduct, connecting the Santa Thereza neighborhood to the downtown area as it has since the 1890s, well before Le Corbusier's visit to Rio in 1929. His first work to be built after he returned from South America, the Pavillon Suisse, revealed in its curvilinear forms and use of raw materials the impact of his experience in the New World.

Le Corbusier's proposals for Rio remained unbuilt, but twenty years later his schemes provided an important source of inspiration for Affonso Reidy's housing complexes, two of which were built. As prominent and visible architectural landmarks, both the Pedregulho and the Conjunto Residential Marques de São Vincente represented the promise of a new, more equitable, and technologically advanced Brazilian society. Thirty years later Le Corbusier's Église Saint-Pierre at Firminy-Vert was inspired by the form of Sugar Loaf Mountain, which then inspired Fonseca's Cathedral de São Sebastiao in Rio, expanding the intercontinental dialogue about topography, infrastructure, and architectural form and enriching the creative exchanges between two cultures.[16] The game of referential counterpoint also revealed the existence of a more subtle and complex dynamic than that implied by the construct of the master European architect and his third world disciples. Le Corbusier's work had a lasting effect on Brazilian architecture and South American culture, but topography and the landscapes of Rio de Janeiro, including both natural elements and the work of human hands, had a profound influence on the work of Le Corbusier. Unexpected connections over a period of three decades reveal that the process of discovery is as complicated as it is stimulating to examine, as unpredictable as the fusion of imagery from disparate sources would suggest, at once multidimensional and deeply creative.

II

CITIES AND WATER

6

Mexico City as Reinvented Geography, Its Looming Environmental Crisis, and Recent Proposals for Regenerative Landscapes

EDWARD R. BURIAN

Agua que no has de beber, déjala correr.
(Water that you are not going to drink, let it run.)
A traditional Mexican proverb used when someone interferes with something which should have been left alone.

The sewer is the conscience of the city.
Victor Hugo, *Les Miserables*

As the capital city of Mexico and home to some 25 percent of its population, Mexico City is one of the largest megalopolises in the world. The environmental conditions endured by the estimated 21.2 million residents of the Mexico City Metropolitan Area (MAMC) are among the worst on the planet, but most recent discussions about contemporary architecture in the MAMC have portrayed an idealized backdrop for innovative visual and formal compositions. The focus of this essay is the largely reinvented geography of Mexico City, largely ignored but responsible for an environmental crisis in desperate need of immediate remedial attention, and three recent proposals for landscape regeneration that offer hopeful prognoses for future interventions in the MAMC.

Mexico City as Paradoxical Reinvented Landscape, Inextricably Linked to Its Topography, Geology, and Hydrology

The Valley of Mexico is a hydrographic basin one and a half miles above sea level surrounded by volcanic mountain ranges with no natural drainage

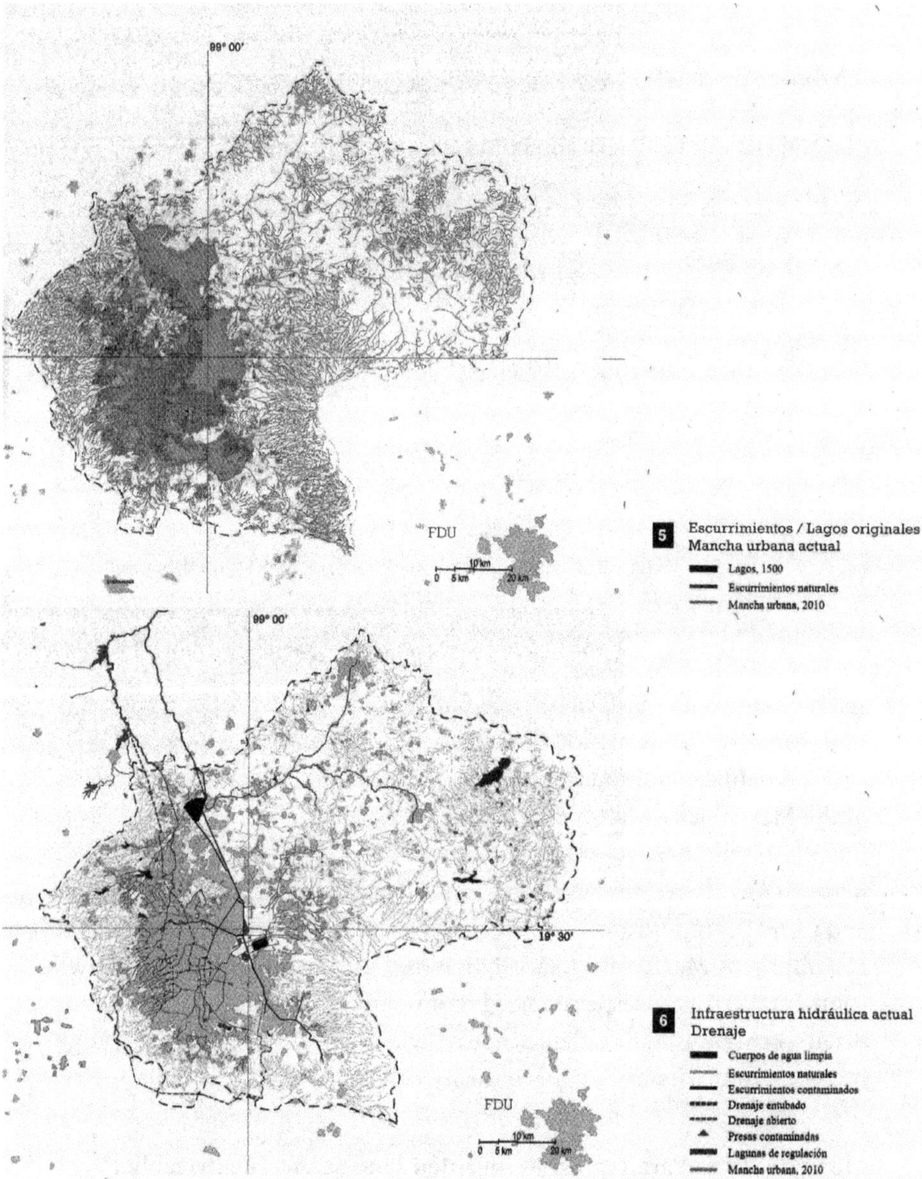

Figure 6.1. Lake, creek, and drainage systems, Mexico City. Courtesy of Alberto Kalach, 2012.

where, over time, five large, shallow lakes were formed by a combination of drainage, natural springs, and mountain snowmelt. Lake Texcoco, the largest of them, extended over a substantial portion of the basin, forming an interconnected system with the other four: Xaltocan, Zumpango, Chalco, and Xochimilco. The valley's high altitude produced a mild climate, with cooler microclimates and more precipitation found at even higher elevations to the west and south (figure 6.1). From 1200 BC until 1521, competing pre-Columbian city-states developed around the perimeter of the lakes. The Mexica, or Aztecs, were wandering newcomers who believed that their god Huitzilopochtli would reveal the location of a new city with the sign of an eagle perched atop a nopal cactus while eating a snake. This prophecy was fulfilled when in 1325 on a small island in Lake Texcoco they founded their capital, Tenochtitlán (Nahuatl for "prickly pears growing among the rocks").

The Aztecs were fierce warriors who eventually dominated the more established tribes around the lakes and ultimately controlled a huge region with a tribute-empire of around 10 million people. Over the course of two centuries, Tenochtitlán and the adjoining island trading city of Tlatelolco became one of the world's largest urban settlements at that time with an estimated 250,000 to 500,000 residents. The dense, gridded city interlaced with canals developed an amphibious "metropolitan" urban culture with natural defenses, irrigated farmland including *chinampas*, small rectangular islands constructed on the shallow lake beds that were extremely fertile, water-based transportation, and extensive trade networks. Tenochtitlán was largely destroyed in the Spanish conquest (1521), but rebuilt over the ruins to symbolize their imposition of a colonial new order and renamed "Mejico."[1]

During the Spanish colonial era (1521–1821), the water in the Valley of Mexico was gradually depleted for ranching, farming, and urban building sites, and the landscape was reimagined to resemble the semi-arid plains of Castile. Waste for the new colonial city was initially discharged through open ditches into the San Lázaro Canal, which emptied into Lake Texcoco. Deforestation of the surrounding hillsides for farmland, firewood, and building construction caused erosion, and large deposits of silt carried by runoff flowed down the barren slopes into the lake.[2] Located less than 6 feet above water level, Mejico flooded numerous times between 1555 and 1604, but proposals that the city be relocated were unsuccessful due to the opposition of influential real estate interests and urban property owners.

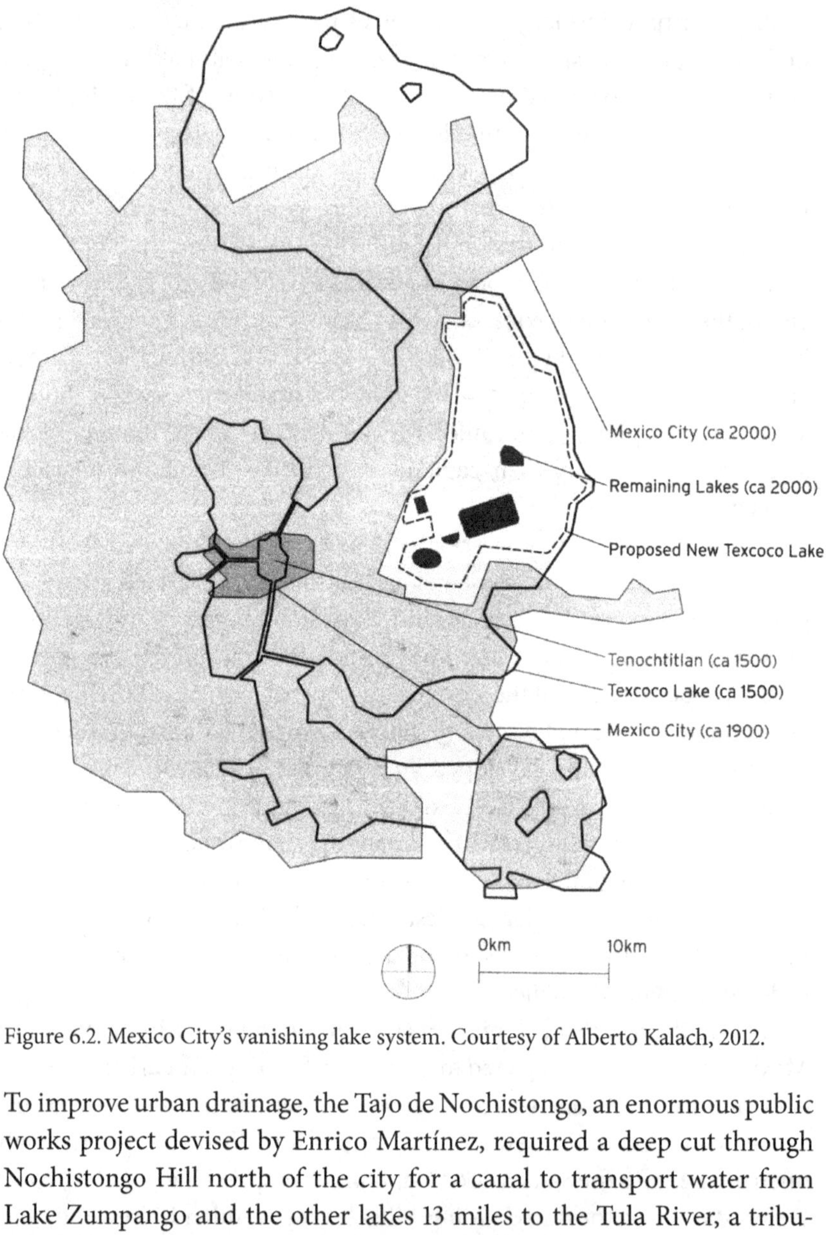

Figure 6.2. Mexico City's vanishing lake system. Courtesy of Alberto Kalach, 2012.

To improve urban drainage, the Tajo de Nochistongo, an enormous public works project devised by Enrico Martínez, required a deep cut through Nochistongo Hill north of the city for a canal to transport water from Lake Zumpango and the other lakes 13 miles to the Tula River, a tributary of the Panuco River which empties into the Gulf of Mexico. Only Lake Xochimilco (*Nahuatl* for "place where flowers are grown") and its *chinampas* gardens were spared, as they provided food for the capital and a place to grow native and imported flower species. Even after the canal was completed, costing huge sums of money and the lives of an estimated

70,000 indigenous laborers, the city was still subjected to flooding, and the process of draining the lakes has continued into the present (figure 6.2).[3] At the end of the nineteenth century, as the city continued to grow, the 30-mile-long Gran Canal was built to control the periodic flooding by collecting both sewage and flood water and diverting it into a 6-mile tunnel, and an aqueduct 16.5 miles long was constructed to supply the capital with water from Lake Xochimilco, hastening its environmental decline.[4]

World War II marked the beginning of tremendous growth for the MAMC; capital flowed into Mexico City to purchase raw materials for the Allied war effort, followed by foreign investment, improvements in healthcare, and reduced mortality rates. The Mexican intelligentsia and politicians advocated a growth strategy based on urban industrialization rather than agricultural development. New factories and industrial sites were built in the least desirable areas of the city, including the former lakebeds of Iztapalapa and Tlalnepantla in the east and the north.[5] This was followed by informal developments in the low-lying areas to the northeast and southwest, including Nezahualcóyotl and Chalco.[6] Today 60 percent of the residents of the MAMC reside in areas informally urbanized, and

Figure 6.3. Valley of Mexico aerial view, Tlateloco Plaza of the Three Cultures, Mexico City. Courtesy of Oscar Ruiz.

some 40 percent are impoverished, living in one-room dwellings shared by an average of five people.

The constant pumping of the aquifer to extract drinking water and the construction of dense urban and industrial fabric on the unstable lake beds caused the city to sink as much as 25 feet in some locations.[7] By 1950, as the city continued to tap its aquifer for diminishing supplies of drinking water, the subsidence and uneven ground settlement began to affect the drainage and waste systems, making it necessary to pump the sewage upward in some locations.[8] To avoid soil subsidence, in 1967 a new 60-mile network of underground deep-drainage tunnels, the Drenaje Profundo, was completed at a depth of between 98 and 820 feet underground, with a central tunnel of 21.3 feet in diameter to channel rainwater out of the basin.

Ironically, the city founded in a lake is now running out of water: about 70 percent of it is pumped from the aquifer up to 1.25 miles below grade, and the remainder is piped up to 250 miles from the Lerma and Cutzamala basins west of Mexico City. The MAMC drainage system currently mixes storm runoff with wastewater, raw sewage, street garbage, dead animals, and hazardous medical wastes. Ninety percent of it is untreated and channeled north out of the city via unlined, open air canals that have overflowed in the past over earth embankments.[9] Seepage from subsurface cracks in the sewage canals also risks contamination of the aquifer, which would result in millions of deaths.[10] Differential settlement has had a devastating impact on water supply infrastructure, routinely causing many older pipes to rupture, losing up to 30 percent of the city's scarce potable water (figure 6.4).

Another critical element of the MAMC's infrastructure is the network of streets and highways clogged with more than 4 million vehicles daily. The Valley of Mexico is enveloped in smog that is interrupted only for a few days after the air is cleansed by seasonal rainfall, and the average visibility of 7 miles in the 1940s is less than a half mile today. At an elevation of 7,500 feet, the basin's oxygen is almost a third less than is available at sea level, and the levels of carbon monoxide and hydrocarbon emissions produced by motor vehicles are nearly twice as high. This condition is further aggravated by the surrounding mountain ranges that trap smog and block the flow of winds that would cleanse the air. The high numbers of vehicles also cause high noise levels, and the continued deforestation of the Valley has made the mild climate hotter and dryer.[11] The basin's

Figure 6.4. Raw sewage spill in Chalco, Mexico. Photo courtesy of Oscar Ruiz, 2011.

air also contains high concentrations of fecal matter from the millions of gallons of sewage dumped into the dried lake beds near the city and waste produced by over 3 million stray dogs, making Mexico City one of the few places in the world where a gastrointestinal disease such as hepatitis or dysentery can be contracted by inhalation. Unoccupied public and private property, including the ravines surrounding the valley which play a crucial role in recharging the aquifer, have been used as a dumping ground for trash and construction debris or taken over by informal housing settlements. Since just after the 1968 Olympic Games up until the present day, public officials in the MAMC have largely ignored the problem of unplanned, uncontrolled growth and avoided the implementation of systematic regional planning, typically superimposed on both formal and informal development only after the fact.[12]

Regenerative Landscapes and the Restoration of Environmentally Degraded Sites: Three Projects

Three recent proposals for landscape regeneration offer solutions to avert an environmental catastrophe in the MAMC that is otherwise all but inevitable. The Xochimilco Restoration Project by Mario Schjetnan and Grupo Diseño Urbano (GDU) focuses on a remaining fragment of the original pre-Columbian lakes declared a UNESCO World Heritage site in 1987. This 7,400-acre restoration project mitigates a number of urgent environmental issues related to the comprehensive deterioration of the *chinampas* and difficult access to those located at the interior of the canal system underutilized for agriculture, sinking of the lake's environs caused by aquifer depletion, water pollution, encroachments by illegal residential developments around the lake's perimeter, increasing storm runoff, and canals choked with aquatic plants.[13] With the exception of the relatively sophisticated water treatment plant, Schjetnan and GDU employed a hands-on, low technology approach to the Xochimilco Restoration Project: polluted water was cleansed at treatment plants before being returned to the lake to replenish water levels, reservoirs were created to retain storm water to prevent runoff, and water was pumped back into the aquifer to stabilize the site. Eroded *chinampas* were stabilized with a mesh of logs filled with dredge, thousands of traditional *salix* trees were planted, horticulture including vegetable and flower cultivation was reintroduced, and some islands were set aside for grazing.[14]

At the edge of the restored lake, a 740-acre park includes agricultural, recreational, and educational uses: a new terraced entry features stone-lined aqueducts that discharge treated water into the lake (figure 6.5); a plaza contains a water tower, and a new interpretive center includes an auditorium and galleries with exhibits featuring regional ecology, archaeology, and agriculture; a roof terrace offers panoramic views over the surrounding lakes and canals, as well as the volcanos Popocatéptl and Iztaccíhuatl, somewhat compromised by the smog that typically fills the city; a pergola leads to a waterside promenade, and an arboretum and flowerbeds represent the productive horticultural activities of the restored *chinampas*. Other areas of the new park feature playing fields, ball courts, and restored wetlands to collect storm runoff. Traditional shallow-bottomed, pole-navigated canoes carry visitors through the cleared canals amid restored *chinampas* and working gardens, while other watercraft offer food for sale and floating entertainment by groups of musicians (figure 6.6). This regenerated "working landscape" is a microcosm of what might be possible for portions of the largely destroyed traditional environment in the Valley of Mexico. Extending well beyond merely scenographic gestures, the project successfully engages environmental, social, educational, and economic issues.[15]

Figure 6.5. Xochimilco Ecological Park, Mexico City. Photo courtesy of Mario Schjetnan.

Figure 6.6. Xochimilco. Photo courtesy of Edward R. Burian.

"Recovering the City of Lakes" by Alberto Kalach and his team, México: Ciudad Futura, is an even more ambitious, broad-based proposal to address issues of public health and environmental degradation within a proactive planning framework including a comprehensive social agenda. The proposal would partially reconstitute portions of the original MAMC lake system to recharge the depleted aquifer, restore humidity to the now arid microclimate, and help to cleanse the air, addressing issues of public health and environmental degradation within a proactive planning framework, including a comprehensive social agenda. This strategy utilizes the current ecological crisis and loss of open space for parks and recreation as an opportunity to rethink the interrelationships of urbanization and infrastructure, as well as anticipate possibilities for the city's future development.[16] Inspired by Nabor Carrillo's 1966 Proyecto Texcoco scheme for reconstructing portions of the city's original lakes to act as natural detention ponds for controlling wastewater, the Kalach proposal would partially restore 10 percent of the Valley of Mexico's original system of lakes while repurposing 7 percent of the MAMC's black water to revive Lake Texcoco—the largest of the lakes that has been almost completely drained—to control flooding and receive the treated wastewater.[17]

The reconstituted lakes would occupy land that floods, is too salty to cultivate, or is too soft to support buildings without extensive reinforcement, thus creating positive voids in the dense urban fabric and stimulating development in the surrounding neighborhoods. The shorelines would be reforested and used for low-rise development including university and public buildings on the eastern shores with revitalization of existing low-income settlements on the western shores. Creation of "green fingers" in restored ravines would recharge the aquifer by filtering runoff water through their porous volcanic rock and channeling it into the lakes.

A much-needed new international airport located on an artificial island in Lake Texcoco and accessed by freeways and mass transit lines crossing the lake's surface would partially finance the proposal while creating a new entrance to the city for those arriving by air.[18] The airport would act as a catalyst for development around the lakes' perimeters, simultaneously contributing to local ecological restoration and enhancing economic relationships with global networks while providing a new identity and social gathering spaces for the MAMC and vital connections to surrounding communities (figure 6.7).[19]

Figure 6.7. Lakes project, Mexico. Rendering courtesy of Alberto Kalach, 2012.

Buildings with floating foundations to distribute their structural loads over wide surface areas on the soft soil would contain diverse programmatic uses, including housing, and employ hybrid technology for water storage, wastewater treatment, and production of electricity for energy independence.[20] Reclamation of Lake Texcoco, creation of vibrant lakefront areas, installation of water treatment facilities, and a new international airport would all contribute to the landscape remediation initiative, reintegrating Mexico City with its natural setting, reconciling the built megalopolis with its topography, geology, and hydrology while also addressing its social and economic needs as a growing urban center. Construction of the project would create many employment opportunities, from highly skilled technical positions to jobs for unskilled laborers. As one of the few proposals that confronts MMAC's ecological crisis, the Lakes Project has brought it to the forefront of architectural discourse in Mexico, along with the systemic deficiencies plaguing local and national transportation networks from highways to transit lines and the urgent need for a new international airport. Unlike many utopian planning proposals intended as universal panaceas, the Lakes Project is a solution for a particular set of local circumstances that responds to the pressures of globalization on a specific site.[21] Whether the proposal will be adopted in whole or in part remains to be seen, but inaction regarding the ongoing depletion of MAMC's aquifer and indifference to the potentially catastrophic inadequacies of its waste treatment system are not viable options for the future.[22]

Also noteworthy are the proposals by Kalach and his team for reforestation of the Valley of Mexico basin, "Urban Reforestation Interventions, and Delimitations of Urban Edges" (2012), published in the *Atlas of Projects for the City of Mexico*, a two-volume compilation of thirty-seven remedial urban infrastructure projects, including initiatives for urban reforestation, regeneration of urban creeks and rivers, creation and refurbishment of public spaces, and construction of social housing.[23] Taken together, these proactive proposals attempt to forge a collective consensus about the need to conserve land and water resources, preserve urban public space, and challenge the shortsighted objectives of most real estate developers who maximize short-term profits by replicating suburban sprawl, as well as bureaucratic planning practices based exclusively on statistics, political favors, and economic imperatives.

These proposals reveal how numerous existing public places and parcels of land in the MAMC could be reforested without large capital outlays. This would benefit the entire MAMC, which could be reforested without large capital outlays, benefiting the entire area by reducing urban heat islands, absorbing dust and pollutants, sheltering wildlife, limiting erosion, improving conservation of water resources while avoiding construction of additional costly drainage infrastructure, providing shade canopies to reduce energy expenditures and improving pedestrian environments on commercial streets, lowering ambient temperatures on pavements while encouraging slower, safer traffic speeds as well as sheltering wildlife and facilitating carbon sequestration.[24]

One such proposal is entitled "Urban Centers Neza York," a much needed initiative to reforest the streets and boulevards of the informally developed Nezahualcóyotl Colonia, with 2 million low-income residents and almost no public space, parks, or street trees. The low-rise commercial buildings that have filled in spaces which were once planned parks and plazas would be relocated to new towers with smaller footprints containing commercial uses as well as offices for public services providers, including health, education, cultural, and recreation programs, allowing the original public open space use to be restored. Additional desperately

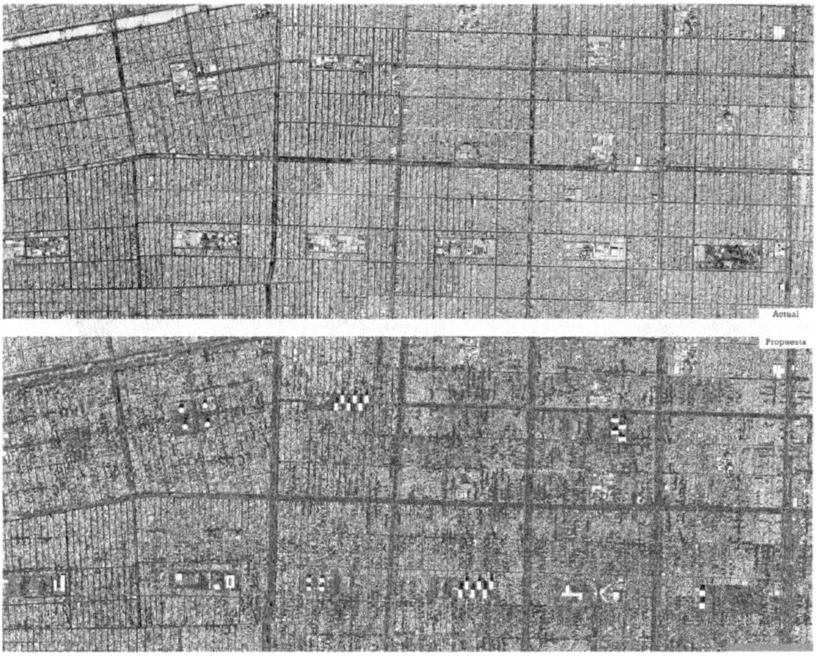

Figure 6.8. Neza York urban intervention. Rendering courtesy of Alberto Kalach and GDU, 2012.

Figure 6.9. Neza York. Rendering courtesy of Alberto Kalach, 2012.

Figure 6.10. Green reforestation of Estadio Azteca and Estadio Olimpico parking lots. Rendering courtesy of Alberto Kalach, 2012.

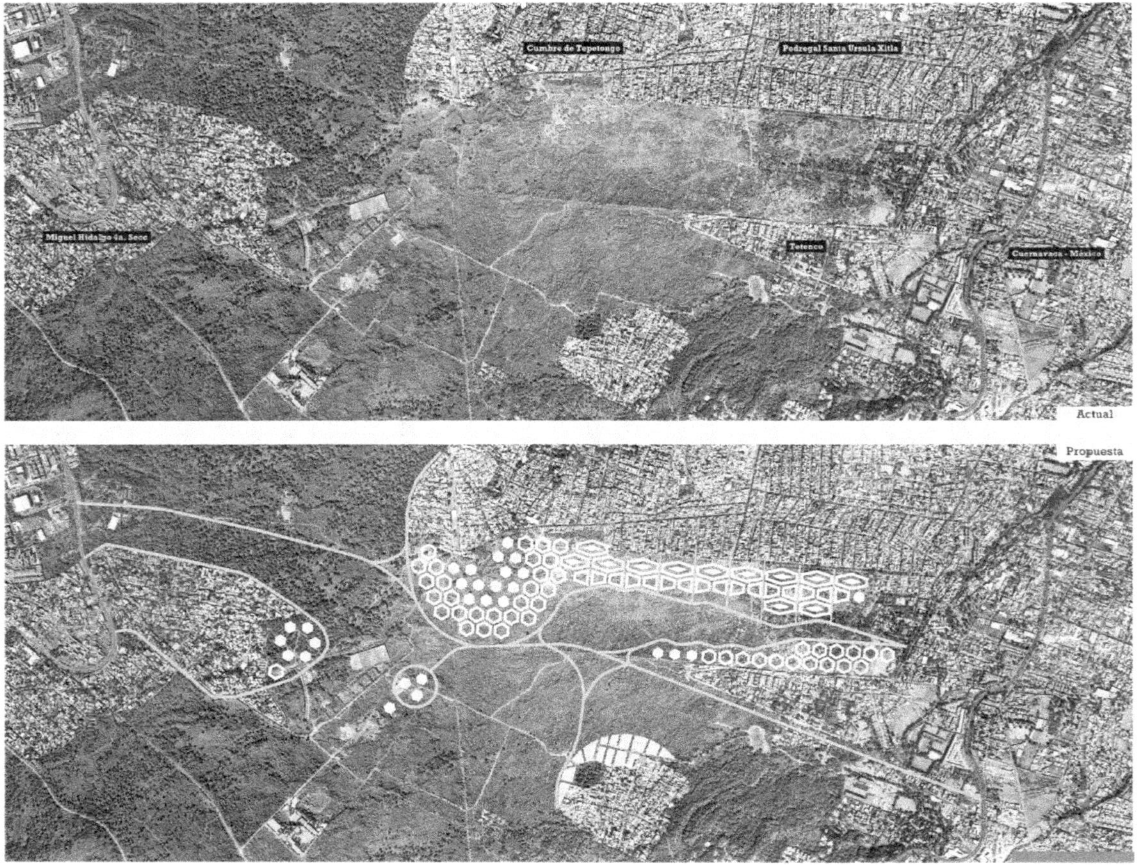

Figure 6.11. Urban edge for Ajusco, Mexico. Rendering courtesy of Alberto Kalach, 2012.

Figure 6.12. Ajusco urban edge intervention. Rendering courtesy of Alberto Kalach, 2012

needed green space would be created by utilizing the existing rooftops of the dwellings of the *colonia* for container roof gardens using recycled materials to create a lush, verdant canopy. Other proposals for urban reforestation involving the large parking areas for the Estadio Azteca, designed by Pedro Ramírez Vázquez and Rafael Mijares Alcérreca (1966) and Estadio Olimpico, designed by Augusto Pérez Palacios, Jorge Bravo, and Raúl Salinas (1950–55), would make a significant impact by cooling the urban environment, helping to recharge the aquifer, and improving the overall quality of life in the city. In his proposal "Urban Edge and Ecological Reserve for Ajusco," Kalach seeks to reverse the cycle of deforestation followed by soil erosion driven by low-density urban sprawl, which relentlessly consumes land at the city's perimeter. This proposal creates a series of high-rise towers with 10,000 housing units surrounded by infill reforestation to define the borders of the sprawling megalopolis while providing an ecological reserve and a vital recharge zone for the MAMC's aquifer.[25]

Environmental Apocalypse and Remedial Interventions

More than interesting shapes and the cool, detached cynicism of formal exercises, MAMC's looming environmental disaster requires an engagement and ethical commitment to create architecture that at the most basic level should sustain human, animal, and plant life while preserving water, air, and land resources.[26] Remedial environmental, infrastructural, and landscape interventions are desperately needed, including the planting of street trees, restoration of creeks and river banks, gray water recycling, implementation of strategies to reduce air pollution, and systemwide refurbishment of infrastructure for water purification, aquifer restoration, and wastewater treatment.[27] The scale and complexity of any one of these projects is enormous, requiring leadership from public officials and the business community, as well as the architecture, engineering, and other design professions, to avert the environmental disaster threatening the MAMC.

Despite the hardships of daily life in the MAMC, from the preindustrial squalor of the *colonias* to the upscale condominium culture of Santa Fé, the family unit endures, and relationships within close-knit extended families are the bonds holding Mexican society together. Traditionally the guardians of family welfare, women are now also assuming prominent roles in the public sector, including the leadership of the "Green" party in Mexico City, and may now be positioned to forge the necessary political consensus and shared sense of common purpose among families across all economic and social groups to confront the MAMC's looming environmental crisis.

7

Mountains, Wetlands, and Public Space in Bogotá

RENÉ DAVIDS WITH JULIÁN ALEJANDRO OSORIO

Since Bogotá's founding 450 years ago, its favorable location between a fertile savannah and the forested slopes of the Cerros Orientales has also been its undoing. The cutting of trees on the mountain hillsides for energy and construction eventually led to erosion of the denuded slopes, and the spoils polluted nearby rivers, wetlands, and lagoons. As Bogotá grew over the centuries, its environmental and social problems increased in severity so that by the end of the twentieth century, it had become a polluted, chaotic, and crime-ridden metropolis. But a dramatic political change in the 1990s halted the downward spiral and began to turn the city's fate around.[1]

Before the Spanish arrived, the central highlands of Colombia were inhabited by the indigenous Muiscas and Bacatá, or Bogotá, peoples. Meaning "planted fields," Bogotá alludes to the fertility of the land that was the center of the native civilization. At an altitude of nearly 9,000 feet, the highland area is a mostly flat, poorly drained savannah traversed by an extensive network of wetlands fed by abundant annual rainfall and streams flowing down from the Cerros Orientales. Surrounded by and dependent upon water, the Muiscas dwelt in *bohios*, or small cabanas, rather than the monumental structures the Spaniards encountered in Mexico, and they offered tributes to the lagoons that were the center of their secular and religious lives.[2]

In 1538, on a plateau in the foothills of the Cerros Orientales, Gonzalo Jiménez de Quesada founded the colonial settlement of Santa Fé de Bacatá, named after his birthplace in Spain, which became the capital of the New Kingdom of Granada, part of the Viceroyalty of Peru. Santa Fé rather than Bogotá was the city's official name during colonial times, but people referred to it as Santa Fé de Bogotá to distinguish the urban center from others with the same name, and it only became Bogotá in 1819 when the Republic of Colombia was founded. The Cerros Orientales provided a strong topographical barrier and effective shield against the prevailing winds from the east, the San Francisco and San Augustin Rivers defined the city's northern and southern boundaries, and the vast savannah extended outward from the west.[3] Later, the city expanded north toward the Arzobispo River and south to the boundary provided by the San Cristóbal River.[4] Water for drinking and irrigation was captured from the rivers through constructed canals. The situation on the foothills meant that traditional low-pressure gravitational technology of the sort developed in ancient Rome and familiar in Spain from at least the time of the Roman occupation would be entirely sufficient to allow the water to flow.[5] The first to be used for domestic purposes was built in the sixteenth century out of stone, lime, and brick and linked the San Agustín River to a public fountain in the main plaza.

Demography, Energy Resources, and Materials

Compared with Mexico City or Lima, Bogotá during colonial times was a relatively modest sized capital, but the precise number of its inhabitants is difficult to determine. According to Spanish historian Juan Flórez de Ocáriz, the prevailing social conventions of the sixteenth century are likely to have excluded indigenous peoples and *mestizos* living in Bogotá from population surveys, rendering them unreliable.[6] Estimates including both the officially recorded and undocumented populations indicate that the number of people residing in Bogotá at the end of the seventeenth century was only in the 10,000 range, but by the beginning of the nineteenth century it had doubled.[7] By midcentury, the demand for wood was so intense that the Cerros Orientales were depicted in watercolors by English foreign-service officer Edward Mark as barren (figure 7.1).[8] On the occasion of the First National Congress of Medicine of Colombia in 1884, Dr. Manuel Cotes reported a scarcity of wood so dire that the poor were forced to cook with manure.[9]

The harvesting of the indigenous *chusque* plants from the hillsides for fuel that commenced soon after Bogotá's founding, combined with the extraction of clay and rock for the manufacture of bricks and roof tiles, eventually caused the erosion of the Cerros Orientales so that by the

Figure 7.1. Plaza Mayor de Bogotá, Colombia. Edward Walhouse Mark, 1846. Watercolor courtesy of Colección de Arte del Banco de la República, Colombia.

mid-nineteenth century their plant cover had been completely removed and the topsoil eroded by water and wind. Unimpeded by vegetation, whenever water flowed down the slopes, the subsoils became saturated, disrupting the hydrological cycle and the San Francisco, San Agustin, and San Cristóbal Rivers, which supplied 90 percent of Bogotá's water and caused landslides in 1770, 1798, 1805, and 1826.[10] From 1853 until the end of the nineteenth century, thirty-three landslides resulted in blockages

Figure 7.2. Cerro Monserrate and Plaza del Periodista, Bogotá, Colombia. Photo by René Davids, 2011.

of the canals that supplied the city's water. The loss of life and related property damage after yet another landslide covered a major highway in November 1890 resulted in a permanent ban on excavations in the Cerros Orientales.[11]

As mills and tanneries already discharged toxins and residents dumped effluents and garbage into it, mudslides worsened the already poor quality of the water supply obtained from the rivers causing the population to suffer a high incidence of gastroenteritis, dysentery, and typhoid fever. Relief did not begin to arrive until the 1890s when a municipal plumbing system was authorized, but its construction was not substantially complete until the 1920s.[12] Quality of life issues were compounded by the absence of a comprehensive sewage and garbage collection system. Bogotá's residents were thus forced to discharge household wastes into open sewers, causing a local press report to describe the city in 1904 as a dirty and stinking place.[13]

To improve the situation even further, the Empresa de Acueducto de Bogotá—the municipal water authority—decided in 1916 to purchase several properties in the Cerros Orientales and reforest them with fast-growing invasive tree species such as eucalyptus and pine, which were believed to have the added advantage of purifying the air with the scent of their leaves. The eucalyptus trees were eventually discovered to be voracious consumers of water, which reduced the amount of runoff returned to the rivers, and their low leaf litter did little to replenish the nutrients they extracted from the soil, further impoverishing it. In 1924, local authorities decided to encourage replanting of native species on the hillsides instead, and the failure of the reforestation project prompted Bogotá's Consejo Municipal (Municipal Council) to acquire the land surrounding the sources of the rivers for construction of Colombia's first water treatment plant in 1929.[14] The other measure that significantly improved public sanitation was the decision by the municipal government beginning in 1917 to pipe the rivers through underground conduits.[15]

In Bogotá's socially stratified and racially divided milieu, impurities in the water supply were not related to general unhygienic practices but perceived by the upper classes to be the consequences of objectionable behavior of the lower classes, including the devastating Spanish flu epidemic of 1918–19, widely believed to have been caused by the low-income residents of the foothills soiling the water that flowed to the elite neighborhoods located downstream, although that particular outbreak of influenza was a pandemic that did not originate in South America.[16]

Beginning in the mid-nineteenth century, the presence of greenery, water, and wildlife began to be perceived as an antidote to the noise, congestion, and environmental degradation afflicting many cities. Toward the end of the nineteenth century, Genáro Valderrama, superintendent of Bogotá's gardens and parks, was inspired by the example of Frederick Law Olmsted, the designer of New York's Central Park and a believer in nature's capacity to relieve the stresses of urban life.[17] He determined that more green space in Bogotá would improve public health, have a salutary effect on the daily lives of the lower classes, and, if designed to the standards of the Bois de Boulogne or Central Park, advance its reputation as a world-class city.[18] By the end of the nineteenth century, colonial squares including Plaza de Bolívar, Plaza de los Mártires, and Plaza de Santander had all acquired vegetation, and new parks with patriotic names honored national achievements with commemorative statues and monuments.[19] Parque del Centenario was inaugurated in 1883 to celebrate the centenary of Simón Bolívar's birth, followed in 1910 by Parque de la Independencia commemorating the country's independence, and Parque Nacional Olaya Herrera in 1934, which simultaneously honored the president who served between 1920 and 1934 and the four hundredth anniversary of Bogotá's foundation in 1538. Believed to be the work of the Austrian urban planner Karl Brunner and Pablo de la Cruz, Parque Nacional Olaya Herrera created a green link between the city and the hills west of the Arzobispo River, with playing fields for sports, recreation, and a program of physical improvement. Also built around the same time were the Gaitán Cortes and Luna landscape parks north and south of central Bogotá, respectively, which contained lakes fed by the rivers and smaller creeks.[20] At a time of incipient industrialization, construction of public works infrastructure including railway lines and municipal services such as electricity, sewage disposal, and underground potable water were all intended to boost national pride and provide physical evidence of the country's progress. Provision of the new amenities helped to assuage the political pain and instability caused by a civil war called la guerra de los Mil Días (1889–1902), which led to the demoralizing loss of the province (Departamento) of Panamá in 1903.[21]

Growth and Contamination

With the construction of plazas, parks, water treatment plants, and municipal sewage and garbage collection systems, sanitary conditions in Bogotá gradually improved, but progress on that front suffered a setback in 1944–46 when Avenida de las Americas and Bogotá's first airfield, the Aerodromo de Techo, were built, dividing the vast El Tintal wetland to the southwest into smaller lagoons. Other highways followed: the Autopista Norte and the Avenida El Dorado, large thoroughfares which enabled the sprawling development that would gradually encroach upon, pollute, and disrupt the ecological balance of the western savannah.[22] Much of the development consisted of informal housing built by refugees from the civil war between Colombian government forces and revolutionary insurgents that began in the 1960s.[23] Polluted, congested, and lacking sanitation, waste management, and water service, the informal settlements quickly became breeding grounds for the spread of infectious diseases, social problems, and crime.[24] The deteriorating environmental conditions adversely affected the quality of life throughout the city, and by the early 1990s, Bogotá's reputation was that of a metropolis in an advanced state of decay.[25]

Alamedas and the Restoration and Reforestation of Wetlands

Bogotá's turnaround began with the 1992 prosecution and imprisonment of Mayor Juan Martin Caicedo for corruption, which triggered reform of the mayoral selection process. While mayors had previously been presidential appointees, since 1992 they have been democratically elected. The democratic process allowed capable leaders to emerge who were able to transform one of the world's most dangerous, violent, environmentally contaminated, and corrupt capitals into a relatively orderly and peaceful metropolis.

Instrumental in enabling the transformation was the approval and adoption of the Estatuto Orgánico de Bogotá in 1993, a set of bylaws that ensured citizen participation in city government and more effective and efficient expenditures of public funds, land use law, and other key legal improvements. The municipality increased the income received from local taxes, improved the procedures used to determine property values, and applied an additional tax on gasoline that allowed Mayor Jaime

Castro (1992–95) to establish a sound fiscal foundation for subsequent mayors. His successors Antanas Mockus (1995–97) and Enrique Peñalosa (1998–2001) invested those funds in ambitious civic improvement programs to enhance public squares and streets, restore deteriorated parks, provide markets for street vendors, and install bollards to prevent illegal parking. The program's best-known achievement was the establishment of the TransMilenio transportation system, which set fixed routes and lanes designated for the exclusive use of buses. Modeled on a system first implemented in the Brazilian city of Curitiba to ease traffic congestion, the TransMilenio also featured a new network of pedestrian overpasses, sidewalks, and bikeways.[26]

Understanding that modifications to the physical structure of the city had to be accompanied by a change in civic attitude, Mayor Antanas Mockus introduced a program of ingenious and thought-provoking street theater performances and cultural events aimed at promoting mutual respect and improved civic behavior among Bogotá's citizens. Unpopular measures such as restrictions on possession of guns by civilians and anti-gun advertising campaigns were also carried out.[27]

Another important tool in the reform of Bogotá was the implementation of the Plan de Ordenamiento Territorial (Plan of Territorial Organization), a set of legislative and planning policies introduced in 1997 to regulate land use, property rights, and environmental protection as well as any physical intervention in the surrounding region, allowing the Peñalosa administration to institute a comprehensive plan to create infrastructure and provide social services in poor neighborhoods by building hospitals, public libraries, and schools; legalizing informal settlements; and resettling those living in areas of high physical risk.[28]

Among the most celebrated of Peñalosa's construction projects are three public libraries. The most remarkable among them is the centrally located Virgilio Barco Library, designed by Rogelio Salmona, Colombia's best-known modernist architect. Built of reinforced concrete and brick, the library is organized around a sequence of courtyards connected by ramps and stairs, with water features reminiscent of traditional Moorish architecture that begins in the surrounding park and culminates in a roof deck.[29] Rogelio Salmona's passion for promenades and water reemerges in his design for the Eje Ambiental de la Avenida Jiménez de Quesada (Environmental Axis Jiménez de Quesada Avenue) (figure 7.3). Conceived in collaboration with Luis Kopec, the Eje, built between 1997 and 2001,

Figure 7.3. Eje Ambiental de la Avenida Jiménez de Quesada, Bogotá. Architects Rogelio Salmona and Luis Kopec. Photo by René Davids, 2000.

transformed the street originally built over the San Francisco River into a brick-paved *paseo* featuring native trees, linear fountains running along its sloping course, benches, and brick pavement for the TransMilenio. The effect was to establish a relationship between public transport and pedestrian traffic while revitalizing the public spaces along the *paseo's* route. Since the San Francisco River continues to be diverted underground, the Eje marks its invisible course and emphasizes the importance of water as a fundamental part of the city's identity.[30]

The Eje and the Parque del Tercer Milenio, in the heart of a zone of the city center that had deteriorated into a slum after its more affluent citizens moved to other neighborhoods in the late 1940s, were the catalysts that reignited investment in downtown Bogotá. As a means of memorializing the past, the Parque del Tercer Milenio offers protection with sound and wind barriers built from the debris of the buildings demolished to make space for its construction. Planted with groundcover and flowering vines, the barriers create a protective, secluded valley providing a refuge for local wildlife and city dwellers seeking a respite from the stresses of urban life.[31] Some critics point out, however, that the oasis was achieved

Figure 7.4. Humedal Juan Amarillo, Bogotá. Photo by René Davids, 2011.

by pressuring homeowners to sell their properties, acquiring a few homes through expropriation, and forcibly relocating 12,000 low-income residents, marginalizing an already vulnerable population with no access to legal representation, social services, or alternative living conditions.[32]

While the removal of derelict housing to build the Parque del Tercer Milenio remains controversial, the ecological objectives achieved through the reforestation of the Cerros Orientales and the restoration of the 233-hectare wetland Humedal Juan Amarillo were undisputed successes. By mitigating the effects of seasonal flooding, absorbing the excess flow of water, the environmental restoration plays an important role in the water cycle and provides a habitat for a rich diversity of flora and fauna. Prior to the restoration of the Humedal Juan Amarillo, the spread of informal housing to the east had reduced its size and degraded the wetlands, threatening both the water supply and wildlife habitats. Restoration efforts included the construction of islands for nesting birds and the restitution of the indigenous flora as well as new walkways, a plaza, and cycling paths around the lake (figure 7.4), elements of a new network of pedestrian and bicycle paths known as *alamedas*, conceived by the Taller del Espacio Público under the supervision of architect Lorenzo Castro Jaramillo (figure 7.5).[33] The new public walkways or promenades shaded with poplar trees, conceived during Mayor Peñalosa's term, were intended

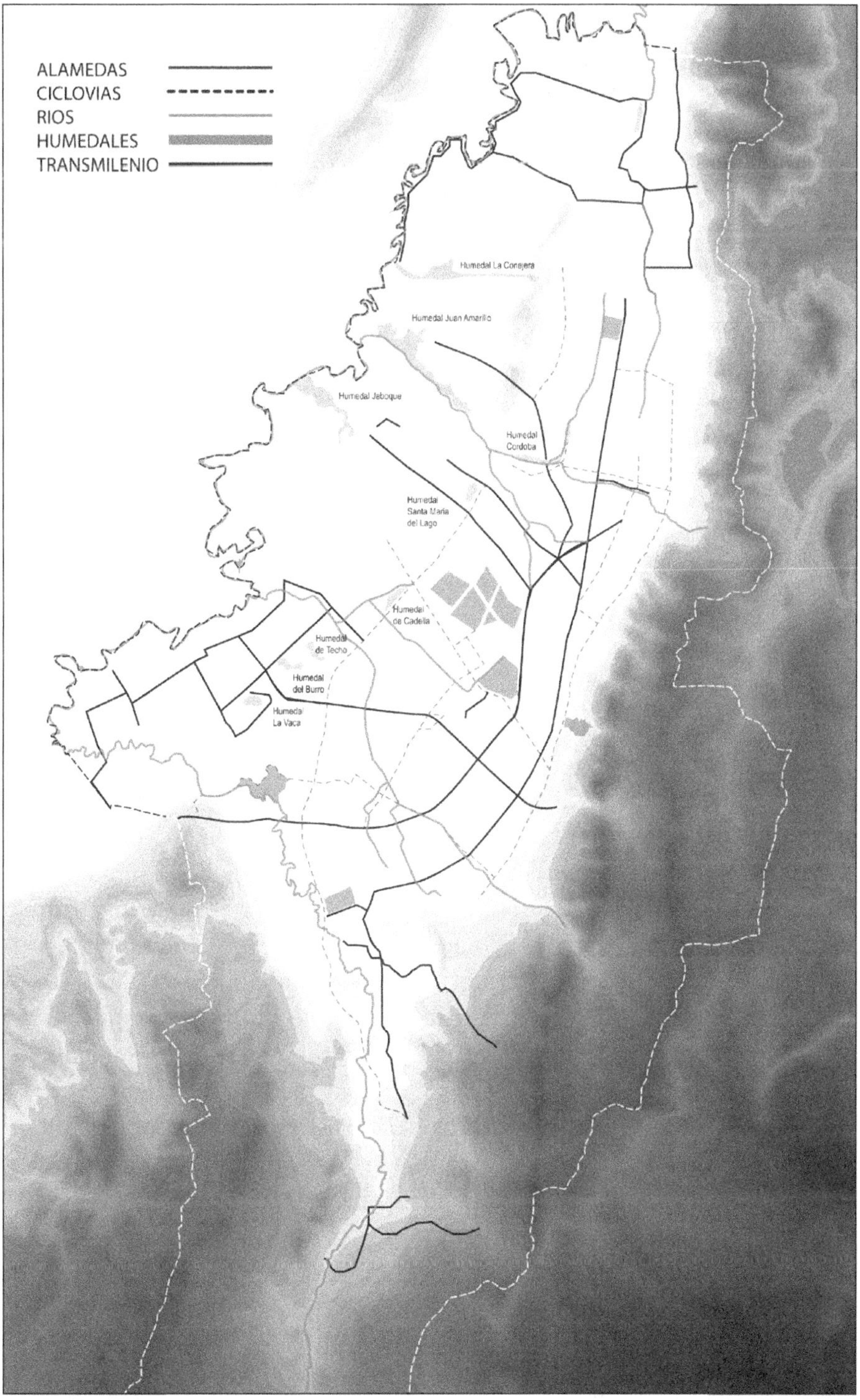

Figure 7.5. Map of Bogotá. Map by René Davids.

Figure 7.6. Alameda del Porvenir, Bogotá. Photo by René Davids, 2011

to reduce the number of cars on the roads by encouraging pedestrian activity and bicycle transport. Peñalosa envisaged a city where green space would be accessible to all, not just those who could afford to belong to private clubs.[34] The first of these, the Alameda del Porvenir, was designed by Felipe Gonzáles Pacheco and constructed in the late 1990s in a low-income area near the city's southwest periphery (figure 7.6). A median of palm trees divides the 17-kilometer path into pedestrian and cyclist lanes and is connected with schools, libraries, community facilities, and the new Library of El Tintal, designed by architect Daniel Bermúdez.[35] The transportation nodes in the districts that the Alameda del Porvenir traverses change dramatically in character along the route, including open fields and the Humedal Tibanica. Many of the Alamedas in the southwest were designed along the drainage canal system to provide public space in areas that tend to flood and lack public space due to the growth of informal housing.

The links established between *alamedas*, wetlands, *ciclovias* (designated bicycle routes), and *ciclorutas* (city streets for cyclists and pedestrians only) in the rapidly urbanizing areas of Bogotá's savannah have created a series of connected public spaces somewhat reminiscent of Boston's Emerald

Necklace, a system of parks and open spaces designed by Frederick Law Olmsted at the end of the nineteenth century to unify Boston's distinct neighborhoods into a civic whole. Both projects preserve vast swaths of natural habitat in their respective cities, clean up polluted tidal creeks and swamps, provide public access to green spaces, and preserve them for future generations. Unfortunately, the success of the Alameda del Porvenir has been compromised by vandalism and poor maintenance,[36] but the Parque del Virrey (figure 7.7), the Canal de Torca (figure 7.8), and the Alameda de la Quebrada de la Vieja (figure 7.9), designed around streams in upscale neighborhoods north of downtown Bogotá, are all well maintained. Before it was diverted in the late 1980s, these streams carried waste into lagoons, wetlands, and ultimately the Bogotá River, contaminating an extensive area of the city. While they have since been cleaned up, both the Canal del Virrey and the Canal de Torca run through concrete culverts, providing no habitats for plants or wildlife, and by narrowing the water's flow, accelerating the speed at which it flows, increasing the risk of floods by preventing percolation into the water table. The Alameda Quebrada de la Vieja includes a short stretch of open water running through a natural canyon before it is diverted into an underground culvert. Their

Figure 7.7. Parque del Virrey, Bogotá. Photo by René Davids, 2011.

Above: Figure 7.8. Canal de Torca, Bogotá. Photo by René Davids, 2011.

Left: Figure 7.9. Quebrada de la Vieja, Bogotá. Photo by René Davids, 2011.

detractors argue that rather than a comprehensive solution to Bogotá's environmental problems, the *alamedas* have increased the sprawl of low-rise development toward the southwest, further damaging the savannah's ecosystem, and toward its periphery, far enough from places of employment that walking or biking to work is impractical, when construction of denser residential neighborhoods would have been a better strategy.

Bogotá's recent transformations can also be understood as part of a broader strategy to improve competitiveness, a crusade to attract foreign investment, and an economic opening to promote social and economic development. When focused on their shortcomings, these projects can be seen more as exercises in image enhancement than genuine social and environmental improvements. While there is some truth to these criticisms, the *alamedas* have significantly improved Bogotá's urban ecology, public space, and civic culture, as well as its overall image as a city, positive effects which in themselves constitute a considerable achievement.

Conclusion

In the 1990s, urban reforms implemented by Bogotá's newly elected political leaders transformed it and represented historic breakthroughs in a city where social classes had been segregated for centuries. The *alamedas* have begun to unite the formal and informal cities into an organic whole, marking a promising new beginning and the end of a schism that had divided the city since its foundation. Taken as a whole, the reform projects have provided new public spaces for many widely dispersed urban neighborhoods, rich and poor alike, and the environmental restoration of degraded wetlands, creeks, rivers, and forests have integrated them with the city as a unified whole. Rather than resources to be exploited or sanitation problems, water and public space have once again become fundamental elements of Bogotá's civic identity.

8

Topography, Hydrology, and the Irrigated Landscapes of Mendoza, Argentina

JORGE RICARDO PONTE,
TRANSLATED AND ADAPTED BY RENÉ DAVIDS

The City in the Oasis

In 1561, the Spanish governor of Chile, García Hurtado de Mendoza, dispatched Captain Pedro Ruiz del Castillo and thirty-nine prospective settlers to the mountainous Cuyo region on the leeward side of the Andes in what is today western Argentina to build a way station for overland commercial traffic between Santiago and the Atlantic port of Rio de la Plata. According to the *Arte de la lengua general del reyno de Chile*, written by Andrés Febres in Lima in 1765, the word *Cuyo* is derived from the Araucanian *cuyum puulli*, meaning "sandy land" or "desert country," as the annual rainfall averages only about 8 inches. Separated from Chile by high mountains blocked by snow for several months each year, Cuyo is a vast semiarid desert where human livelihood depends on the availability of water in the forms of runoff from snow-capped mountains or water drawn from wells in the ground (figure 8.1). Cuyo was inhabited by the indigenous Huarpe people, who had been conquered by the Incas less than a century before the arrival of the Spaniards, and the Valle de Huantata was the southern terminus of Qhapaq Ñan, the Inca road that ran the length of the continent through alpine grasslands and mountain valleys to Quito, Ecuador, the backbone of the empire's political and economic power.

On the east bank of a branch of the Rio Mendoza now known as the Canal Zanjón Guaymallén Cacique, Capitan del Castillo founded Mendoza del Valle de La Nueva Rioja to honor his patron, but seven months later

Figure 8.1. Andes crossing between Mendoza, Argentina, and Valparaíso, Chile. Photo by René Davids, 2011.

there was a new governor in Santiago, Francisco de Villagra. Concerned that official approval for Mendoza might be withdrawn by the current administration, del Castillo designed a layout for the settlement intended to forestall any future formal or legal challenges before he departed for Peru. Although a subsequent expedition sent by Governor Villagra in 1562 relocated Mendoza 200 yards to the southwest, del Castillo's grid of five regular blocks and perfectly centered plaza survived to become one of the most widely copied urban plans in the Spanish colonies, but Cuyo's rugged terrain and Huantata's gravity-fed water supply posed significant challenges to its realization (figure 8.2).[1]

The Valle de Huantata was not a topographical basin but rather a plane sloping gradually northeast and bounded on one side by a branch of the Rio Mendoza, which collected water from snow melt.[2] In Huantata, the Spanish encountered a poor region with a functioning irrigation system of shallow, fast-moving alluvial streams running eastward from the Andes, intersected by an elongated grid-like network of canals running north to south across the sloping terrain and smaller channels with outlets for diverting water to individual properties and dwellings. These the Spanish

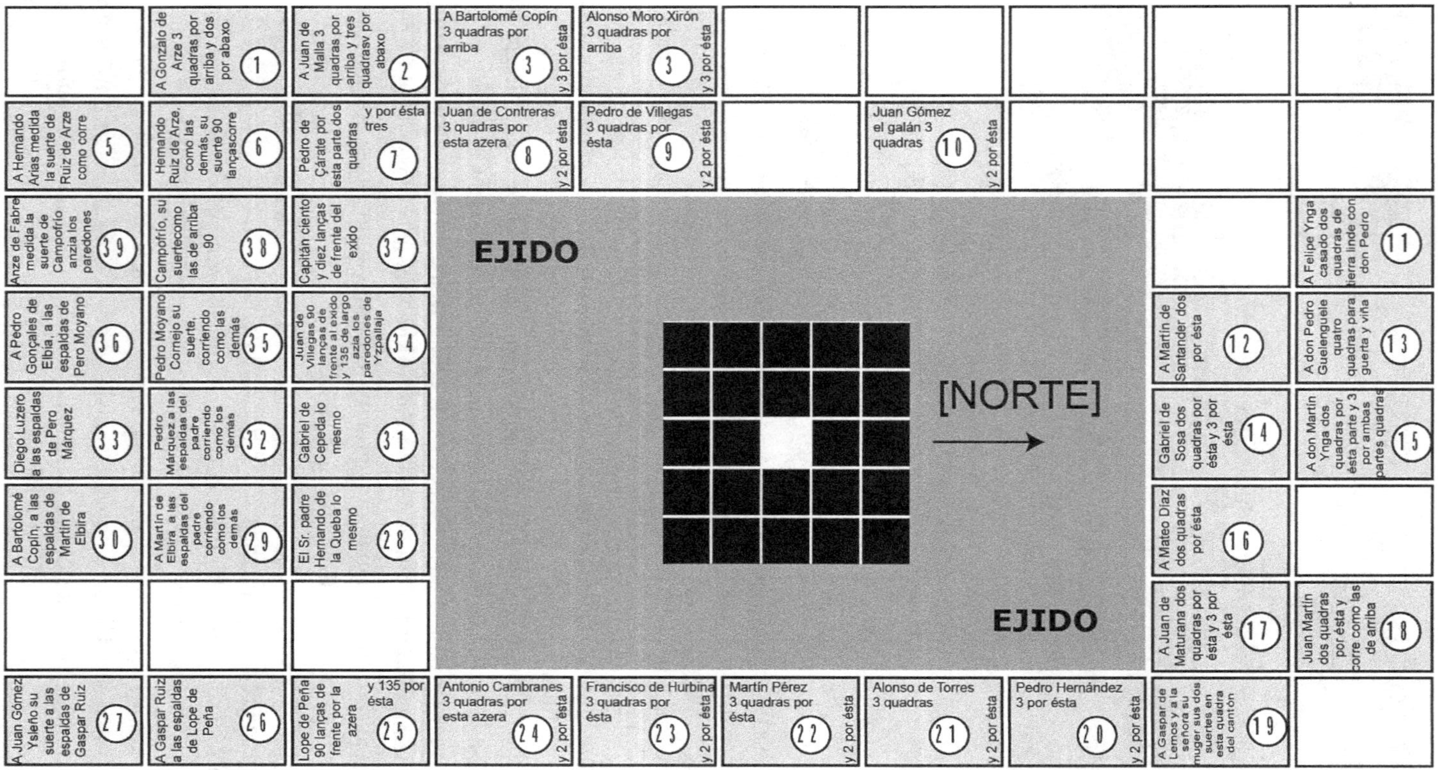

Figure 8.2. Ideal plan of Mendoza, 1561. Image courtesy of Jorge Ricardo Ponte.

called *acequias*, derived from the Arabic *as-sāqiya*, or water conduit for their similarity to the community-operated watercourses introduced by the Arabs to Spain in the Middle Ages. These were installed throughout their colonies in the New World, everywhere except in Mendoza, where the existing indigenous irrigation system would prove more consequential for its future development than anything built by the conquistadores (figure 8.3).

Foundation Plan

Documentation pertaining to Spanish settlements in the Americas tended to exclude information about the existing context, topography, and populations in favor of the idealized urban forms the colonizers wished to impose as templates of civilizing order on the perceived chaos of the New World. Typically annotated by a clerk who registered lots and property boundaries, Spanish maps ignored realities, substituting idealized images of places that the colonizers intended to create as a bulwark against the perceived disorder and chaos of the indigenous world, which they represented as mostly uninhabited.[3] By presenting images of imagined perfection rather than actual places, city maps and perspective views encouraged the perception of a wilderness devoid of human settlement where such abstractions could be realized without obstacles or interference. Capitan del Castillo is likely to have preferred an idealized plan for another reason: to avoid penalties for ignoring explicit prohibitions in the Laws of the Indies against the construction of new colonial cities over existing indigenous settlements. Further removing the necessity to create precise documentation of landholdings in Mendoza was the return to Chile soon after their arrival of nineteen prospective settlers out of the thirty-nine notables who had set out with del Castillo in 1561. As farming rather than mining of precious metals provided the only source of income, the notables had little incentive to stay, and at best left subordinates behind to look after their affairs. Demands that the settlers return to assume their obligations as landowners were ignored by the Captaincy General of Chile in Santiago, to which Mendoza belonged until the creation of the Viceroyalty of the Rio de la Plata in 1776. A new expedition led by Captain Juan Jufré in 1562 moved the settlement southwest to a site less vulnerable to flooding.

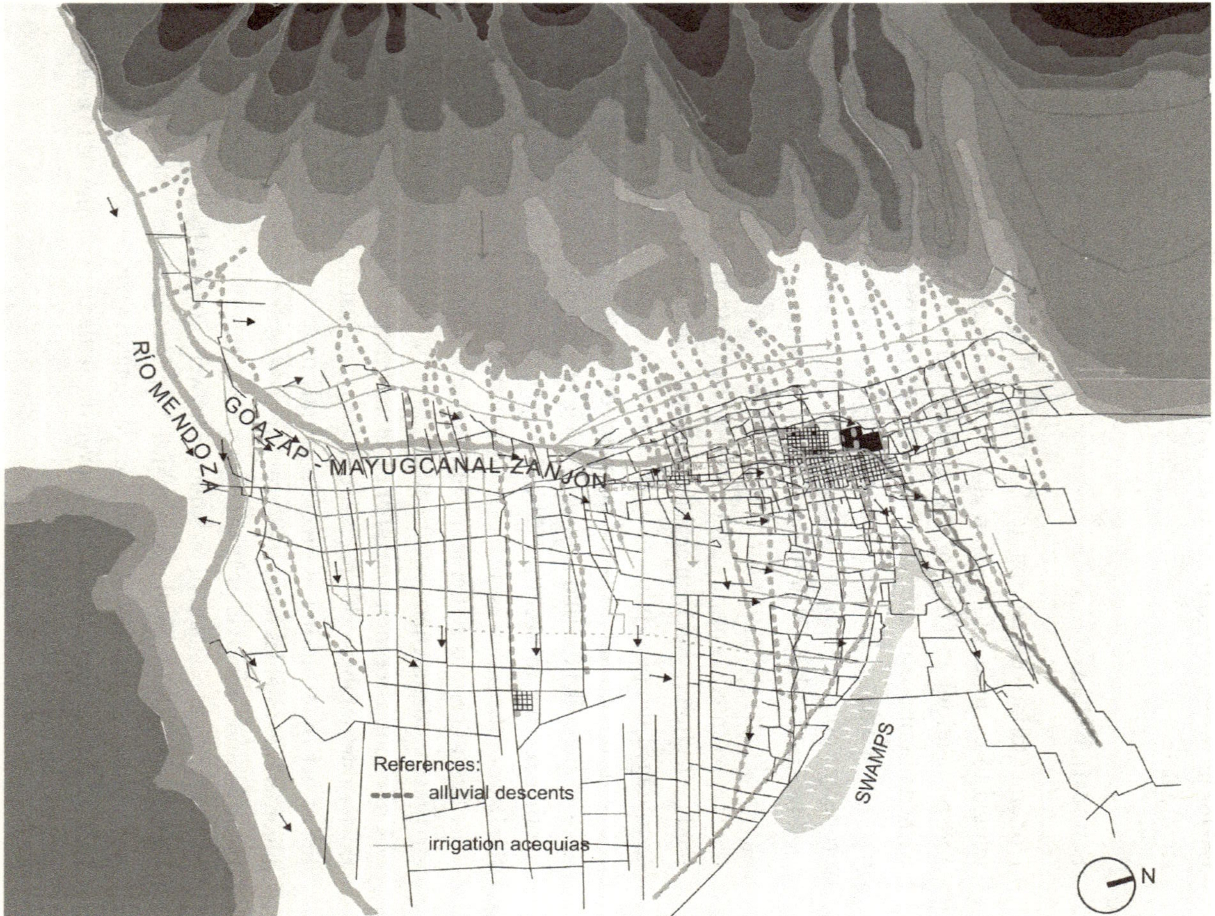

Figure 8.3. Network of alluvial descents and *acequias*, Mendoza, 1896. Image courtesy of Jorge Ricardo Ponte.

The absence of precise survey information in Mendoza's foundation documents provoked and aggravated property disputes, which the Spaniards initially adjudicated by appealing to the Huarpes, on whose land Mendoza had been founded. To resolve one such conflict, the Acta Capitular de Caciques Comarcanos of 1574 (County Chiefs Act) was drafted.[4] It was Mendoza's first recorded document and, until the middle of the eighteenth century, the only one with cadastral information—survey maps showing the extent, ownership, and use of landholdings pertaining to the foundation plan, as well as the semi-urban and rural parcels surrounding it.[5]

The urban core in typical Spanish settlements consisted of a gridiron town center surrounded by an *ejido*, a transitional community-owned zone between town and country used for grazing animals. In 1561, Pedro del Castillo laid out Mendoza's first *ejido* separated from the five-block-square urban core on the east and west sides by a division of the canal known as the Acequia de Tabalqué into Acequia Grande de la Ciudad, its original course now the Canal Zanjón (running through what is now Calle Salta) and the Acequia de la Ciudad (running through what are now Calles Alberdi and San José).[6] First established as a category of land area in 1566, the ideal *ejido* was defined as a regularly dimensioned area of agricultural plots, orchards, and ranches surrounding the urban core.[7] But the form of Mendoza's *ejido* was elongated to take best advantage of the local water sources, measuring roughly 3 by 6 kilometers with an estimated area of 52,420 hectares, 12 times larger than the urban core, and surrounded by 1,071.27 hectares allocated for *chacras*, or farms 33 times larger than the *ejido*, and 245 times as large as the core.[8]

Nothing in Mendoza's early history indicated that it would eventually become one of the largest, most prosperous cities in Argentina. Because many of the prospective settlers departed soon after their arrival, del Castillo's twenty-five block layout was excessively large for those who remained. According to an *informe del cabildo*, or council report, issued in 1567, the population amounted to only "twelve or thirteen men," meaning landowners with legal and voting rights rather than the number residing in Mendoza. In *Descripción y Geografía Universal de la Indias Occidentals* compiled between 1571 and 1574, geographer and historian Juan López de Velasco ranked the 260 Spanish settlements in the New World according to the size of their populations. Mexico City with 3,000 *vecinos*—property-owning married men of good repute—was the largest, a first-rank city (*de primer rango*) in 1st place; Santiago de Chile with 375 *vecinos* was a third-rank city in 15th place; and Mendoza with 30 *vecinos* was a fourth-rank city in 132nd place.[9] At the turn of the sixteenth century, early visitors to Mendoza remarked on the fertility of the land and the abundance of fruit trees and vineyards but also that the few existing buildings were collapsing with no one to rebuild them after most of the indigenous population was forcibly removed by the Spanish to work in Chile.

Mendoza Plan of 1754

According to Abbot Molina, by the middle of the eighteenth century, Mendoza's population had increased to 6,000 residents, but even after the passage of two centuries, it remained a cluster of one-story adobe brick houses, several churches, a *cabildo*, and a few unpaved streets.[10] The only cadastral document recorded in the eighteenth century, superseding the Acta Capitular de Caciques Comarcanos of 1574, showed that the original five by five block urban core had grown to an eleven by thirteen block grid, and four lots captioned "plaza" were marked with a cross in the upper middle portion of the plan, slightly southeast of the center but approximating ideal central placement. Like the urban grid itself, the terrain of suburban properties just outside it followed the slope of the land from southwest to northeast. Those located east of the Acequia Grande de la Ciudad included spaces between them which were likely intended to accommodate the flow of alluvial streams running down from the Andes foothills. The Calle Corrientes, which still exists, carried the caption "royal road leading to the provinces of Tucumán and Buenos Aires" and was the only road linking the city center with the periphery at that time. While Mendoza looked settled on this plan, after heavy rainfall, alluvial streams would wash out the orthogonal street grid. To avoid having to rebuild the local roads after every storm, their layout likely diverged from the Spanish formal model to follow the practice of the Huarpes, who located them next to water courses and irrigation canals.

In a similar departure from the conventions of the Laws of the Indies, the layout of plots in the *ejido* was adapted to the vagaries of local hydrology. Analysis of the *ejido's* boundaries confirms that the Spaniards analyzed the terrain carefully. The Acequia Principal del Cacique Tabalqué and the Acequia de la Ciudad, or del Molino, determined the north-south axis of the original settlement. The northern boundary of the *ejido* was most likely established at the inflection point of the Acequia Principal del Cacique Tabalqué, and the southern boundary was moved as far as possible from the old courses of the Zanjón Frias or del Escarpe. As no bridges are indicated anywhere on the plan, the crossing points for these watercourses are unknown. The significance of the well-proportioned landscape plan of 1754 (figure 8.4) lies in its confirmation that the Spaniards had adapted Mendoza's original layout to the existing *acequias*.[11] While it lacked a scale, the document contained sufficient cadastral information to accurately describe the *ejido's* outlines, identifying with captions the ownership of the forty semirural properties and their uses as houses, vineyards, or both. Superimposition of the 1754 plan on a later version produced in 1888 and comparisons with recent hydrological information from other sources confirm that the spaces between properties on the plan indicated the courses of existing water channels, as did the spaces between properties along the southern route where the Calle San Vicente Luján runs today (figure 8.5).[12]

The New City

Despite adjustments to the original layout to accommodate alluvial flows and the vagaries of the water cycle, well into the nineteenth century Mendoza remained a sparsely settled town with poorly constructed houses and numerous gardens. In the aftermath of an earthquake in March 1861 that killed 4,300 of its 12,000 people and destroyed most of the buildings, including the *cabildo*, some wealthier residents decided to rebuild higher up in the foothills southwest of its foundation site with cooler air and cleaner water, leaving behind the dusty streets and primitive, haphazardly constructed buildings of the ruined colonial core; it never recovered and remains the city's poorest area. Because of lingering postcolonial resentment of Spanish cultural hegemony, Mendoza's elites looked to Paris for design inspiration, but only the width of the new city streets, increased to enable safer egress during earthquakes, resembled Baron Haussmann's boulevards. While the appearance of the new buildings differed markedly from the old white stucco Spanish colonial fabric, they were much lower than their Parisian counterparts, and their pastel colors seemed more Italianate than French. With streets running on north-south/east-west axes converging on the Plaza Independencia, and the four smaller plazas situated at the corners of the square of roads surrounding the town center,

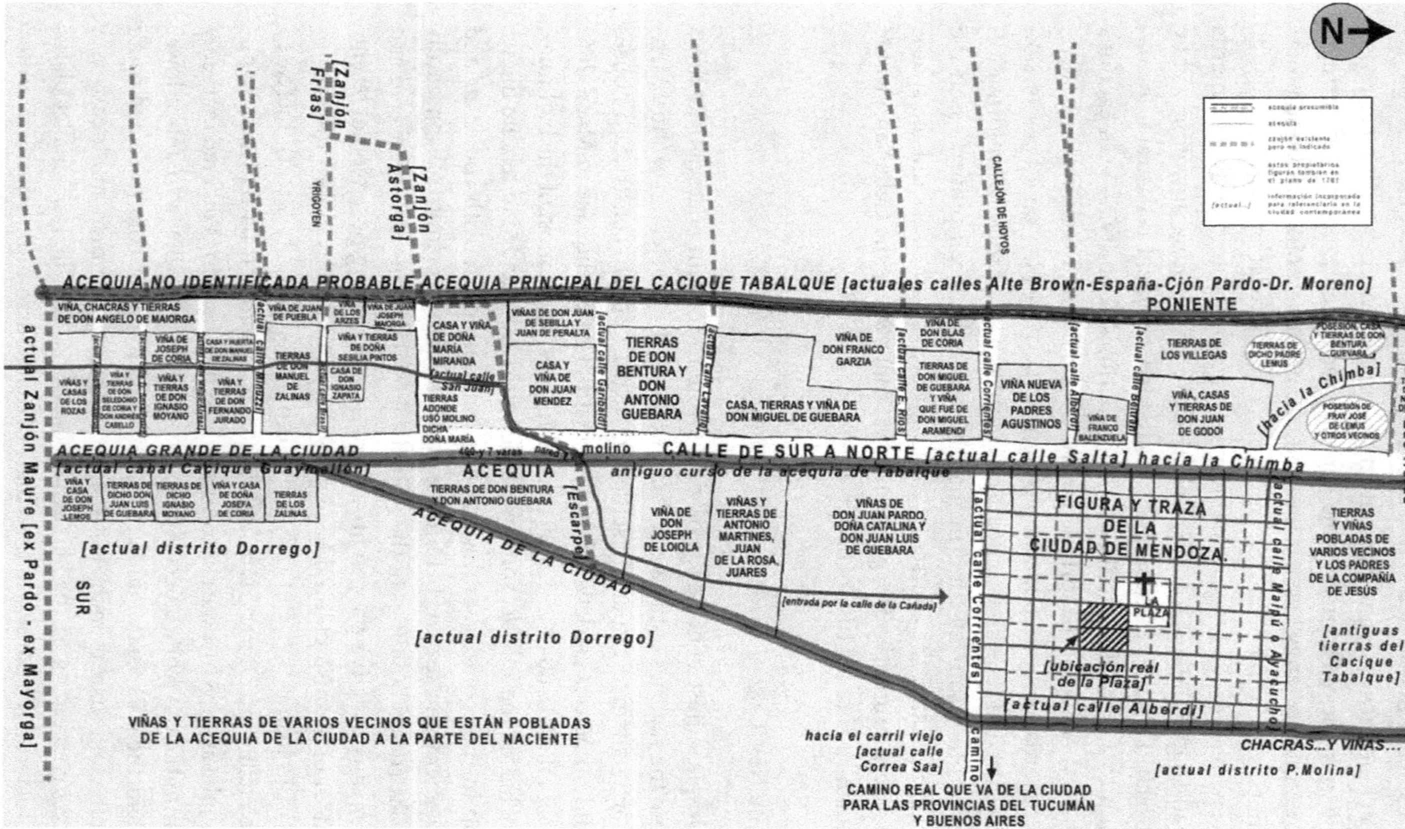

Figure 8.4. Plan of Mendoza, Mayorga Jurado, 1754. Image courtesy of Jorge Ricardo Ponte.

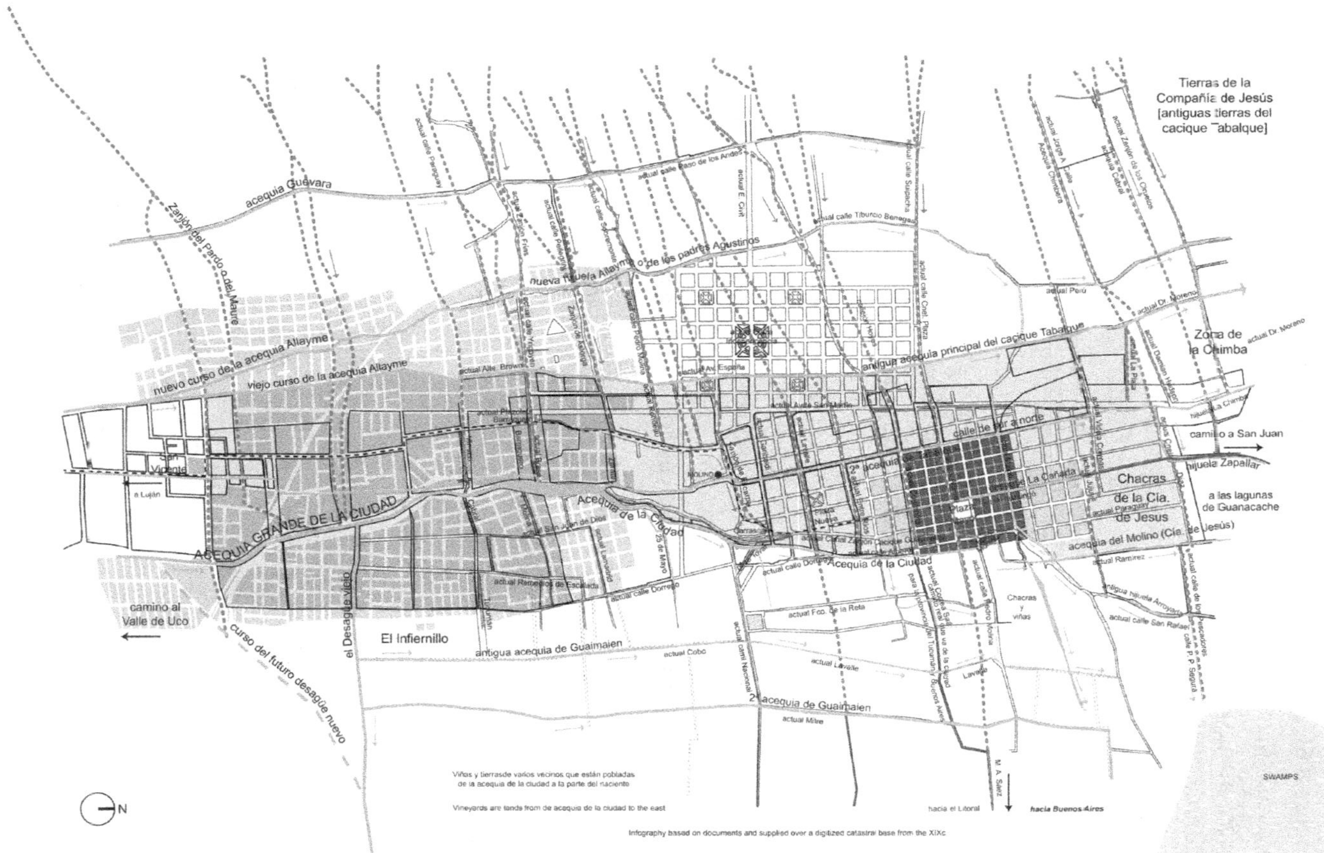

Figure 8.5. Plan of Mendoza, Infography, 1754. Image courtesy of Jorge Ricardo Ponte.

Mendoza's new plan resembled that of a typical Spanish colonial town (figure 8.6). But it was the Avenida San Nicolás, later renamed the Avenida San Martín, the extension of the *alameda* created in 1808 as a public *paseo* alongside the Tajamar Canal (1764) (figure 8.7), that became the commercial center, the first street in Mendoza to be paved and lighted.[13]

The extensive earthquake damage sustained by the canals in the highland areas west of Mendoza made its water supply and distribution an even more critical concern. Construction of the del Oeste Canal in 1880 helped increase the amount of water available in southwest areas of the city. In the early 1900s, lining the Zanjón Canal with reinforced concrete allowed its flow to be closely regulated, tripling its capacity and relieving chronic water shortages. Construction of *acequias* in the new city commenced in 1872, but unlike the existing canals which allowed water to follow its natural course, they were laid out orthogonally to facilitate clear subdivision of properties and provide fresh potable water as well as irrigation for the large shade trees that would eventually line both sides of every street in Mendoza. To accommodate their extensive root systems, wide pavements known as *veredas* extended from edges of the *acequias* to the street curbs. Together the ensemble of *acequias*, street trees, and

Figure 8.6. Plaza San Martín, Mendoza. Photo by René Davids, 2011.

Figure 8.7. Alameda, Mendoza. Photo by René Davids, 2011.

veredas constitutes Mendoza's most memorable urban feature (figures 8.8 and 8.9).

The splendor of tree-canopied streets irrigated by *acequias* suggested wealth of a sort that would have been unimaginable in the immediate aftermath of the earthquake or at any time during the preceding three centuries. But in the late nineteenth century, after Mendoza's reconstruction was substantially complete, its economic fortunes began to improve. Grazing pastures for cattle crossing the Andes and flour mills, both watered by the *acequias*, had long been the mainstays of the local economy. But in the mid- to late nineteenth century, Mendoza's irrigation-dependent industries began to be outperformed by naturally irrigated competitors in northeast Argentina, at about the same time that the arrival of the railroads in 1885 enabled the efficient distribution of goods and people throughout the region. The railways established commercial links from Mendoza to the rest of Argentina and through Buenos Aires to Europe, carrying immigrants who would be employed in the new food processing and bottled wine industries. At approximately the same time, the introduction of local tramways stimulated expansion and development to the southeast. Enactment of the Ley General de Aguas, or General Water Law,

Figure 8.8. Pedestrian Mall Sarmiento, Mendoza. Photo by René Davids, 2011.

Figure 8.9. New city street showing *acequia*, Mendoza. Photo by René Davids, 2011.

in 1884 organized surface irrigation throughout Mendoza Province under the control of the Departamento General de Aguas, today the Departamento General de Irrigación, which began the construction of dikes and dams to better control water delivery and enable a more orderly expansion of cropland. The Ley General de Aguas also regulated all permanent and future rights to use surface water and groundwater in accordance with actual usage at the time it was accepted. Because there was no groundwater pumping at the time the law was passed, the legal and regulatory loophole resulted in unlimited exploitation of the aquifer for agricultural uses, rather than a more balanced allocation that would ensure long-term protection of a precious resource for a broader range of uses, including urban water supply.[14]

Mendoza's prosperity increased with industrialization, population growth, and urban expansion, but the rapid pace of economic development caused pollution levels to rise in the already contaminated *acequias*, the only water source for the poorest residents of the old colonial core and widely believed to be responsible for chronic public health problems. Following an outbreak of cholera in the summer of 1886–87, popular pressure forced the authorities to consider alternatives to the *acequias* for potable water, and public demands intensified for the installation of an underground municipal water system with sanitary sewers. A campaign was begun to eradicate the street trees, whose shade was claimed to be oppressive, so that the *acequias* could also be removed, but the counterargument which ultimately prevailed maintained that without the dense shade provided by the trees, summer heat in Mendoza would be unbearable, and sanitary sewers were soon installed to protect the *acequias* from contamination with untreated wastes.

Protection of Mendoza's water supply also figured prominently in the development in 1896 of the 971-acre Parque del Oeste, known today as the Parque San Martin, which extended from the western city limit to the foothills of the Andes. With its extensive lawns, wide tree-lined avenues, botanical garden, and artificial lake designed by Argentine landscape architect Carlos Thays, the Parque del Oeste was a synthesis of English and French landscape traditions similar to other urban parks built throughout the world at the end of the nineteenth century as refuges for city dwellers from congestion and pollution. To mitigate the effects of unsound agricultural practices, poor land management, and extensive cattle grazing that had eliminated plant cover on the hillsides, leaving precious topsoil vulnerable to erosion from wind and water, the Parque del Oeste included a tract of 50,000 trees to serve as a flood control barrier. Replacement vegetation was installed on the barren slopes to stabilize them and prevent contamination of surface water from runoff following summer storms.

Metropolitan Mendoza

By the turn of the twentieth century, the once dusty low-rise agricultural settlement of Mendoza had become a large industrial city, and challenges to its water quality and environmental equilibrium increased as pressures for further development intensified. Disorganized, poorly planned growth resulted in the incorporation of irrigation and drainage infrastructure into the urban fabric and increased the amount of pollutants of various kinds dumped into the *acequias*, including industrial and household effluents, that damaged the health of those residents for whom they remained the primary source of water. Because the land slopes eastward, the water-borne pollutants were transferred by the *acequias* to rural areas outside the city, causing environmental and landscape degradation along the way, contaminating crops, and diminishing the quality of life for both urban and rural inhabitants.[15]

Widespread disposal of solid wastes clogged the *acequias*, and their beds were partially blocked by the construction of bridges built to encourage pedestrian traffic in commercial areas of Mendoza, causing overflows that flooded city streets, highways, and agricultural land with polluted water. During brief periods of intense rain, surface flows triggered landslides in urban and suburban areas, and the capacity of the *acequias* to contain the overflow was exceeded and caused flooding and crop losses in agricultural areas. Excessive exploitation of the upper aquifer for irrigation has compromised its capacity to recharge with freshwater and a widespread reversal of the natural vertical hydraulic gradient, forcing salinity down into the lower aquifer and threatening its suitability for irrigation of salt-sensitive crops such as grapes and other fruit.

International wine production and export firms relying solely on groundwater arrived in the 1990s and situated their water demands upstream of irrigated agricultural land, reducing the amount of irrigation water available to farmers at lower elevations, who constructed increasingly deeper wells to compensate for the deficit. As a result, the aquifer is being depleted due to excessive exploitation at an alarming rate.[16]

Proposals have been made to control aquifer salinization and substantially reduce pumping of groundwater by requiring irrigators to relinquish groundwater extraction rights; backfilling and sealing the numerous poorly constructed wells that accelerate the downward migration of saline groundwater to the deeper layers of the aquifer; and improving the efficiency of the *acequias* and/or replacing them with conduits.[17]

Mendoza's recent growth has been possible because over the course of many centuries, *acequia*-based irrigation systems substantially modified its original semiarid ecosystem. While necessary or desirable in some locations, impervious linings and conduits may compromise the benefits that *acequias* provide to metropolitan Mendoza's ecosystem by transforming the hydrology that supports many of its functions and significantly altering the landscapes between *acequias* and their supplying watercourses whose vitality depends on the interactions of surface water and groundwater. Researchers investigating seepage from a traditional *acequia* and the groundwater response along the Rio Grande in north-central New Mexico found that as water seeps into the *acequia's* bed and banks, it causes nearby groundwater levels to rise, sustaining riparian vegetation alongside it.[18] The flow caused by ditch seepage may dilute contaminants in shallow groundwater and protect deeper groundwater by flushing contaminants away from it. *Acequias* are functionally similar to natural riparian systems that act as transition zones between aquatic and dry land environments, with vegetation responsible for attenuating floodwater damage, filtering contaminants, maintaining bank stability, recharging groundwater, and protecting water quality while supporting wildlife habitat for species reliant on *acequia*-associated riparian vegetation for nesting habitat, cover, and refuge. Lining *acequias* or replacing them with conduits to reduce seepage would also reduce the recharge to shallow groundwater already contaminated by salinization as well as the volume of groundwater return flow to the Mendoza River. The research indicates that *acequia* systems can prove ecologically beneficial, supporting agricultural production while minimizing its negative effects on the environment and natural resource base.

In the early twenty-first century, agriculture, industry, and urban development compete for a diminishing water supply in metropolitan Mendoza, with the fourth largest population in Argentina of well over a million, 95 percent of whom live on the 3 percent of the land that is irrigated. To ensure its economic survival, the growing demand for water as well as the increasing amount of salinity, pollution, and waterborne wastes must result in an increased awareness of the importance of water resources for life throughout the province. New landfills and waste transfer stations have been built east of Mendoza, but discharge of household and industrial wastes into the canals continues to degrade them, and despite more stringent environmental controls, *acequias* are still used as landfills.

A recent study by researchers from the Universidad de Cuyo to assess the extent to which residents value and use the *acequias* and the success of initiatives by government agencies to educate the public about their vital environmental role revealed that they are not valued as essential to Mendoza's quality of life, and efforts by provincial and municipal agencies to raise public awareness about the importance of protecting water sources were not sufficient to change destructive behaviors, more prevalent in neighborhoods of lower socioeconomic status, where most waste accumulates in the *acequias*.[19] Most believed that Mendoza's economic success was due to the perseverance of an industrious local workforce rather than the presence of water resources and systematic irrigation, although the former is very much dependent on the latter.[20] These results are attributed to the absence of integrated and sustainable environmental policies throughout Mendoza province, as well as a decline in the quality and quantity of provincial and local services available to those of lower socioeconomic status.

The *acequias* of Mendoza belong to an environmental legacy that predates the arrival of the Spanish by several millennia, forged as dry land river basin communities in the Andes adapted their settlements to the local topography and the hydrological cycle and developed water-management regimes based on social order to control common usage of a precious resource. Ignoring specific directives in the Laws of the Indies, Pedro del Castillo appropriated the irrigation network built by the indigenous Huarpes into his foundation plan for Mendoza, adjusting the layout of its *ejido* to take advantage of their canals and *acequias* that channeled runoff from mountain streams. During the colonial period, water use in Mendoza was based on the pre-Colombian practices of the Huarpes and Arab community water rights traditions brought to Argentina by the Spanish. Both systems emphasized cooperation among water users with special provisions to accommodate the needs of individual areas as determined by their natural settings. Like its predecessor, the new city of Mendoza, rebuilt higher up in the foothills after the catastrophic earthquake of 1862, was deferential to the existing irrigation system, whose *acequias* continue to water the poplars and acacias that form dense canopies of shade over all of Mendoza's streets.

Despite the degradation to which they have been subjected, the *acequias* are fundamental to Mendoza's regional and urban identity, as well as its economic future. Without the *acequias*, the oasis of Mendoza could exist in its present form, but their survival is in the balance, dependent on increasing public awareness of and appreciation for their essential role in maintaining its livability. In most cities, water is invisible, piped through underground conduits that remove it from public view. Elsewhere in Latin America, with the exception of some rural areas where they have been repurposed for irrigation, *acequias* have been covered or filled in, but in Mendoza they provide visible traces of a continuity with the land use traditions of an ancient past, as well as an affirmation of the life-giving presence of water in a desert, a celebration of abundance amid scarcity.

III

HILLS, INFRASTRUCTURE, AND SOCIAL ORDER

9

Santiago de Chile and the Changing Meaning of Its Hills

RODRIGO PEREZ DE ARCE,
TRANSLATED AND ADAPTED BY RENÉ DAVIDS

For the first two-thirds of the nineteenth century after Chile declared independence from Spain in 1810, the capital city of Santiago de Chile remained an unprepossessing town with almost no public green spaces (figure 9.1).[1] By the 1870s, with increasing wealth derived from agriculture and mining, a major program of transformation was begun in the Chilean capital, influenced by Emperor Napoleon III's vast program of public works in Paris. The Quinta Normal, a botanical precinct, became a formal public garden, the dusty old Champs de Mars was transformed by European landscape designers into Parque Cousiño (today Parque O'Higgins), and the island hill of Cerro Santa Lucía became an urban park (figures 9.2–9.7).[2]

Although sited on mostly level ground, Santiago seems hilly because of the proximity of the Andes Mountains and foothills. Positioned like a fallen meteorite a few blocks from the Plaza de Armas, the Cerro Santa Lucía was both the most enigmatic and familiar of Santiago's hills, an isolated outcrop surrounded by a mass of alluvial debris offering privileged views in all directions. Its transformation into a park was Mayor Benjamín Vicuña Mackenna's most cherished enterprise during his term of office from 1872 to 1875, which he believed would have a positive impact on the city's poor hygienic conditions, provide a safe place to promenade when seasonal rains flooded flatter areas of town, and give Santiago a park comparable to the best he had seen in Paris. Not by coincidence, the design for the Cerro's remodel was laid out in association with French nationals: architect Lucien Henault and engineer Ernesto Ansart, with native-born

Figure 9.1. Plan of Santiago de Chile in 1600. Sketch by Luis Thayer Ojeda. Courtesy of the archive of Memoria Chilena, Biblioteca Nacional de Chile.

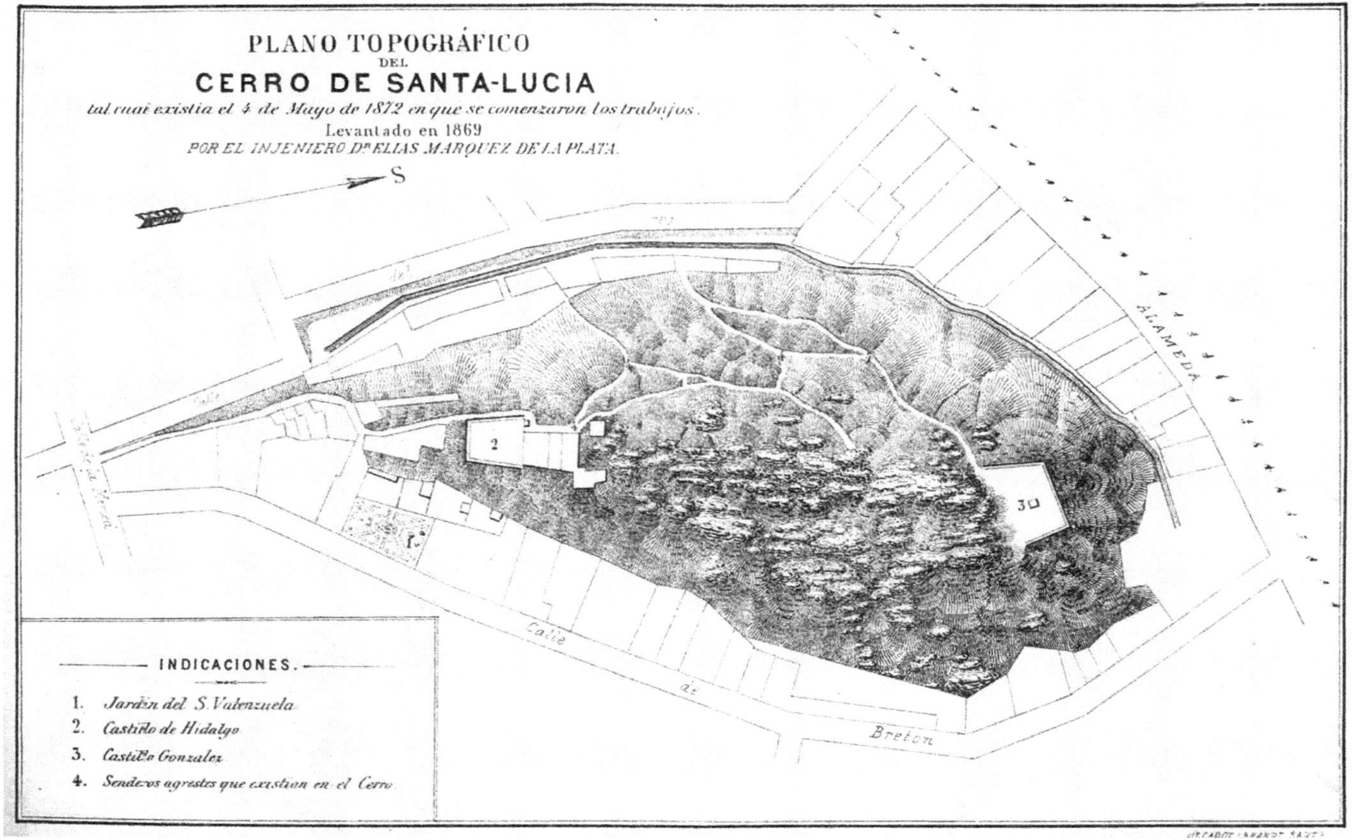

Figure 9.2. Plan of Cerro Santa Lucía, Santiago de Chile, 1869. Image from Benjamín Vicuña Mackenna's Álbum del Santa Lucía (Santiago, 1874). Courtesy of the archive of Memoria Chilena, Biblioteca Nacional de Chile.

Figure 9.3. Southwest side of Cerro Santa Lucía, Santiago, 1874. Image from Benjamín Vicuña Mackenna's *Álbum del Santa Lucía* (Santiago, 1874). Courtesy of the archive of Memoria Chilena, Biblioteca Nacional de Chile.

Figure 9.4. Cerro Santa Lucía taken from Monjitas. Image from Benjamín Vicuña Mackenna's *Álbum del Santa Lucía* (Santiago, 1874). Courtesy of the archive of Memoria Chilena, Biblioteca Nacional de Chile.

Figure 9.5. Cerro Santa Lucía, Santiago. Photo by René Davids, 2011.

Manuel Aldunate, the architect's disciple.[3] Financing for this enterprise was supplemented with private donations, including reportedly Vicuña Mackenna's own funds, and construction was under way from 1872 until the park's inauguration in 1874, with the assistance of miners, masons, and free prison labor.[4]

Before the remodel took place, the Cerro Santa Lucía had been used as a criminal hideout, a quarry, and a garbage dump as well as a burial ground for "dissidents" (Protestants and Jews) on the eastern slope. The new park linked two large terraces, Hidalgo and Marco, which had been erected as defensive positions during the Chilean struggle for independence (1814–18).[5] The first significant arrival points on the Cerro Santa Lucía, these terraces were located at approximately the same elevation on opposite sides of the hill (figure 9.5). Farther up the slopes were a viewing pavilion, Chile's first museum, a restaurant, and a theater. To connect the park with the neoclassical landscape tradition, Vicuña Mackenna imported numerous French sculptures of figures from Greek and Roman mythology that were mounted on pedestals at various locations in the park, along with other sculptures of historical figures associated with the struggles for independence of former Spanish colonies, evidence of his national and regional pride. The hilltop was crowned by an observation

Figure 9.6. Balcón Volado, Cerro Santa Lucía. Image from Benjamín Vicuña Mackenna's *Álbum del Santa Lucía* (Santiago, 1874). Courtesy of the archive of Memoria Chilena, Biblioteca Nacional de Chile.

pavilion that further emphasized its extraordinary profile when viewed from other areas of the city. Vicuña Mackenna sought to identify the buildings in the park with various historical periods he regarded as appropriate: the west-facing slope of the hill was reconfigured to resemble a medieval fortress, a chapel was built in neo-Gothic style, and a gardener's cottage was in Swiss alpine style.[6] The Cerro Santa Lucía became a prominent showplace that Isabel Anderson described in *Circling South America* as "the most perfect hanging gardens in the world for those who could afford the entry charge" (figure 9.6).[7]

Like the construction of Parc des Buttes Chaumont (figure 9.8) in Paris, designed by Jean-Charles Adolphe Alphand and built between 1864 and 1867, the refurbishment of Cerro Santa Lucía was in part the product of a preoccupation with hygiene shared by many urban reformers in the second half of the nineteenth century.[8] Vicuña Mackenna described his project for the Cerro Santa Lucía as a place of "recreation and art" but also "health and hygiene."[9] The argument that the hill park would improve urban sanitation was not without its detractors, as its transformation cost

Figure 9.7. Western side of Cerro Santa Lucía. Photo by René Davids, 2011.

Figure 9.8. Parc des Buttes Chaumont. Jean-Charles Alphand, Paris, 1864. Photo courtesy of Marc Treib.

an amount almost equal to Santiago's entire annual operating budget. In challenging those who criticized his ambitions as inappropriate for a city with modest resources and pervasive social inequalities, Vicuña Mackenna argued that the park was essential to promoting democracy, seemingly oblivious to the fact that the Cerro Santa Lucía was only accessible to a small segment of the population.[10] Like other members of the Chilean upper classes, Vicuña Mackenna did not necessarily believe that democracy was suitable for everyone, and he planned to divide Santiago with a green beltway—*camino de cintura*—that would create a *cordon sanitaire*, separating the "enlightened, Christian, and opulent city" where the Cerro Santa Lucía was located from the outlying districts that he considered to be an infectious sewer of vice, crime, and disease, a "horse stable of death."[11] His other argument—that the provision of a high place would provide conditions conducive to exceptional health, along with what he referred to as "a not too small health hospital"—was a recurring theme in Santiago's professional circles.[12] Outbreaks of smallpox, cholera, and typhoid were common, and highly visible populations of vagrants, prostitutes, and other delinquents helped to sustain the local obsession with hygiene. Another desirable consequence of the transformation of former urban wilderness areas such as Buttes Chaumont and the Cerro Santa Lucía were the handsome profits accruing to those who owned real estate in the vicinity of the redeveloped parks.[13]

While underscoring the distinction between the more and less healthy areas of the city, the winding paths and ascending stairs installed on the Cerro Santa Lucía also provided a stark contrast with Santiago's straight gridiron streets. The system of paths was created to support different kinds of movement: walking, climbing, riding in horse-drawn carriages. Frequent bends in the paths produced a succession of rapidly changing vistas that produced a kind of visual *staccato*, a continuously refreshed stimulation of visual perception. The designs of Buttes Chaumont and the Cerro Santa Lucía were in marked contrast to eighteenth-century landscape parks such as Stowe and Stourhead which were structured around a series of tableaux intended to be appreciated at a contemplative strolling pace. The increasing popularity of train travel in Europe during the latter half of the nineteenth century coincided with the development of urban parks that offered changing views of the landscape in rapid succession, establishing a new link between the city and the countryside.

Because of its significant role in advancing Chile's economic progress, the display of new technology used to create the Cerro Santa Lucía park provided a spectacle as compelling as its landscapes and outlooks. Both Parc des Buttes Chaumont and Cerro Santa Lucía used horse-powered hydraulic pumps to lift water to the upper areas of the parks. But in the Parisian park, the technology was carefully concealed while at the Cerro Santa Lucía, the pumps were located in a wheelhouse at the foot of the hill, a few feet away from the Alameda, Santiago's most important avenue, with a sign prominently displayed on the pediment advertising its function.[14] Certain types of contemporary technology such as the suspension bridge were conspicuous in Parc des Buttes Chaumont but more mundane products of engineering such as plumbing and hydraulics were concealed to sustain the illusion of the park as a wholly natural landscape, with no visible evidence of the advanced earth-moving machinery and technology required to create it. The Cerro Santa Lucía was a rugged outcrop whose transformation required the construction of sturdy masonry retaining walls and paths carved by blasting with dynamite through the rocky terrain. The role of technology in the creation of the park was reinforced by other symbols of progress, such as the gas lighting installed throughout and others desired by Vicuña Mackenna that were never installed: a monumental clock, an aerial railway, and a lighthouse that would have made an ever-present light show visible throughout the city.[15]

The Cerro Santa Lucía was an isolated urban set piece in Santiago, whose overall standard of development was aptly characterized by an English diplomat as rudimentary at best: "Chileans call their metropolis the (South) American Paris, in reality Santiago is only a little fragment of Paris inserted in an Indian village."[16] Nineteenth-century Paris was considered to be the epitome of modernity and refinement, a model for everything from fashion to architecture and linked to revolutionary democracy rather than a legacy of Spanish colonization and oppression. The design of the Cerro Santa Lucía was only superficially "Parisian" as was evident in the unabashed evidence of the technology required to mitigate the coarseness of its topography, a striking contrast with the smoother landscapes and sophisticated illusions of Parc des Buttes Chaumont. But for the general public that had little if any contact with Europe, the Cerro Santa Lucía was as good as anything to be found in Paris, a jewel that was both an expression of urban progress and a platform from where development in the surrounding city could be monitored and enjoyed. In 1901, writer Sanhueza Lizardi reported that "the eager eyes got charmed at 630 meters above the sea of the Cerro Santa Lucía looking down at a beautiful panorama of the Mapocho Valley with its capricious houses extending below through a wide green carpet embraced by a belt of very high mountains covered with a cloak of snow and a blue sky; a panorama that inspires and inflames the mind." From the summit the view could also inspire a more somber reflection, as the same writer found evidence in the landscape of the cruel Spanish domination of the indigenous people who had originally inhabited the valley.[17]

Vicuña Mackenna regarded the successful transformation of Cerro Santa Lucía as a model to be emulated in provincial capitals,[18] and soon afterwards Cerro San Cristóbal, Santiago's other important island hill, also become a park, with supporters making similar claims about purer air, health, and public hygiene benefits that it would bring to Santiago's citizens. An article in the popular magazine *Zig-Zag* claimed that the park would be "a great lung for Santiago" and a place of pilgrimage for those who "searched for leafy trees and the pure beneficent oxygen of the mountains." Like the Cerro Santa Lucía, the Cerro San Cristóbal was inhabited by criminals and vermin that lived in its caves and had also been used as a quarry for stone with which to pave Santiago's city streets and line the culvert built for the Mapocho River.[19] When the French government donated the resources to build a sanctuary and sculpture of the Virgin Mary to celebrate the fiftieth anniversary of the doctrine of the Immaculate Conception in 1908, it replaced a Christian cross that had crowned the hill since 1561 but was difficult to maintain.[20] An observatory was built on Cerro San Cristóbal in the mid-nineteenth century because the air surrounding the hill was relatively clear.

The transformation of the hill owed much to the efforts of Alberto Mackenna Subercaseaux, the mayor of Santiago from 1921 to 1927 and an admirer of Baron Haussmann's work in Paris.[21] A strong proponent of modernization, Mackenna feared that Santiago was being overtaken by cities he regarded as lesser capitals, such as La Paz, Bolivia.[22] He strongly supported a plan drawn up by the Sociedad Central de Arquitectos in 1912 that proposed cutting a series of diagonal avenues connected by traffic circles similar to the Parisian boulevards laid out by Haussmann through Santiago's relentless gridiron plan.[23] With the exception of an entrance plaza in front of the Cerro San Cristóbal, the plan was not implemented,

Figure 9.9. View of Cerro San Cristóbal from Cerro Santa Lucía. Photo by René Davids, 2011.

but the park itself became the mayor's favorite and best-known project. The transformation of the Cerro San Cristóbal began in 1917 after the hill was expropriated from private ownership, and work continues today. The renovation of Cerro San Cristóbal, unlike that of Cerro Santa Lucía, involved many professionals among those who contributed to its design, including French landscape architect Carlos Thais, a disciple of Alphand and creator of the botanical garden in Buenos Aires (figure 9.9). A four station watering program and irrigation channels were installed to mitigate the hill's arid climate. Roads were built in 1921, followed by the construction of a zoo, whose mediocre design was best described as a *conventillo*, or tenement, for animals.[24]

Luciano Kulczewski, a Chilean architect of Polish descent, received the commissions for the park's most important built works, including the funicular's lower terminal, the restaurant and its adjacent terrace on the summit, and other minor buildings.[25] Kulczewski's work often displayed an idiosyncratic sense of form with influences from Art Nouveau and the designs of Victor Horta, the Belgian architect who was perhaps the best-known architect working in that idiom, but his stylistic vocabulary was more angular, eclectic, restrained, influenced by the neogothic style more than Horta. Searching for an architectural idiom and suitable style for rugged terrain of the Cerro Santa Lucía, Kulczewski designed the lower funicular terminal to resemble a medieval Roman castle built with stone extracted from the quarries on Cerro San Cristóbal. The brick arches, stained glass windows, and use of stone in both the terminal and the restaurant buildings on the Cerro San Cristóbal summit exemplified Kulczewski's penchant for a rich material palette.

Despite the dramatic and expressive design decisions, Kulczewski's work on Cerro San Cristóbal was no match for Catalán architect Antoni Gaudí's Parc Guell in Barcelona, to which it is occasionally compared.[26] It is unclear whether Kulczewski was familiar with Gaudí's work, but one hundred years after Chilean independence, as a way to counteract what was perceived as the increasing influence of North American pragmatism, Chile's cultural elite began a search to reconnect with their Spanish roots, and finding inspiration from a Spanish architect might have been part of this trend.[27] Whether or not the references were intended, Santiago's climate and topography are similar to those of northern Spain, and Kulczewski's use of stone from local quarries produced an idiosyncratic style strongly evocative of Parc Guell.

As the city expanded eastward toward the foothills of the Andes, the Cerro San Cristóbal became an increasingly popular place "to get out of the oven of Santiago, refresh the brain and soul with breezes and the enlivening spectacle."[28] Beyond fresh air, the attraction was the ascent by funicular or car to the summit of the hill and views that miniaturized the city—one observer called them toy houses whose streets were being used by insects[29]—and offered returning visitors a platform from which to view and assess the changing urban panorama. As the highest accessible place in Santiago, the top of Cerro San Cristóbal was an important new vantage point from which to assess its continuing progress.[30] The city's development relative to that of other international urban centers was a local concern bordering on obsession and a frequent subject of newspaper articles. By the early decades of the twentieth century, the generally unfavorable commentary about Santiago from foreign visitors of fifty years earlier had become mostly complimentary, partly because its more miserable areas were overlooked, but not by Santiago's most important newspaper, *El Mercurio*, which relentlessly cataloged its deficiencies, describing one neighborhood as an "immense worm pit of vice and poverty,"[31] none of it visible from the summit of Cerro San Cristóbal. After an extended visit in 1929 and 1930, French town planner Jacques H. Lambert thanked his host, Mayor Alberto Mackenna, with a tribute to Santiago: "In remembrance of a peregrination to one of the most beautiful wonders of the world, in the heights of a capital, queen of a unique place."[32]

Conclusion

In the late nineteenth and early twentieth centuries, two island hills in Santiago were transformed from barren wastelands to monumental landscapes as city leaders built public spaces expressive of civic ideals into symbols of technological progress based on European precedents, affirming its status as a modern capital. The parks had a strong appeal for Chileans anxious to achieve a European standard of living, but they were also expressions of the search for an original, independent creative identity. The refurbished Cerros Santa Lucía and San Cristóbal provided stage sets for the elite to display their cultural sophistication and viewing platforms from which to admire Santiago's progress while contributing to its changing identity and growing stature as one of the world's most progressive cities.

10

Valparaíso

A Future in the Balance

RENÉ DAVIDS

During the nineteenth century, the port of Valparaíso, Chile, was transformed from a colonial outpost into a thriving cosmopolitan center of global commerce before the opening of the Panama Canal in 1914 eliminated the need for a voyage around Cape Horn to travel between the Atlantic and Pacific Oceans. The end of its status as a center of international trade began a seemingly permanent economic decline until Valparaíso received a UNESCO World Heritage Site designation in 2003 for its well-preserved port infrastructure, bringing new capital investment and an improved outlook for the future. If Valparaíso is to recover its former prosperity without sacrificing its cultural identity, a balance must be achieved between the interests of business leaders and politicians relying on development of the tourist industry to boost the local economy with the concerns of longtime residents protective of their urban heritage.

Founded on a precarious site in one of the world's most earthquake-prone countries, Valparaíso's history has been one of an organic process of urbanization periodically interrupted by natural disasters. Sited on a narrow coastal plain, encircled by steep hills rising to a height of almost 2,000 feet, with unstable terrain, occasional earthquakes, wildfires, and landslides, its harbor battered by prevailing winds and surging seas from the north, Valparaíso's most attractive feature was its proximity to Santiago, Chile's capital. Although founded in 1544, Valparaíso only expanded three centuries later after the development of elevator and earth-moving technology in the mid-nineteenth century overcame the barriers to growth presented by the hills and marshy sediments in the harbor, which had prevented large ships from using it. After docks and quays were built, Valparaíso soon became the most important port on the South Pacific coast after passage through the Strait of Magellan, attracting trade and international immigrants.[1]

As Valparaíso grew, its strategic location, challenging site, and the cultural diversity of its population profoundly influenced its urban form. Unlike most Spanish colonial cities whose layout and organization were proscribed by policies originating in sixteenth-century Madrid, Valparaíso was never formally planned, but expanded organically when more space was needed, shaped mainly by the nineteenth-century European planning principles imported with the new immigrants, loosely adapted to its topographical irregularities. A shortage of flat land on El Plan, the narrow strip of land on the shoreline, resulted in two city-building initiatives: an ongoing project to enlarge the coastal plain using rubble and fill quarried from the hills, eventually quadrupling its area, and expansion into the hills themselves, many with unstable ground and scored by ravines.[2] The urban fabric around the harbor has a vernacular grid with public spaces fanning outward from the port to the foothills, where individual builders improvised their own techniques for managing the difficult terrain: massive retaining walls, narrow, winding streets, stairways, bridges stringing the isolated hills together, plazas, *paseos*, and *miradores*, the outlooks that serve as the main public spaces of hillside neighborhoods. Lightweight multistory dwellings similar to North American balloon framing and small, densely packed houses were built in a variety of imported architectural styles, typically constructed of wood, adobe infill, and metal cladding, as well as repurposed salvage materials such as the corrugated sheet metal from shipping containers.

To overcome the hardships of daily commutes over steep, unpaved paths to the commercial center and enhance the appeal of the developing residential neighborhoods, individual entrepreneurs installed thirty inclined funiculars of various sizes, known locally as *ascensores*, between 1883 and 1912, linking the hillsides with the coastal strip, some of which became a public utility service in 1915 (figure 10.2). The combination of the *ascensores* and the existing streetcar network operated on the coastal strip provided Valparaíso with one of the most efficient municipal transit systems in South America, allowing relatively quick and effortless commutes between the hills and the commercial center on El Plan (figures 10.3 and 10.4).[3] Not only did the *ascensores* solve a transportation problem, but

Figure 10.1. View of Valparaíso, Chile. Photo by René Davids, 2011.

their top and bottom stations also became nodes of social and commercial activity for the new hillside neighborhoods, where the sweeping panoramas previously visible only from private dwellings were now available for all of Valparaíso's residents to view their city as an integrated whole.

Technological innovation enabled Valparaíso's rapid growth in the nineteenth century but also hastened its decline in the twentieth. The spectacular engineering triumph of the Panama Canal in 1914 was the single most important factor responsible for the collapse of Valparaíso's international trade-based economy. As ships traveling between Europe and the West Coast of the United States were no longer required to navigate the long, treacherous passage around Cape Horn, Valparaíso's strategic position as the first port of call on the Pacific coast became irrelevant. Soon there was no longer sufficient economic activity to draw new immigrants, businesses relocated north to the beach town of Viña del Mar or east to Santiago, the middle classes departed, drastically reducing the tax base, and Valparaíso seemed doomed to a long twilight of urban decline. At the end of the twentieth century, even as liberalized trade policies and modernization of its banking system brought dramatic improvements to Chile's economy, Valparaíso remained impoverished, but with its nineteenth-century industrial infrastructure largely intact, if somewhat

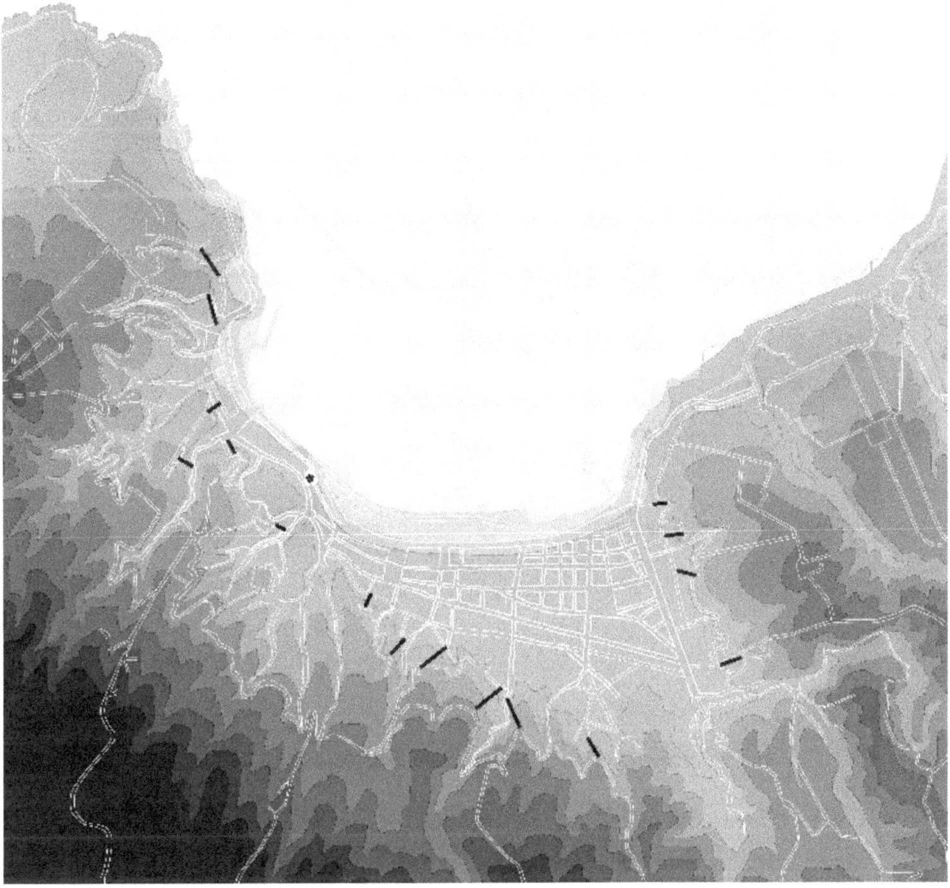

Figure 10.2. Plan of Valparaíso with location of *ascensores*. Drawing by René Davids.

dilapidated.[4] In 2003, the area around the harbor, part of the coastal plain, and several hills were designated a UNESCO World Heritage site, the "Historic Quarter of the Seaport City of Valparaíso," an exceptionally well preserved example of an urban port during an early phase of globalized commerce.[5]

Nurtured by Valparaíso's pluralistic culture, the creativity and entrepreneurial spirit of its immigrants overcame the environmental challenges and physical obstacles presented by its difficult topography, producing a distinctive urban fabric that remains an enduring part of its civic identity, a synthesis of natural and constructed form. The documents submitted by the Chilean government in support of Valparaíso's World Heritage list

Left: Figure 10.3. Ascensor Mariposa, Valparaíso. Photo by René Davids, 2011.

Below: Figure 10.4. Ascensor Las Monjas, Valparaíso. Photo by René Davids, 2011.

nomination referred to "an indefinable quality which makes this city, with its light and shadows, to be highly esteemed by its inhabitants, to inspire a deep admiration in both Chileans and foreigners, and to transcend in artistic works of exceptional value" as well as the effects of geography and topography on its architecture and urban design; the spatial and visual cohesion afforded by its amphitheater-like setting, ravines, and public spaces; an urban layout based on topographic conformation rather than planning; architecture responsive to its context with spaces for socializing and savoring the spectacular views; and a unity which is a synthesis of diversity.[6]

After it was listed as a UNESCO World Heritage city, Valparaíso's community and business leaders along with local government officials focused on the creation of new initiatives to attract tourists, catalyze private and public investment, revitalize civic infrastructure, generate jobs, and improve the quality of urban life for its residents. In 2005, the government of Chile received a loan from the Inter-American Development Bank (IDB) that would eventually fund the Programa de Recuperación y Desarrollo Urbano de Valparaíso (Program for the Recovery and Urban Development of Valparaíso, or PRDUV), a management agency supplemented with Chilean government funds for the implementation of a comprehensive strategy to reclaim areas with historical value and economic potential through investments in civic infrastructure and both public and private real estate. Project funds were used to finance street and sidewalk renovation including lighting installations, rehabilitation of some historic residences that had fallen into disrepair, refurbishment of parks and public buildings, painting and restoration of residential facades, and repairs to some of the *ascensores*.[7]

One of the largest and most important initiatives to receive a major stimulus from Valparaíso's World Heritage designation was the Proyecto del Borde Costero (Coastal Edge Project), intended to improve the public access to a waterfront historically reserved for port activities.[8] Its first project was the transformation of the 230 × 30 meter wood and concrete Muelle Barón, a pier built by an English firm for the state railway service to facilitate the handling of coal between 1912 and 1917, into a new *paseo*, or a public promenade, with a small marina. Muelle Barón has a wood viewing deck raised over a public meeting room and café, a popular venue for evening strollers and a spectacular vantage point from which to take in the panoramic views of the Pacific and the surrounding hills (figure 10.5).

Figure 10.5. Muelle Barón, Valparaíso. Photo by René Davids, 2011.

Two of the old dock cranes were retained to provide vertical definition, and lighting installed overhead and at ground level emphasizes the linearity of the promenade and distinguishes it from the other port facilities. Often used as a venue for art exhibitions and other large-scale public events, Muelle Barón's enthusiastic reception prompted the construction of another two *paseos*, Paseo Wheelwright (2005–8), the longest of the three, and the Paseo Altamirano (2007), located on Valparaíso's northwest coast, featuring a series of pavilions with sweeping views of the sea cliffs.[9] Together the three projects represent the most recent examples of Valparaíso's centuries-old typology of promenades, outlooks, *miradores*, and viewing platforms (figure 10.6).

Other projects have struggled with pressures to meet the elevated expectations presumed to accompany a World Heritage designation. After it was announced that the Centro Cultural Ex-Cárcel de Valparaíso would be built on the site of the old city prison to mark the bicentenary of Chile's independence from Spain in 2010, the project's sponsors at the Ministerio de Obras Públicas de Chile (MOP) were delighted when celebrated Brazilian architect Oscar Niemeyer offered to donate a design that all parties expected would attract worldwide attention, even possibly replicating the success of Frank Gehry's Guggenheim Museum in Bilbao. When Niemeyer's proposal was discovered to be a variation of his earlier design for a cultural center in Avilés, Spain, it generated strong local opposition among those who believed that Valparaíso was entitled to a building appropriate for the context.[10] The proposal was finally rejected after Niemeyer declined to include any of the site's existing historic structures.[11] Following an MOP-sponsored design competition in 2009, the commission was awarded to a firm of young Chilean architects whose winning entry proposed to repurpose substantial parts of the old prisoners' gallery, sections of the perimeter walls, and the gunpowder magazine (figures 10.7 and 10.8).[12] The central raised portion of the prisoners' common was transformed into a public park for outdoor recreation, large enough to host concerts and festivals.[13] Conceived as a metaphorical Valparaíso hill, the Centro Cultural Ex-Cárcel is a bridge beam supported by columns that straddles the adjacent ravines. Connected to the common/park/plaza level and surrounding streets, the rooftop terrace is used as a parking deck and provides access to spaces below for dance and music recitals as well

Figure 10.6. Paseo Altamirano, Camino la Pólvora, Valparaíso. Photo by René Davids, 2011.

Figure 10.7. Parque Cultural Ex-Carcel, Valparaíso. Jonathan Holmes, Martin Labbé, Carolina Portugueis, and Osvaldo Spichiger, 2011. Photo courtesy of the architects.

as another deck that serves as a foyer for the auditorium and leads to the galleries.[14] The former prisoners' gallery contains five conditioned spaces for resident artists, practice and rehearsal rooms for musicians and dancers, and a workshop. The small square penal windows, metal window bars from the old prison repurposed as a balustrade, bricks covered with old prisoner graffiti, and the gunpowder magazine built by the Spanish prior to Chile's independence all provide a striking visual contrast with the new glass, metal, and concrete additions and insertions into the existing

Figure 10.8. Parque Cultural Ex-Carcel, Valparaíso. Photo by René Davids, 2011.

Figure 10.9. Cerro Concepción. Ascensor Reina Victoria, Valparaíso. Photo by René Davids, 2014.

shell. Unlike Niemeyer's proposal, which would have removed all historic buildings from the site, the new Centro Cultural Ex-Cárcel is carefully integrated with the remains of the old prison and Valparaíso's existing network of *paseos*, viewing terraces, and plazas. Rather than a high-profile attraction for international tourists, the new facility is intended to provide a training, performance, and exhibition venue for local artists and a cultural and recreational amenity for the people of Valparaíso.

Debate regarding the Centro Cultural Ex-Cárcel was resolved in favor of those who view the World Heritage designation as an opportunity to repurpose and restore Valparaíso's existing fabric, and to create new buildings that, while modern, are compatible with it, but the fate of another controversial project has yet to be determined. The Mall Plaza Puerto Barón project, a large regional shopping mall, is planned for a

12-hectare parcel of disused port land, including 840 meters of public waterfront, adjacent to Muelle Barón. The site has been leased for thirty years to the Chilean multinational development company S.A.C.I Falabella, whose Mall Plaza brand generates revenue through a diversification of its tenant mix. When the lease expires, control of the site may revert to the Empresa Portuaria de Valparaíso (EPV), Valparaíso's port authority, but at that point S.A.C.I. Falabella also has an option to buy the land outright. The mall buildings will occupy 5 hectares of land and envelop the historic Bodegas Simón Bolívar, which will lose approximately one-quarter of their existing area and be visible only from the mall's interior. While the mall's eventual tenants have not been disclosed, the developer's promotional literature indicates that in addition to retail and parking, restaurants, cinemas, a supermarket, and a luxury hotel will be included in the mix. Realization of the Mall Plaza Puerto Barón complex would regenerate a decayed area of the waterfront, create a large number of jobs, raise tax revenues for a city that clearly needs them, and provide an important boost to the local economy. But ever since plans for the project were announced in 2002, public opposition has intensified, with objections similar to those that scuttled the preliminary plans for the Centro Cultural Ex-Cárcel: an unsuitable project imposed on Valparaíso's complex urban fabric.[15] The developers have expressed their intentions to serve the public interest by stimulating tourism, but their proposal for Mall Plaza Puerto Barón is a generic mass-market product that fails to respect Valparaíso's social, economic, and physical realities, and further compromises the connection of the city with its waterfront, from which it is already separated by rail tracks and a raised highway.[16]

S.A.C.I. Falabella was not required to produce an Environmental Impact Report for Mall Plaza Puerto Barón, and there have been no scientific or academic studies assessing its potential impact on the waterfront, immediate environs, or the city as a whole. As the property is not included in the World Heritage site or the surrounding buffer zone, there has been no attempt to evaluate its effects on either one, so responsibility for the project's environmental impact analysis has been assumed unofficially by concerned citizens of Valparaíso and activist organizations representing the public interest such as Puerto para Ciudadanos. Objections to the project are focused on its proposed bulk, including building heights up to 60 meters, which would further disrupt Valparaíso's visual relationship with the waterfront, as well as possible limitations on public access. While

65 percent of the site, including the waterfront, is supposed to remain open to the public "to realize the local dream" of partaking in the country's economic boom, there are fears that it will be regulated according to social status.[17] The glassy corporate architecture and oversize public spaces depicted in the developer's promotional literature are incompatible with the port's historic fabric. As an attraction intended mainly for tourists, Mall Plaza Puerto Barón will likely be occupied by the same multinational retail tenants renting space in the developers' other projects; any new companies will compete with Valparaíso's struggling small businesses, traditionally the structural base of the local economy. The entire concept of Mall Plaza Puerto Barón compromises the unique identity of Valparaíso that makes it worthy of inclusion on the World Heritage list.

At the invitation of the Chilean government, the UNESCO World Heritage Committee (WHC) undertook a mission to Valparaíso in November 2013 to assess the current state of conservation, management, and protection efforts, as well as ongoing and planned projects impacting the World Heritage site. Regarding the Mall Plaza Puerto Barón, the WHC representatives expressed concern that the people of Valparaíso and visitors alike will lose the possibility of fully appreciating the Bodegas Simón Bolívar and the other significant remains of the old port unless their facades are preserved,[18] and that despite its apparent compliance with Valparaíso's master plan, the design of the Mall Plaza Puerto Barón represents a rupture in the existing urban fabric.[19]

The controversy surrounding the Mall Plaza Puerto Barón project reveals the consequences of a decision-making process narrowly focused on economic considerations. As a part of the continuum of Valparaíso's urban landscape, the World Heritage site shares its geographical and topographical settings shaped by the same nineteenth- and twentieth-century history, technology, and infrastructure, but the Mission found that any research produced by Valparaíso's management plan for the World Heritage site was restricted to the buildings and the public spaces within its physical limits and those of the buffer zone with no consideration of the important relationships between the protected area and the rest of the city, including the port.

There has been no study of the possible future use and occupation of Valparaíso's waterfront, the remnants of Puerto Barón, the surviving *ascensores* beyond those few located within the World Heritage site's perimeter, or scrutiny given to the impact of development in other parts of the city on the site. Because the cultural identity of Valparaíso resides not only with the World Heritage property but the entire city and the port in particular, the WHC mission emphasized that efforts must intensify to conserve surviving architectural elements located outside its perimeter. It is recommended that a study be undertaken to produce an Environmental Impact Report assessing the effects of the Mall Plaza Puerto Barón development on the waterfront, the World Heritage site, and the rest of the city, evaluating alternative land uses on the shoreline, and revise the project consistent with the report's findings.[20]

In its summary, the WHC report emphasized the need to embrace a broader approach to the management of the World Heritage property, noting that the existing Management Plan does not take into account the important relationships between the World Heritage site and the rest of the city, including the port. Once again, the WHC noted the crucial need for a broader consensus to reconcile development proposals with the conservation of the attributes of the World Heritage site, in particular that decision-making be coordinated among national and municipal authorities, including the EPV, as well as with representatives of other interested parties, and that this improved coordination have the force of law to ensure that the coordinated management arrangements are sustained in the future.

While the debate over the future of Valparaíso's waterfront continues, public protests over the decrepit state of the *ascensores* have achieved limited results.[21] Whether due to neglect or insufficient maintenance, the mechanical failure of the *ascensores* contributed to the isolation of entire neighborhoods left without affordable public transportation. Concerned about what they perceived to be the authorities' preoccupation with expenditures on tourist infrastructure while ignoring local needs, angry residents rallied around slogans such as "Too many stairs hurt our hips and taxis hurt our wallets"[22] and "Provide us with more reality and fewer postcards."[23] In 2012, the Chilean government finally agreed to purchase ten of the fifteen surviving *ascensores* with the intention of repairing and returning them to service; seven are now operational. But in 2014 for the first time since 1996, the *ascensores* appeared on the World Monuments Fund Watch List, published every two years as a call to action for cultural heritage sites around the globe at risk from natural, social, political, and economic events, to emphasize the continuing need for their restoration.

In the past, the *ascensores* provided Valparaíso's hillside neighborhoods with an essential mode of public transportation—the fastest, cheapest, and most agreeable way to travel from the hills where more than 90 percent of the city's 300,000 residents live. In 1998, the Chilean government declared the *ascensores* to be national historic monuments, but for a variety of reasons—ownership issues, administrative turf wars, the high cost of repairs, their alleged unprofitability, bureaucratic incompetence, and lack of will—little was done to keep them running.[24] The *ascensores*' mechanical systems are nineteenth-century relics, repairs are expensive, they do not operate on a fixed timetable, leave their stations only when full, and are not officially considered public transportation, putting them beyond the reach of safety standards and regulations.[25] A government-commissioned study by Valparaíso's Universidad Técnica Federico Santa María found that the *ascensores* "do not comply with basic safety standards. . . . In general, there is a total lack of investment in conservation and maintenance. Without greater intervention and investment, the *ascensores* are doomed to disappear."[26] In order for the *ascensores* to survive, it is essential that they be incorporated into an integrated public transport system combining horizontal and vertical conveyances, not only to improve their safety and economic sustainability but also to reinforce their significance beyond that of a tourist attraction, as a means of transportation that is still needed and used by residents of Valparaíso.

While the *ascensores* symbolize the dilemma of Valparaíso's historic past, the picturesque decay of its present, and the uncertain impact that future redevelopment will have on its identity, they also raise questions about the actual benefits accruing to the city from the World Heritage designation. Valparaíso's distinctive identity is now recognized on the World Heritage list, but remains threatened by economic deterioration, blighted infrastructure, a waterfront cut off from the city, and widespread poverty among its residents, many of whom live in precarious informal settlements on the hillsides. More than a decade after Valparaíso acquired a UNESCO World Heritage site designation, several of the *ascensores* have been repaired and returned to service, and investment by the PRDUV has enabled the repair of broken pavements, restoration and upgrading of buildings and facades, more reliable public sanitation and waste collection, installation of street lighting, new urban signage, and service equipment in public spaces.[27] The number of tourist visits has increased from 15,000 to roughly 85,000 annually. The greatest impact of the World Heritage designation has been felt within the boundaries of the World

Figure 10.10. San Blas neighborhood, Cuzco. Photo by René Davids, 2014.

Heritage site itself, in the higher income hillside neighborhoods of Cerro Alegre and Cerro Concepción, where large numbers of houses have been refurbished and transformed into boutique hotels and restaurants.

While the restoration of some urban infrastructure including several *ascensores*, the realization of a well-integrated Centro Cultural Ex Carcel, new *paseos*, and other public works projects completed beyond the boundaries of the World Heritage site suggest that the creation of a tourist precinct similar to those installed in other World Heritage cities can be avoided in Valparaíso, other indicators point in the opposite direction.[28] Work opportunities have been slow to materialize, the focus on redevelopment for the hospitality and service sectors has led to a loss of residents within the boundaries of the World Heritage site and its buffer zone, and escalating real estate prices have caused the gentrification process to spill over into adjacent neighborhoods such as Cordillera and La Cárcel.[29] Meanwhile, other districts such as Zona Puerto, the oldest part of Valparaíso, are neglected, the city continues to lose population overall, and the large sums spent since the creation of a World Heritage site have had little if any effect on the lives of most Valparaíso residents.[30]

There is widespread agreement that the key to Valparaíso's economic survival is the preservation of its cultural heritage, but there are increasing concerns that the process of redevelopment to promote tourism could compromise its authenticity and overwhelm its distinctive character. Ongoing debates are focused on the course that future development should take: will the 23-hectare World Heritage precinct and the surrounding 45-hectare buffer zone become a historic district patronized mainly by tourists, encircled by a periphery that services it, or will the eclectic character of Valparaíso's urban fabric as well as the physical and social cohesion that has famously characterized its past be preserved? When designated a World Heritage City in 1983, Cusco, Peru, sought to reinvent itself as the national tourist capital through a partition, one area of the city reserved for longtime residents, another for visitors where all new projects are required to be built in neo-Inca and neocolonial styles, a preservation of the past through imitation which effectively transforms Cusco's historic precinct into a themed environment.[31] With a much more recent and heterogeneous past, imposition of a single style would not be feasible for new building projects in Valparaíso, and the government's application to the WHC in support of Valparaíso's nomination to the World Heritage list emphasized the appeal of its eclecticism, successfully challenging the requirement for homogeneity traditionally imposed on historic city candidates. Valparaíso has so far avoided the cynical two-track urbanism that segregates visitors and local residents, but the appeal of large-scale hospitality and retail projects with an immediate commercial return may be its undoing. Massive commercial redevelopment projects such as Mall Plaza Puerto Barón can raise large amounts of capital, but they risk destroying the city's cultural heritage in the process, and it would be sadly ironic if twenty-first-century technology and entrepreneurship manage to destroy the physical and social environment created by similar forces in the nineteenth and early twentieth centuries.

11

Topography and Civic Order in Latin America

RENÉ DAVIDS

Historical Segregation

There are many complex relationships between the formal and informal cities in Latin America, but most literature on the subject emphasizes social, economic, historical, geographical, and political processes in isolation, rather than as integral parts of a dynamic urban history. The evolution over four centuries of the original Spanish colonial grid and plaza settlements to mega-cities with sprawling informal neighborhoods located in close proximity to natural and human-created hazards that threaten to destroy them is a dramatic story of urban transformation. Spanish colonization practices in the Americas determined that settlements be located near water sources and fertile agricultural lands exposed to favorable winds, but no accommodations were made for variations in local topography.[1] The gridiron plans were intended to be located practically anywhere, even on difficult terrain, to enable the rapid foundation and expansion of colonial cities; these also contained built-in assumptions about the location of inhabitants according to social and economic status.[2] Portuguese colonial settlements were less rigidly ordered than those of the Spanish and were often based on models derived from existing cities in Portugal rather than abstract diagrams; scholars have argued that although the Portuguese process of site selection was more flexible, it also adhered to coherent principles of spatial order that were eventually synthesized with a variant of the Spanish orthogonal gridiron plan during the later stages of colonization.[3]

Spanish colonial towns in the Americas were designed to be symbols of civilization and served as instruments to convert, impose order on, and civilize the indigenous population.[4] From the beginning of the European conquest, the gridiron city symbolized the ordered Christian civilization intended to contrast with what the conquerors regarded as the disorder of the indigenous settlements; that they deliberately ignored the precedents of European medieval towns was, as George Kubler has pointed out, likely evidence that the new colonial order served as much to reassure them as to impress the conquered peoples. In Mexico, the grid and plaza designs represented not an invention but variations of a settlement order in place before the conquest.[5] In a few cities such as Cuzco and Tenochtitlan, the Spanish imposed their own layouts on existing grids, even as many buildings were razed so that the materials could be reused in new construction.

Because many informal or squatter settlements originally began as occupations of vacant land, they are regarded as recent phenomena, a notion further reinforced by their absence from city maps. In actual fact, the economic and racial segregation regarded as typical of informal cities—the existence of gated communities in formal cities, and the separation of residential enclaves according to race and class—date back to the beginning of the European conquest.[6] The conquered peoples were not allowed to live in the newly created colonial cities, and Ciudad de México, the most important Spanish city in the Americas, was described at the time as surrounded by "casual dense agglomerations of huts and shelter."[7] Separate settlements known as *reducciones* built to civilize and evangelize the indigenous population and provide a source of cheap labor were located close to but apart from the new Spanish colonial towns; the Cercado de Lima was the best known among them.[8]

The separation of Spanish and indigenous residential areas began to collapse as both groups gradually transgressed each other's boundaries. Many second and third generation descendants of the first Spaniards to arrive in Ciudad de México lacked the financial resources of their forebears and as a consequence were forced to settle in the indigenous quarters while native peoples began to inhabit the colonial city as domestic laborers for wealthier families.[9] Miscegenation eventually made physical distinctions between the two groups more difficult to sustain, but class distinctions that intersected with racial ones were maintained through a less overt system of urban segregation. Beginning in the second half of the nineteenth century, new modes of transportation allowed people with sufficient means to live farther away from the traditional business center.[10]

As newly independent Latin American countries attempted to define their postcolonial identities, poorer residents were often driven away from locations regarded as too prominent or visible to foreign visitors. When the Avenida Central in Rio de Janeiro, inspired by Haussmann's Paris, was built by Mayor Pereira Passos (1902–6), it became the center of urban life. The new boulevard intensified the political motivation to eradicate the cramped alleys with their precarious dwellings and disease-ridden populations in the city center, to eliminate all remaining physical traces of the colonial past, and to make Rio de Janeiro's infrastructure the equal of prominent cities around the world. Many colonial buildings were subsequently destroyed, and the occupants who were left homeless found refuge in the surrounding hills, where they built new communities from scratch, creating informal housing settlements that became known as *favelas*.[11] Even more dramatic was the demolition of the Morro do Castelo in 1922, the hill on which Rio had been founded, in order to eliminate significant vestiges of its colonial past and a poor neighborhood that was directly visible to ships approaching the city's harbor. Vicuña Mackenna, the Chilean urban reformer and mayor of Santiago from 1872 to 1875, proposed a ring road around the capital city to separate what he regarded as the prosperous Christian center from the poor barbarians on the periphery.[12] The road was never built, but the urban elites eventually established a sort of de facto segregation by moving out of the central city to the suburbs. During the middle decades of the twentieth century, slum clearance followed by a transfer of impoverished people to modernist housing estates was the favored means of eliminating squatter settlements, but this strategy failed because governments were unable to construct enough new buildings to meet demand, and those that were built were unpopular for various reasons including social dislocation, lack of public services, and discomfort with the architecture. Recent efforts to improve the housing estates have emphasized upgrades that are more responsive to residents' needs.

Topographical Segregation

During the nineteenth century, free-market policies stimulated economic growth in newly independent Latin American countries, but increasingly complex economic, social, and cultural imperatives and the topographical obstacles that frequently surrounded the original colonial settlements often made urban expansion difficult. Toward the end of the nineteenth century, when advances in mass transportation—railroads, trams, and eventually automobiles—enabled them to do so, the upper social classes in Andean Latin American cities such as Quito, Ecuador, Lima, Peru, Santiago, Chile, and Caracas, Venezuela abandoned the historic town centers for new homes on higher ground near the more sparsely settled peripheries. The heights provided the usual advantages of better views, cooler temperatures, cleaner air, privacy, and physical separation from the lower classes, as well as a greater sense of security for wealthy homeowners because access to their properties was more difficult than in the city centers, where rich and poor often lived in close proximity. Migration was encouraged by the technology developed to improve geologically unstable terrain, move large quantities of earth, regrade vast areas of land, construct high retaining walls and terraces, pump water out of saturated soils and channel water flows and drainage, as well as the recent availability of flood, fire, and earthquake insurance. Technological advances allowed the racial, ethnic, and cultural divisions in society to find clearer physical expression in the cities' spatial configurations. Where higher ground was accessible from city centers, local differences in geologic or climatic conditions and the existence of transportation links to the business district generally determined the order of settlement according to race, class, and economic status.

Rio de Janeiro was founded on a narrow strip of level land at the base of steeply sloping terrain, but was relocated to higher ground on the Morro do Castelo for purposes of civil defense and to escape the disease-breeding swamps of the flatlands. By the end of the seventeenth century, settlement had reached the lower slopes, but the hilltops were reserved for churches and convents. When the Portuguese established the royal court in Rio de Janeiro at the beginning of the nineteenth century, efforts to expand residential development in the hills acquired new momentum.[13] The foreign community had a preference for living on the hillsides: the French and the English claimed the hills of Gloria and Catete, while the Germans colonized Santa Teresa. The development of Santa Teresa was further boosted by its relative isolation during the cholera epidemics that decimated a large percentage of the population of Rio de Janeiro in the second half of the nineteenth century. In the next few decades, Santa Teresa's best homes

Figure 11.1. Favela Andarai, Rio de Janeiro. Photo courtesy of Kristen Belt.

would often be positioned to take advantage of privileged views of Rio de Janeiro and Guanabara Bay. When the elites began to move to the coast at the beginning of the twentieth century, Santa Teresa experienced a period of decline from which it has only recently begun to recover as colonies of artists have moved in. During the eighteenth and nineteenth centuries, the hilly areas around Rio also served as refuges for runaway slaves who established independent towns there; with the abolition of slavery in Brazil in 1888, newly emancipated slaves joined them. Today there are elegant neighborhoods of single-family mansions with spectacular views on some of the hillsides, such as Gavea, while others are occupied by the informal housing settlements. Flat areas near the beaches of Ipanema and Leblon are now generally considered to be the most desirable residential neighborhoods (figures 11.1 and 11.2).[14]

There are also elite neighborhoods in some foothills surrounding Lima and Caracas similar to those of Rio de Janeiro and also some of its poorest (figure 11.3). Immigration from the Venezuelan countryside caused the formation of the first informal settlements where a large percentage of the population now lives. Caracas developed along the contours of a narrow fertile mountain valley in northern Venezuela, 20 miles from the port of

Figure 11.2. Favela Rocinha, Rio de Janeiro. Photo by René Davids, 2001.

Figure 11.3. Informal housing on Cerro San Cristóbal, Lima. Photo courtesy of Brian Allen, Smith / Allen Studio, 2010.

Figure 11.4. Metro Cable, San Agustín. Urban Think Tank, Alfredo Brillembourg, and Hubert Klumpner, Caracas. Photo courtesy of Adriana Navarro-Sertich, 2010.

La Guaira and separated from the coast by the steep central highlands of the Cerro Avila; its central plaza is located in an ideal spot above a wide bend in the Guaire River. Maps show that the original city grid was only interrupted by streams carrying runoff from the mountains to the Guaire, rather than modified to accommodate their courses.

Adaptation of the city fabric to the local topography began to take place when the discovery of vast petroleum reserves in the early twentieth century transformed the Venezuelan economy, and an influx of national and foreign immigrants in search of jobs and a higher standard of living forced the expansion of Caracas's boundaries to encompass the entire valley and extend into the surrounding foothills.[15] *Barrios*, or squatter settlements consisting largely of unreinforced masonry buildings located in the most geologically vulnerable and therefore least desirable areas of the city—ravines with steep, unstable sloping sides, dry river beds, or residual spaces between freeways and canyons—grew simultaneously with the upper-income residential districts to eventually contain 50 percent of the population of Caracas. With multifamily structures as high as five stories built on structurally unsound foundations, the *barrios* are similar to the *favelas* of Rio de Janeiro, but because Caracas sits astride the boundaries of the South American and Caribbean tectonic plates, they are also threatened by seismic hazards, as well as violent tropical storms. The vegetation that once provided some protection from mudslides has been stripped from the hills, making Caracas an unfortunate example of an instance where geological and climatic hazards have been exacerbated by human intervention (figure 11.4).[16]

In Buenos Aires, where the terrain is mostly flat, subtle variations in topography have nevertheless affected settlement patterns. Buenos Aires was founded on the south bank of the Rio de La Plata, with a typical colonial gridiron plan as prescribed by the Laws of the Indies and a fort situated on slightly higher terrain overlooking the river that allowed the arrivals and departures of ships to be monitored; La Casa Rosada, the official seat of the executive branch of the government of Argentina, is still located on the same spot. Topography was of little interest to early twentieth-century planners, but it has had a major impact on most of Buenos Aires's informal settlements, the so-called *villas miserias*, the Argentinian equivalent of the Brazilian *favelas* and the Venezuelan *barrios* where impoverished populations live in densely crowded areas that typically lack utilities or urban amenities and present significant risks to public health, for their residents as well as for the city as a whole. Six percent of the population of Buenos Aires now lives in these informal developments located in floodplains, beneath the undersides of bridges, or in proximity to urban infrastructure that exposes the inhabitants to noise, water, and air pollution.[17] Numerous informal settlements are located along the Matanza-Riachuelo River, the most contaminated river basin in Argentina. The housing in these settlements is of poor quality, built of scavenged materials offering inadequate protection from the elements and susceptible to invasion by disease-carrying rodents and insects (figure 11.5).

The degradation of the Matanza-Riachuelo began in the nineteenth century when meat, leather, and wool were processed on and exported from its banks, and slaughterhouses dumped wastes directly into the river. With twentieth-century urbanization and industrial growth, pollution levels steadily increased and domestic effluents were discharged directly into the river. The Matanza-Riachuelo also floods during the rainy season,

Figure 11.5. Villa miseria, Buenos Aires. Photo courtesy of Ivan Valin, 2010.

spreading the river's highly polluted waters throughout the informal settlements, further exposing the inhabitants to dangerous contaminants.[18]

Racial and Economic Segregation

Although racial and class definitions differ among Latin American countries, the vast majority of indigenous people, those of African origin, or with mixed blood from either group, belong to the lower economic and social classes, while direct descendants of the Spanish conquerors and more recent immigrants from Europe belong to the upper strata of society. The Amerindian population is mainly concentrated in the highland areas of countries around the Pacific Rim, from Mexico to northern Chile, the black population in Brazil and the Caribbean basin, and those of European descent in the southern South American countries of Chile, Argentina, and Uruguay.[19] Although it followed an indigenous tradition that was centuries old, the rediscovery of slopes as places for habitation in the twentieth century was led by newly arrived European settlers and descendants of earlier European immigrants. Where higher ground was accessible from city centers, local differences in geologic or climatic conditions and the existence of transportation links to the business district generally determined the order of settlement according to race and class.

The *favelas* are typically built of concrete frame structures, with brick infill and metal sheeting, growing over time with the addition of mass illegal invasions and migrations from the poorer north of Brazil, as well as successive generations born in the *favelas*.[20] With narrow, dark streets that admit little light or fresh air to the dense concentrations of dwellings on either side, little or no infrastructure or sanitary services such as sewers or garbage disposal, precariously built housing, and high crime rates, the *favelas* of Rio de Janeiro have become symbols of extreme urban poverty throughout the world.[21] Although *favelas* are infamous for their violence and are often viewed as separate enclaves, there are many relationships between the formal and informal sectors of the city, as some *favela* residents travel outside to temporary or permanent low-wage jobs and others manufacture goods consumed by the metropolis as a whole. After years of neglect, the Brazilian government has ceded de facto control of the *favelas* to gangs of highly organized drug traffickers who enforce order, provide some social services, adjudicate disputes, and engage in frequent dramatic clashes with government armed forces. Despite the poverty, it is common to find neatly arranged interiors, small courts, and terraces with carefully painted doors and windows, as well as tight social supportive networks. Contradictions abound as many of the *favelados* enjoy the cooler breezes, proximity to ocean beaches, and panoramic views of Guanabara Bay prized by the elites.

Integrating the City

A number of ambitious new infrastructure projects have been implemented and others initiated to urbanize the squatter settlements and overcome existing divisions between the formal and informal cities. These projects are intended to facilitate movement within the informal city, create links to the city center, address health and environmental concerns, and improve the sociological and economic status of the settlements. Since 1995 the architect Jorge Mario Jáuregui has been working in the Favela-Bairro Project in Rio de Janeiro, turning blighted areas into functioning neighborhoods. Jáuregui's design initiatives have included the construction of community centers offering recreational activities and job training, daycare facilities, communal kitchens, and new streets and pedestrian walkways. In the Manguinhos district of Rio de Janeiro, the architect devised a comprehensive development plan, as well as a specific proposal for the Avenida Leopoldo Bulhões, currently bisected by a railroad line that would be elevated.

The project consists of a new linear public landscape inspired by the Ramblas in Barcelona that will connect the various informal residential neighborhoods. To transform the street from a physical barrier into an urban connector, a landscaped promenade will be flanked by housing on either side of the Avenida Leopoldo Bulhões and be served by a new multimodal 24/7 transportation interchange with links to train and bus lines and supportive infrastructure for taxis, vans, and bicycles. The project is intended to serve *favela* residents as well as the general public and is carefully structured to meet the needs of all segments of the population with public facilities for sport, cultural activities, and job- and income-related counseling. There is a special emphasis on attractions for children and teenagers to integrate them into the community and prevent them from being absorbed by the drug trade, the primary source of employment in Rio's low-income areas.[22]

As in Rio, some recent interventions proposed by architects are intended to improve conditions in the *barrios* of Caracas. These include proposals by Urban Think Tank, a Venezuelan architectural firm with strong connections in New York led by Alfredo Brillembourg and Hubert Klumpner, for small-scale interventions and insertions that respond to community needs, funded in part by the German Federal Cultural Foundation. In order to overcome the lack of infrastructure, a major problem in the *barrios*, Urban Think Tank designed five stations for the Metro Cable on a 1.3-mile loop that would extend Caracas's metro system to the San Augustín district (figure 11.4). A standardized concrete structure based on a module with a steel roof deck allows the stations to be tucked into crowded urban neighborhoods without displacing the residents.[23]

Some of the most successful neighborhood upgrades are located in Medellín, Colombia, a former haven for drug traffickers. With its informal settlements clinging to the surrounding mountain, working-class neighborhoods, and elegant residential towers, Medellín is now a dynamic metropolis, and a series of small-scale strategic urban interventions have helped to transform what was once considered to be the world's most violent city. A major magnet for migration from the countryside in northwest Colombia as well as refugees from the ongoing low-grade civil war, Medellín has grown rapidly since the mid-twentieth century. Although the local economy successfully absorbed most of the in-migration, it was not able to provide enough jobs to keep up with the population surge, and the resulting widespread unemployment allowed the Medellín Drug Cartel, official and unofficial paramilitary groups, guerrillas, and various other criminal organizations to establish strongholds in low-income neighborhoods. Given the circumstances, President Andrés Pastrana established a special program in 1998 to address the violence, overcome the lack of government control, and eradicate social degradation in low-income neighborhoods. The election of visionary mayor Sergio Fajardo in 2003 and the implementation of small works projects carried out with the assistance of community members helped to further reduce the crime statistics.[24]

Like many other cities in South America, Medellín is located in a geologically unstable area, spreading over hillsides and gorges. Existing informal communities were improved surgically by carefully clearing canyon rims and redeveloping them into linear parks, then connecting them with pedestrian bridges and erecting small-scale housing projects without displacing area residents. With the provision of spaces for community gatherings, such as squares and streets with sidewalks and the construction of schools and libraries as prominent beacons to a brighter future, the lives of many poor residents improved significantly.

Facilities and services previously lacking in neighborhoods were provided, and people's economic prospects rose through education. The most striking of these buildings is Parque Biblioteca España in the Santo Domingo Savio *barrio*, a stark formal contrast to the makeshift dwellings surrounding it, a building whose iconographic presence promises renewal (figure 11.6). Designed by the architect Giancarlo Mazzanti, the complex includes a library, auditorium, classrooms, and administration areas in the form of three discrete, boulder-like shapes intended to resemble the surrounding rugged mountainous terrain. The monumental building is a landmark that has helped to give the neighborhood a new identity: no longer the area with the highest crime rate but the location of the most iconic building in all of Medellín.[25]

The most important features of all of these designs are the linkages established between the infrastructures of access and circulation, the creation of public spaces, and the construction of facilities for the provision of social services. The ongoing transformations of informal Latin American

Figure 11.6. Santo Domingo Savio Biblioteca España. Giancarlo Mazzanti, Medellín, Colombia. Photo by René Davids, 2011.

cities allows them to be perceived as syntheses of diverse neighborhoods that together constitute integrated wholes, rather than agglomerations of segregated entities.

Conclusion

Since the beginning of the nineteenth century, the growth of Latin American cities has been far less predictable than their founders anticipated. Rather than the ideals of rational well-ordered gridiron cities that inspired urban planning diagrams in Renaissance Europe, their haphazard nature resembles the medieval squalor those diagrams were intended to replace. Hillside settlement patterns vary from country to country and city to city, affected by local topographic, cultural, social, and economic factors. Many of the most geologically unstable urban areas in Latin America and those sites least suitable for building—river banks, steep slopes, flood plains, garbage dumps, or the undersides of freeways—are those most likely to be colonized by informal housing. These areas typically also face the greatest environmental challenges and are most likely to be permanently damaged or destroyed by the negative impacts of prolonged squatting on fragile ecosystems. Their continuing degradation by informal settlements in many cases removes vital natural defenses and increases the likelihood that disasters will one day overcome the settlements entirely. Poverty limits the capacity of informal settlement dwellers to take measures that might lessen their exposure to a whole range of environmental hazards. Paradoxically, as awareness of the ecological sensitivity of marginal urban lands grows along with the importance of protecting the natural processes that sustain the environment, the stewardship of these fragile ecosystems is left to the most vulnerable populations.

In recent years, strategies for addressing the concerns raised by informal settlements have shifted away from the large-scale slum clearance and relocation that have caused massive social disruption to on-site upgrades and improvements, with the goal of eventually integrating them with their larger urban contexts.[26] As the examples of Medellín, Rio de Janeiro, Caracas, and Buenos Aires illustrate, a responsive architecture that combines local commitment with political and professional leadership can overcome physical and cultural obstacles to significantly improve community life and the city as a whole. Informal settlements have become inseparable parts of many metropolises in Latin America and should be perceived as such when issues related to their topographical, social, and economic organization are considered, from both a theoretical and practical standpoint. The dialectic of formal versus informal may have run its course, since 60 percent of cities such as Lima and Caracas now consist of informal settlements. Formal and informal cities are inextricably linked through shared infrastructure, utilities such as water and electricity that are often illegally obtained, transportation networks and roads, labor and services, and the often unregulated commerce that flourishes in the city streets, a common history, and an interdependent process of urban evolution.[27]

12

Demolishing Urban Hills

Establishing New Identities

RENÉ DAVIDS

Demolishing Urban Hills

Up until the nineteenth century, builders overcame the challenges of rugged terrain using traditional construction techniques with ingenuity and skill, making efficient use of available materials and causing minimal disruption to the land itself. With the arrival of industrialized technology, commerce and urbanization evolved rapidly, and economic considerations began to overcome previously insurmountable physical barriers to settlement. Hillside locations began to be valued for their distance from urban congestion, their proximity to industrial production, and eventually their dramatic views.[1]

Despite advances in engineering and technology such as the steam-powered shovel and new earth-retaining techniques like concrete and masonry gravity walls, the process of building on hillsides remained difficult, dangerous, and controversial. In cities where steep hillside slopes presented significant obstacles to their development, debates raged on whether to raze them. In San Francisco, citizens who favored conservation eventually won the argument on economic grounds (razing the hills would have been prohibitively expensive) rather than ethical grounds, and the justification used was aesthetic, to preserve the city's scenic beauty.[2]

In spite of the preservation efforts, many hills were gradually cut or diminished. First settled in 1849, Telegraph Hill located on the eastern edge of San Francisco was greatly reduced during the late nineteenth and early twentieth centuries, but most tourists visiting Pioneer Park on its summit today are unaware of the hill's original size. The continued growth of the city toward the end of the nineteenth century created demand for crushed rocks to be used for paving, concrete manufacture, and fill. For about three-quarters of a mile, the east and north faces of Telegraph Hill were used for extraction. The quarry activity (some of it recorded by photographer Eadward Muybridge) threatened houses that were built on top of the hill, and one house even fell to the bottom of the cliff. The blasting finally stopped in 1914, after several broken injunctions, two deaths, and mounting public pressure.[3]

Located between Central Basin and the Bay, Irish Hill in San Francisco was altered even more drastically. Accessed by a flight of wooden stairs 250 feet high, in the late 1800s Irish Hill was home to thousands of immigrant foundry and mill workers, its slopes crowded with boardinghouses and saloons, but most of it was excavated for the expansion of Bethlehem Steel during World War II, and all that remains today is an overgrown industrial waste heap.[4]

While contemporary sensitivities might be offended by hillside demolitions, the city of San Francisco would arguably not have prospered or developed without at least some alterations to its topography. The infamous "Second Street Cut" between Howard and Bryant Streets in the Rincon Hill area in 1869 made a level connection to the waterfront, which was then a vital part of the city's economy and source of income for the working poor (figure 12.1).[5] In fact some of the piers provided thoroughfares that stretched for almost 2 miles over the waters of the bay. William T. Sherman reports that by 1850 some had become streets, and the space between them was filled with sand, debris coming from the demolished hills. The filling of these water lots created a new beachhead on the newly completed land. "Half of the city in front of Montgomery Street was built along the old shore line becoming the heart of the new business district."[6] The Rincon area, which had been the fashionable district of San Francisco, suffered a further blow when the railroad was pulled into the city just south of it. Not only did the area became topographically altered but its lifestyle was sacrificed in the name of progress.

Another North American city that rebuilt its topography was Boston. Of the three original hills that restricted its growth, only one remains

Figure 12.1. Construction on Second Street, San Francisco, 1869. Photo courtesy of California History Room, California State Library, Sacramento.

(figure 12.2). Hills were not the only obstacles, however. The Shawmut peninsula on which the town originated had a narrow connection to the mainland through an isthmus. By often overflowing, it made the town a virtual island. To achieve its development ambitions, Boston therefore had to modify its topography, and it did so by drastically changing its shoreline and hillside profile. When during the mid-twentieth century the process had been completed, the original peninsula had become unrecognizable. Rather than a small town on a peninsula surrounded by rugged water, the city of Boston became a largely flat metropolis that featured some hills and waterways.

As in San Francisco the consolidation of a hill or its demolition was determined by social, economic, and geographical conditions. For example, the siting of the Massachusetts State House on top of Boston's famous fancy neighborhood of Beacon Hill was the result of a deliberate attempt to promote the area. The leveling of Fort Hill, by contrast, was a large-scale enterprise set up with the intention of eradicating a slum.[7] Once home to merchants, the Fort Hill area soon decayed because of its proximity to the

Figure 12.2. Map of hills in Boston, including Beacon Hill (demolished 1807) and Pemberton Hill (demolished 1835). Drawing by René Davids.

business district. The old mansions and warehouses were converted to house Irish immigrants, and the quarters became overcrowded, expensive, and unhealthy. In the fall of 1866, the city began clearing the Fort Hill area, and in 1872 the entire hill was leveled and the spoils used to fill the new Atlantic Avenue.

In South America where the poor didn't just stand in the way of development but where race and identity considerations interfered with self-image, the practice of relocating the poor could adopt a far more radical turn. Until the beginning of the seventeenth century, most Portuguese settlements in Brazil were situated on top of easily defensible hills from which access routes could be controlled. Situated at the edge of the magnificent Guanabara Bay, Rio was settled in 1567 on Morro do Castelo (Castle-Hill) in an area surrounded by hardwood forests, good arable land for the cultivation of sugar cane, swamps, and abruptly rising green hills (figure 12.3). In addition to Morro do Castelo, the colonial settlement was demarcated by two other hills controlled by religious orders and a third topped by a fortress. The siting of these first stone monuments on secure hilltops overlooking the settlement emphasized the commanding positions these institutions held in "civilizing" the African slaves and aboriginal Indians.[8] This underclass was left to inhabit the areas subject to flooding such as the swamps' edges and coastal fringes.

Because it was closer to the mining region of Minas Gerais than Salvador, the harbor of Rio was a more convenient location from which to launch gold shipments back to Europe, and in 1763 it became the capital of colonial Brazil while still a relatively modest city of simple single-story houses and narrow streets. Adapting swiftly to its new status as the seat of

Figure 12.3. Morro do Castelo, view from the Church of the Third Order of Carmel, Rio de Janeiro. Photo by Juan Gutierrez. Courtesy of Marc Ferrez / Thiele / Coleção Gilberto Ferrez / Instituto Moreira Salles Collection.

the court and residence of the viceroys, Rio implemented a series of embellishments, including an opera house and its first theater. New streets were opened, fountains installed, and plazas inaugurated. Although the hills were thought to interfere with air circulation by blocking the cooling breezes from Guanabara Bay, the most significant public health problems were the swamps and marshes, which increased the humidity in the intense heat and provided ideal breeding environments for disease-spreading miasma, insects, and other pathogens (figure 12.4).[9]

Among the places altered to mitigate these conditions was the Boqueirão da Ajuda, an ocean backwater that had become a swamp and was known for its unpleasant stench. After a fever epidemic that infected most of Rio's population was blamed on the swamp's deplorable condition in the mid-eighteenth century, the Boqueirão da Ajuda's 20 hectares were filled in with spoils from the adjacent Morro das Mangeuiras (Hill of the Mango Trees). Transformed into flat terrain, the area was made into the Passeio Público (1783), the first public pleasure garden in Brazil. Where there had previously been only domestic vegetable and flower gardens,

Rio's Passeio Público came to represent a triumph of civilizing culture over nature and identified with tasteful, luxurious entertainment.[10]

After 1815, following the transfer of the Portuguese royal court to Brazil during the Napoleonic invasions, and when it subsequently became an independent kingdom in 1822, Rio de Janeiro experienced a surge of new growth. Many new buildings were erected, others restored, streets paved, lighting installed, new roads opened, public fountains built, and new civic and cultural institutions established, including the Royal Press, the Royal Library, the Theatre of Saint John, the Academy of Fine Arts, the Botanical Garden, and the Bank of Brazil.

The abolition of slavery in 1888 followed by the transformation of Brazil's government from a monarchy to a republic in 1889 stimulated foreign immigration as well as increasing internal migration from the countryside to urban centers, both factors in Rio's continuing population increase. To accommodate the new surge, city authorities implemented many important urban landscape and infrastructure projects to advance their dream of creating a metropolis that would surpass other South American capitals and equal European capitals such as Paris and Berlin.[11]

During the prefecture of Pereira Passos (1903-1906), Rio's central business district was renovated and sanitation improved with the installation of new water, plumbing, and gas utilities.[12] Rubble removed from the Morro do Senado (Senate Hill), the second hill to be demolished in Rio, was used to fill in coves and straighten the shoreline, extending the city farther into Guanabara Bay and modifying the shores where the poorest

Figure 12.4. Rio de Janeiro and Botafogo Bay c.1885. Photo by unidentified photographer, courtesy of Thiele / Coleção Gilberto Ferrez / Instituto Moreira Salles Collection.

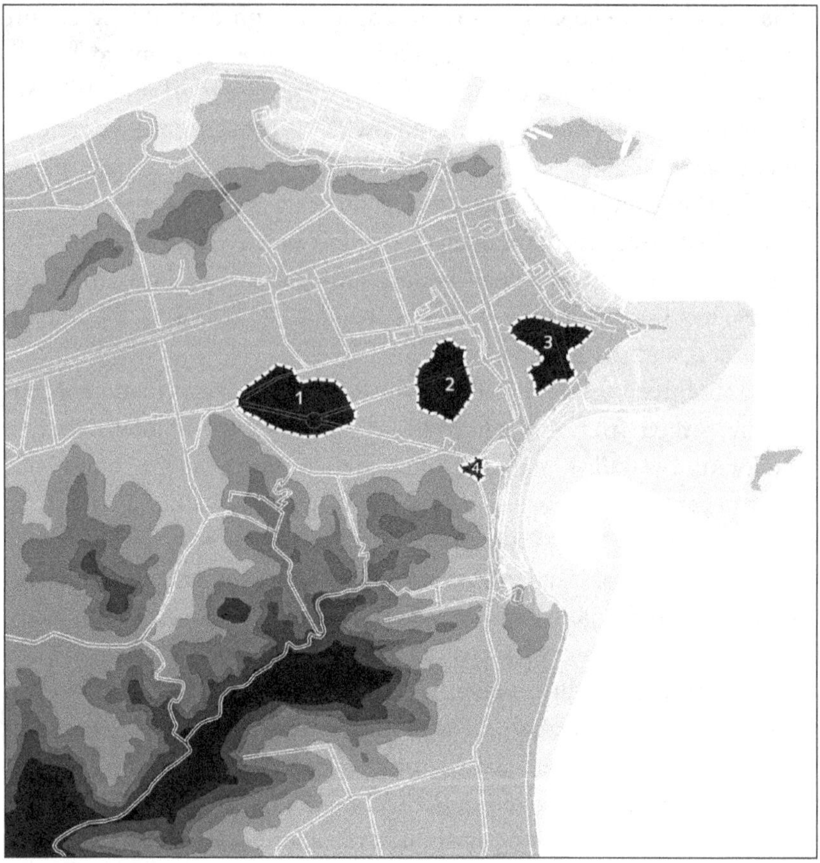

Figure 12.5. Map of demolished hills (in black), Rio de Janeiro. Drawing by René Davids.

citizens of Rio, called Cariocas, fished and bathed. The port installations were modernized and upgraded to accommodate large cargo and passenger ships. In the manner of Baron Haussmann, new streets were cut through existing urban fabric to facilitate the transport of goods. In the process of transforming the narrow, filthy streets of neighborhoods near the port, Mayor Pereira Passos also removed their populations, regarded as unsanitary by the elite. Areas of landfill were turned over to speculators for real estate development, traffic arteries, and parking lots. A neighborhood with a circular square at its center, with several radiating streets in a manner strongly reminiscent of Baron Haussmann's Parisian traffic roundabouts, rose where the Morro do Senado had once stood (figure 12.5).

With the increase in maritime commerce, Rio's center of gravity shifted away from Morro do Castelo to the flat areas around the port. As the hill lost its primary position in Rio's urban landscape, the lower strata of society who lacked the resources to maintain the colonial buildings gradually moved in and the resulting deterioration led to the first calls for razing the whole neighborhood. Because Morro do Castelo was located at the edge of the Guanabara Bay, residents of Rio who wanted to retain it argued that the hill acted as a windbreak or that the colonial buildings had historical value, while those who favored its demolition maintained that the hill blocked cooling sea breezes from the east and was an eyesore, a rotten tooth that should be extracted. Other arguments for demolition stressed commercial development of the port and the elimination of buildings from an unpopular period of Brazilian history.[13]

In the article "O Morro do Castello e esthetica" (*O Malho,* no. 989, August 27, 1921), an anonymous journalist arguing in favor of demolition disagreed with those who believed that Rio's beauty lay in its exuberant topography, maintaining that Buenos Aires was also a beautiful city built on flatland and that their lush vegetation, not landforms or architecture, gave Brazilian cities their sense of excitement. The article reminded its readers that the hills of Santa Theresa and Gloria remained, so there was no reason to fear that Rio would become flat, and the new space created by the demolition would allow for further commercial expansion of the port and eliminate disagreeable vestiges of the colonial past.

As Needell has pointed out, the colonial infrastructure of the old city was not merely inefficient but also inconsistent with the desire to project an image of modernization and economic power to the world.[14] Despite the controversy, city officials were finally persuaded to proceed by the invitation to host the International Exhibition celebrating a century of Brazilian independence in 1922 and flattened the Morro do Castelo the previous year (figure 12.6).

The land cleared by the demolition of Morro do Castelo was conveniently located within the city so that visitors coming to Rio by ship could enjoy the exhibition buildings and spectacle from the sea. Opening its doors to the international community, the exhibition displayed all of Brazil's cultural, agricultural, commercial, and industrial products,

Figure 12.6. Demolition of Morro do Castelo, Rio de Janeiro, 1922. Courtesy of Juan Gutierrez / Thiele / Coleção Gilberto Ferrez / Instituto Moreira Salles Collection.

establishing a sense of *brasilidade* ("Brazilianness") or Brazilian identity through its multiculturalism.[15] The exhibition was housed in monumental neocolonial building pavilions that replaced the original Portuguese colonial fabric with new and improved versions of the old buildings. A night photograph from 1922 shows an impressive spectacle with structures appropriately scaled for Rio's grand ambitions bathed in the glow of artificial light (figure 12.7).

The neocolonial style was intended to evoke the Portuguese colonial architecture while also expressing a modern Brazilian identity by incorporating new technologies and adapting to the lifestyles of the early twentieth century. A typical structure built for the centenary exhibition was the small industry pavilion inspired by the São Francisco convent in Salvador, Bahia, Brazil's first colonial capital. Decorated with Portuguese tiles covering its rococo facade and borrowing liberally from the religious baroque, the building featured two lateral galleries reminiscent of Franciscan cloisters and was bookended by towers that featured voids to facilitate a good circulation of air, demonstrating that the style could be adapted to different climates, modern programs, and technologies.

Exuding a sense of confidence and pride, the homogeneous collection of Brazilian neocolonial buildings for the Centennial Exhibition contrasted visibly with the eclectic nature of the foreign pavilions.[16] Somewhat paradoxically, given that the new neocolonial architecture had literally replaced the foundation fabric of Rio, the style also reignited interest in the colonial buildings from which it had borrowed. By the time Rio de Janeiro demolished a large section of the centrally located Morro de San Antonio to make space for ceremonies of the XXXVI International Eucharistic Congress of 1950, interest in preserving colonial architecture had gained momentum; while providing material for the construction of Parque Eduardo Gomes in the Flamengo Beach area, colonial buildings on the Morro de San Antonio, the Monastery of St. Anthony, and the church of the Third Order Regular of St. Francis of Penance were saved from demolition. Also spared was the Arcos da Lapa aqueduct that joined the hills of San Antonio and Santa Teresa. The substantial part of Morro de San Antonio that was razed improved the connections between the city center and the southern part of Rio and provided a sports and recreation park for a densely populated area of town.

Figure 12.7. International Exhibition of the Centenary of the Independence of Brazil, Rio de Janeiro, 1922. Photo courtesy of Juan Gutierrez / Thiele / Coleção Gilberto Ferrez / Instituto Moreira Salles Collection.

Figure 12.8. The Monastery of Saint Anthony on Morro de Santo Antônio, Rio de Janeiro. Photo by René Davids, 2001.

Less than thirty years after the Centennial Exhibition was erected over the ground where the colonial fabric of Morro do Castelo once stood, similar monuments became regarded as worthy of protection. Compared with the *tabula rasa* proposals of the modernists, such as Le Corbusier's Plan Voisin of 1925, which would have eliminated an important part of central Paris, the dramatic alteration of the ecology and topography in Rio affected the landscape more radically, if perhaps less extensively.

In the same decade that Rio's population, industrial production, and financial strength were surpassed by São Paulo, Brasília was built, and the role of representing Brazil's modernity, progress, and national identity was transferred from Rio to the new capital. Liberated from the burden of having to embody Brazil's modernity and progress, Rio's colonial period became a celebrated subject of research publications and exhibitions.[17] The passage of five hundred years has seen Rio de Janeiro transformed from a fortified outpost on the rim of an unknown continent into one of the world's great cities whose recorded past is tied exclusively to the legacy of the colonialism on which it was founded. No longer perceived as an embarrassment, Rio's colonial past is now respected as a precious heritage and asset used to promote the city in the global market.

In many cities, infrastructure projects are driven by economic imperatives, but in Rio, the demolition of hills also represented an attempt to rewrite history and reconstruct an urban identity. During the last few decades in response to increasing homogenization of urban environments, architects have considered strategies through which regional, cultural, and site-specific conditions can inform their work. The example of Rio de Janeiro suggests that ideological excesses involving wholesale conservation or elimination of historic fabric are both problematic: the first by risking economic and social stagnation, the second by isolation from the past. The attempt to redefine Rio's identity by eliminating significant topographical features and a substantial amount of its colonial fabric may seem extreme by contemporary standards, but the tendency for cities to selectively re-create historical environments by highlighting some periods and diminishing or obscuring others is as familiar a phenomenon in Rio as elsewhere. Faced with the opportunity to host other important international events such as the World Cup in 2014 and the Olympics in 2016, Rio chose once again to present a more acceptable face to the world by demolishing *favelas* and relocating the poor.

Notes

Introduction

1. Eggener, "Placing Resistance"; Fernandez Cox, "Hacia una Modernidad Apropiada"; Loomis, *Other Americas*. Critical regionalism was called Otra Arquitectura by architect Enrique Brown and Postmodernismo Latinoamericano by historian Silvia Arango. Both concepts take on an interest in the local as well as the international movement.

2. It is now believed that an advanced civilization was flourishing along the Amazon in pre-Hispanic times as well. See Mann, *1491*, 315–68.

3. Kubler, *The Art and Architecture of Ancient America*.

4. Butland, "Frontiers of Settlement in South America"; Squier, *The States of Central America*.

5. Magasich-Airola and Beer, *America Magica*.

6. Denevan, "The Pristine Myth"; Butzer, "The Americas before and after 1492"; Caviedes and Knapp, *South America*; Price, "Prehispanic Irrigation Agriculture in Nuclear America"; Denevan, *Cultivated Landscapes of Native Amazonia and the Andes*.

7. Carlson, *Geography of Latin America*; Hardoy, *Pre-Columbian Cities*; Bodmer, "The Armature of Conquest"; S. Miller, *An Environmental History of Latin America*, 4; Bonavía, "Ecological Factors Affecting the Urban Transformations in the Last Centuries of the Pre-Columbian Era."

8. Bákula, Minelli, and Vautier, *The Inca World*; Mann, *1491*.

9. The Americas contain more pyramids than the rest of the continents combined. Civilizations like the Olmec, Maya, Aztec, and Inca all built them to house their deities and sometimes to bury their rulers. The best-known pyramids are the pyramid of the Sun and the Moon in Teotihuacán, del Castillo at Chichén Itza in the Yucatán, the pyramid at Cholula, and the pyramids of the Sun and the Moon built by the Mochica in the Moche Valley close to Trujillo, Peru.

10. Denevan, "The Pristine Myth"; Caviedes and Knapp, *South America*; Price, "Prehispanic Irrigation Agriculture in Nuclear America"; Bonavía, "Ecological Factors"; Crouch, Garr, and Mundigo, *Spanish City Planning in North America*.

11. Margarita Serje, "The National Imagination in New Granada," in *Alexander von Humboldt*.

12. As opposed to the Spaniards, the Indians used the slopes extensively with varying intensiveness to link the highlands with the lowlands. These landscapes were a central

referent for both their social and spatial social organization. Relph, *The Modern Urban Landscape.*

13. Relph, "Modernity and the Reclamation of Place."

14. J. Larraín, *Identity and Modernity in Latin America*; Vargas Llosa, "The Paradoxes of Latin America."

Chapter 1. Mythical Terrain and the Building of Mexico's UNAM

1. Readings, *The University in Ruins.*

2. Carlos Novoa, president of the Universidad Nacional Autonoma de Mexico, is quoted by Keith Eggener in *Luis Barragán's Gardens of El Pedregal* as presenting the issue of the university siting in the Pedregal region as a matter of great significance, one that went well beyond issues of economy or expediency. University rector Luis Garrido declared in 1952, "The University City is rising in a place marked by destiny. It was the seat of an ancient civilization, and now it will be the seat of the culture of the future."

3. Mabry, *The Mexican University and the State Student Conflicts.*

4. Eggener, *Luis Barragán's Gardens of El Pedregal*; Carrillo Trueba, Portilla, and Rzedowski, *El Pedregal de San Angel.*

5. See Pani and Moral, "The Overall Plan of Ciudad Universitaria."

6. Ortíz Macedo, *Un destino compartido.*

7. In "El Futuro Radiante: La Ciudad Universitaria," Manrique believes the UNAM plaza recalls the Calzada de los muertos in Teotihuacán. Or see Martinez in his essay "La Búsqueda de una Identidad," where he agrees in considering the treatment of the open spaces of the University City as well as the murals present in several buildings such as Juan O'Gorman's library map of the country in the Olympic swimming pool by Felix T. Nuncio and the Alberto T. Arais *frontones,* as a national search for pre-Hispanic roots. Jorge J. Crespo de la Serna, on the other hand, sees the El Pedregal subdivision as an example of new residential Mexican architecture whose Mexicanness and Mexican soul is embedded in the lava upon which it is built. ("El Fraccionamiento Jardines del Pedregal inaugura, franca y característica, la nueva arquitectura residencial, que sin perder, sin renunciar en lo absoluto, a nada de las comodidades que la modernidad exige, establece dominante y seguro de si el estilo arquitectónico más mexicano, levantando en esa extensión de lava hierática, que por sus mismas condiciones, refleja el alma de Mexico, la nueva ciudad cuajada de reminiscencias y portentosa en su futuro.") According to José Antonio Alderete Haas, Mexican architects used three strategies to Mexicanize the architecture of the international movement: the use of local materials, the incorporation of formal references from the pre-Columbian past, and the employment of symbolic murals in buildings. González Gortázar, *La Arquitectura Mexicana del siglo XX*; De la Serna, "Jardines en el Pedregal"; Alderete Haas, "The Search for Roots in Mexican Modernism."

8. Celia Ester Arredondo Zambrano cites the Italian architectural critic as having ridiculed the UNAM's murals as *"grottesco messicano"* in "Modernity in Mexico: The Case of Ciudad Universitaria."

9. Pani and Moral, "The Overall Plan of Ciudad Universitaria."

10. Pérez Palacios, *Estadio olímpico, Ciudad Universitaria, México.*

11. Gallo, *Mexican Modernity.*

12. Le Corbusier and Boesiger, *Le Corbusier: œuvre complète.*

13. See de la Serna. "Jardines en el Pedregal."

14. Curtis, *Le Corbusier: Ideas and Forms.*

15. Wreke and Adams, "From the Virgilian Dream to Chandigarh."

16. See, for example, Burian, "Politics and Architectural Language": "At last, the two aspirations of the 1930s of expressing modernity and Mexicanness were reconciled through the use of murals and urban design. This project was designed with the intention of reflecting the values of national identity as derived from the pre-Hispanic past, and applied them in buildings that made use of both modern materials and composition principles." Or see Arredondo Zambrano's essay, "Modernity in Mexico."

17. Burian, "Politics and Architectural Language," 83. For Antonio E. Méndez-Vigatá, for example, the two aspirations of the 1930s of expressing modernity and Mexicanness were reconciled through the use of murals reflecting the values of national identity as derived from the pre-Hispanic past, and applied them in buildings that made use of both modern materials and composition principles.

18. Kalach, "Architecture and Place." While the extent of Barragán's participation in the landscape design of CU is unclear, the gardens of El Pedregal set the tone and the formal vocabulary for the landscape strategy at the CU.

19. Barragán, "Gardens for Environment—Jardines del Pedregal."

20. Zanco and Vitra Design Museum, "A Setting for Solitude: The Landscape of Luis Barragán," 133. Marc Treib misses in Barragán's large public spaces the depth of involvement and mastery of space and materials characteristic of his residential work and small plazas.

21. Zanco and Vitra Design Museum, "A Setting for Solitude."

22. Pani, *La Construcción de La Ciudad Universitaria del Pedregal.*

23. Pani and Garay Arellano, *Historia oral de la ciudad de México.* In reference to the old downtown university, Pani states that it lacked common spaces; these were the city streets, taverns, or pool halls.

Chapter 2. Universidad de Panama: Designing on the Outside Edge of the Periphery

1. Hitchcock and Johnson, *International Style.*

2. Hitchcock and Johnson, *Latin American Architecture since 1945.*

3. Curtis, "Towards an Authentic Regionalism," 24. See also Benévolo, *History of Modern Architecture.* Also see Curtis, *Modern Architecture since 1900.* In the chapter "The Problems of Regional Identity," he writes that the modern movement was considered the intellectual property of certain countries in Western Europe, the United States, and some parts of the Soviet Union.

4. Giedion, "The State of Contemporary Architecture: The Regional Approach." 115, 132–137.

5. Kirby, Jones, and MacFadden, "Isthmus of Panama Formed."

6. Sources for the history of Panama were McCullough, *The Path between the Seas*; Mena García, *La Ciudad de Panamá en el siglo XVIII;* Robin, *Enclaves of America*; and Wilson, "Imperial American Identity at the Panamá Canal."

7. I am indebted in this chapter to conversations I had with Eduardo Tejeira-Davis.

8. Tejeira-Davis, "Roots of Modern Latin American Architecture."

9. Szok, *La Última Gaviota*, 62, 43.

10. Gutierrez, *Arquitectura Actual de Panamá, 1930–1980*, 125, 160.

11. Cárdenas, "Bolívar y el urbanismo." "Parece que si el mundo hubiese de elegir su capital, el istmo de Panamá sería señalado para este augusto destino, colocado como esta en el centro del globo, viendo por una parte el Asia y por otra el Africa y la Europa." Translated by the author.

12. Cantón, *Desenvolvimiento de las ideas pedagógicas en Panamá*, 203-4. "A la entrada misma del canal que el genio de dos razas ha abierto a través del corazón de un país altruista, sacrificio hecho pro mundi beneficio, la Universidad Bolivariana será colossal faro de luz de un continente, a cuyos rayos todos los pueblos del Nuevo mundo se sentirán hermanos y los hombres de todas partes comprenderán la virtud del amor, de la paz, del trabajo y de la solidaridad. Estupendo sueño de Bolívar, ese sublime visionario; la más completa justificación de la independencia de Panamá in 1903."

13. Tejeira-Davis, *Roots of Modern Latin American Architecture*, 364.

14. Rubio, *La Ciudad de Panamá*, 2:218.

15. Good sources for the University of Panama are Bermúdez and Gutiérrez, "Panorama Histórico de la Ciudad Universitaria de Panamá"; "Panama University Planned Like a Modern Acropolis"; "Université de Panamá."

16. Olgyay and Olgyay, *Solar Control and Shading Devices.*

17. "Vista desde el campus" in *Módulo* 7: Órgano de la Escuela de Arquitectura, Universidad de Panamá (December 1951): 29.

18. Hitchcock, *Latin American Architecture since 1945.*

19. "Université de Panama," 78, and "Panama University Planned Like a Modern Acropolis."

20. The whole issue of *Módulo* 7 is dedicated to the building of the university. On page 7 it states: "La ciudad Universitaria ha de ser, lo es ya, la fragua donde se forja el acero puro de nuestro destino nacional, la cultura por la que ha de llegar a convertirse cada ciudadano Panameño en un hombre libre y digno, capaz de vivir sin miedos inhibitorios en páz y armonía con los demás hombres de la tierra. Lo que ya hemos hecho y lo que inmediatamente seguiremos haciendo son picas que ponemos contra las fuerzas disociadoras, antidemocráticas, retardatarias, regresivas, materialistas, que se revuelven con fauces de Moloch en nuestras calles cosmopolitas, puentes de tránsito de toda clase de comercios."

Chapter 3. Topography and Ideology: The Museum of Modern Art and the Helicoide de la Roca de Tarpeya

1. Situated in the north of Venezuela 20 miles from the port of La Guaira and separated from the coast by the steep central highlands of the Cerro el Avila, Caracas was laid out in 1567 by Captain Diego de Losada, a Spanish conquistador, along the contours of a narrow mountain valley. Visitors marveled at the contrast between the climatic conditions in the hot humid lowlands bordering the Caribbean and the temperate valley of Caracas only 10.5 miles away. William Eleroy Curtis commented at the turn of the

century that the valley of the Guaire in which Caracas was situated, a dry lake bed whose water was believed to have drained into the sea after an earthquake, was "one of the most beautiful as well as one of the most fertile in the world." See Meza Suinaga, "Proyectos del Taller de Arquitectura del Banco Obrero (TABO) para el Plan Nacional de la Vivienda en Venezuela (1951–1955)"; Villanueva, *Caracas en tres tiempos*; Curtis, *Venezuela: A Land Where It's Always Summer*, 24, 46.

2. Coronil, "The Magical State," 40–41; Reynaldo Díaz, "Revisión de políticas urbanas impulsadas en la ciudad de Caracas durante las cuatro primeras décadas del siglo XX," Escuela de Historia Centro de Investigaciones Históricas de América Central Postgrado Centroamericano en Historia Número especial de Diálogos. Revista electrónica de Historia, 2008, http://historia.fcs.ucr.ac.cr/dialogos.htm.

3. Lombardi, *Venezuela: The Search for Order, the Dream of Progress.*

4. Mustafa F. Hassan provides an overview of Venezuela's economic development, stating, "Among the special features that characterize the process of economic development in Venezuela is the high rate of growth of the economy over a comparatively long period of time of about 25 years. Venezuela registered the highest growth in Latin America in the postwar period." According to Charles I. Jones, in the 1960s Venezuela had the third richest economy in the world with an income equal to 84 percent of U.S. income. See Hassan, "High Growth, Unemployment, and Planning in Venezuela"; Jones, *On the Evolution of the World Income Distribution.*

5. Hitchcock and Johnson, *Latin American Architecture since 1945.*

6. Henry Luce and Briton Hadden, "Shapes of the Future," *Time*, April 22, 1957.

7. Barrios argues that the MAM was a "key piece within the context of Caracas as a museum city in the representation of the global collection of modern architecture and abstract art." While she does not define "museum city," the MAM was clearly an attempt to market the new development of Bello Monte as well as an attempt to redefine Caracas' identity as an avant-garde modern city. Inasmuch as the museum implies visual contemplation or perhaps even consumption, the notion of Caracas as a museum city is more difficult to defend. The Universidad Central de Caracas by Carlos Raúl Villanueva, for example, is recognized as an architectural masterpiece, but it is very much part of students' everyday life as opposed to a showpiece. See Barrios, "El Museo de Arte de Niemeyer," 78.

8. "Musée d'art Moderne, Caracas, Venezuela."

9. Ponti, "Proposta per Caracas," 295.

10. Information on Niemeyer can be found in Fils, *Oscar Niemeyer: Selbstdarstellung, Kritiken, Oeuvre*; Niemeyer, *Minha arquitetura: 1937–2005*; Papadaki, *Oscar Niemeyer: Works in Progress*; Underwood, *Oscar Niemeyer and Brazilian Free-Form Modernism.* In an interview conducted by Christian Hornig in Munich in 1981, Niemeyer considered Le Corbusier somebody who exerted a powerful influence on him.

11. Underwood, *Oscar Niemeyer and Brazilian Free-Form Modernism*, 39. Even though David Kendrick Underwood's book has been criticized for its lack of scholarship, see Underwood and Evenson, "Oscar Niemeyer and the Architecture of Brazil," which contains some poetic images/views of Niemeyer's work.

12. Ksiazek, "Architectural Culture in the Fifties."

13. "Art: Last Monument," *Time*, November 2, 1959.

14. Vossoughian, "The Language of the World Museum: Otto Neurath, Paul Otlet, Le Corbusier."

15. Alofsin, "Frank Lloyd Wright and Modernism."

16. Levine, *The Architecture of Frank Lloyd Wright.*

17. Lapunzina, "The Pyramid and the Wall."

18. Ockman, *Architecture Culture, 1943–1968.*

19. Segawa, "Oscar Niemeyer: A Misbehaved Pupil of Rationalism."

20. Coronil, "The Magical State"; Mumford, "Monumentalism, Symbolism, and Style."

21. Gerencia de Asuntos Públicos y Relaciones (Venezuela), ExxonMobil de Venezuela, *Santiago de León de Caracas, 1567–2030.*

22. Fraser, *Building the New World.*

23. For general information on shopping centers, consult Mennel, "Victor Gruen and the Construction of Cold War Utopias," and Jackson, "All the World's a Mall."

24. Cohen, "From Town Center to Shopping Center."

25. "Einkaufszentrum Helicoide de la Roca de Tarpeya"; "Projekt zum Einkaufszentrum mit Industrieausstellung 'Helicoide' in Caracas"; Niño Araque and Mendoza, *1950: El Espíritu Moderno*; Leopoldo Martinez, "Nuevo Helicoide de Caracas."

26. Cleary and Wright, *Merchant Prince and Master Builder.*

27. Drexler and Rudovsky, "Roads (from an Exhibition at the Museum of Modern Art)."

28. Ponti, "Proposta per Caracas."

29. Coronil, "The Magical State," 4.

30. Fernando Coronil reports, "Pérez Jiménez pieced together a doctrine and called it the 'New National Ideal,' first introduced in 1955 at a celebration commemorating the tenth anniversary of the overthrow of President Medina." Ibid. The New National Ideal was an "ideological composite" of Venezuelan liberalism, positivism, traditional militarism, and Democratic Party rhetoric. Avendaño Lugo, *El militarismo en Venezuela: la dictadura de Pérez Jiménez.* To explain the regime's purpose, this doctrine asserted that the military's higher "destiny" was to eliminate political strife and channel social energies toward the "material construction of the fatherland. . . . A clear demonstration of our national consciousness is the materialization of the abstract concept of fatherland in works of great scope, whose importance will be self-evident." Pérez Jiménez, *Cinco discursos del general Marcos Pérez Jiménez, presidente de la República, pronunciados durante el ãno 1955.*

31. Ewell, "The Extradition of Marcos Pérez Jiménez."

32. Coronil, "The Magical State," 42.

33. For a continuing debate about modern architecture being constructed in support of repressive regimes with poor human rights records, see "Herzog on Building the Olympic Stadium: 'Only an Idiot Would Have Said No,'" September 2, 2010, http://www.spiegel.de/international/world/a-569011.html.

Chapter 4. São Paulo's Topography and the Utopian Democracy

1. Godfrey, "Revisiting Rio de Janeiro and São Paulo."

2. Niemeyer, *The Curves of Time.*

3. José Carlos Durand and Elena Salvatori, "Por uma nova agenda de pesquisa em torno de Oscar Niemeyer."

4. Niemeyer's early work is influenced by Le Corbusier, Brazilian vernacular, and other modern masters, most notably Mies van der Rohe, whose curvilinear glass skyscraper for Berlin from 1922 can be felt in the form for the Sede do Banco Mineiro da Produção designed in Belo Horizonte in 1951. In an article published in *Architectural Review,* no. 116 (1954), 235–50, Niemeyer cites Jean (Hans) Arp, Le Corbusier's Obus plan for Algiers, and the Crescent at Bath as the influences on his organic forms.

5. Quezado Deckker cites Vilanova Artigas in *Brazil Built*: "Today, Brazilian Modern architecture is progressing in such a way as to serve as propaganda for any commercial villainy . . . while at the same time reinforcing the penetration of imperialism, giving it cover to enter without being noticed through the doors of cultural movements. . . . For the progressive architects in Brazil, the language of Le Corbusier, in this book, is the language of the worst enemy of our people, American imperialism. It is up to us to reject it."

6. Styliane Philippou, "Challenging the Hierarchies of the City: Oscar Niemeyer's Mid-Twentieth-Century Residential Buildings," Conference Proceedings Hosted by TU Delft Library, 2005, accessed February 27, 2014, http://repository.tudelft.nl/view/conferencepapers/uuid%3A8c5979ee-0e89-4fff-b66b-ed84fcb0f07b/.

7. Ibid.

8. Lévi-Strauss, *Tristes Tropiques.*

9. José Geraldo Simões Jr., *Anhangabaú: história e urbanismo.*

10. Prestes Maia, *Estudo de um plano de avenidas para a cidade de São Paulo,* 74. "O viaducto do Cha, suppoese reconstruido: nao mais a estructura actual, reticulado de palitos, mas um grande arco de cimento armado, material que permittirá uma silhuetta monumental mas sufficientemente esguia para nao obstruir a vista."

11. Le Corbusier, *Precisions on the Present State of Architecture and City Planning.*

12. Bardi, *Lembrança de Le Corbusier.*

13. Andreoli and Forty, *Brazil's Modern Architecture*; Artigas, *A funcão social do arquiteto*; Artigas, *Caminhos da arquitetura*; translated by the editor from "Architecture and Construction," in Ferraz et al., *Vilanova Artigas.* "A partir da habitacao, teria o homem primitivo transposto sua nao menos primitiva 'solera' para apropiarse do espaco da habitacao em escala mais amplia. A outra margem de um rio passa a fazer parte do espaco do habitacao, a traves de uma ponte."

14. Spiro and Mendes da Rocha, *Paulo Mendes da Rocha.*

15. Artigas and Wisnik, *Paulo Mendes da Rocha: Projects, 1957–2007.*

16. Ibid.

Chapter 5. Le Corbusier, Rio de Janeiro, Topography, and Housing: A Cross-Cultural Exchange

1. Benévolo, *History of Modern Architecture.* For new literature on streams of influence between Europe and South America, see Frampton, "Le Corbusier and Oscar Niemeyer"; Brillembourg, *Latin American Architecture, 1929–1960.*

2. See Quezado Deckker, *Brazil Built,* and Sisson, "Rio de Janeiro, 1875–1945," 144.

3. Cavalcanti, *When Brazil Was Modern.*

4. Bannen Lanata and Pérez Oyarzún, *Le Corbusier y Sudaméric: viajes y proyectos,* 39–40.

5. Le Corbusier, *Precisions on the Present State of Architecture and City Planning.*

6. Lucan, *Le Corbusier, une encyclopédie*; W.J.R. Curtis, *Le Corbusier.*

7. Mary McLeod, "Le Corbusier and Algiers," 55.

8. Bonduki et al., *Affonso Eduardo Reidy: arquitetos brasileiros.*

9. Cavalcanti, *When Brazil Was Modern.*

10. Bruand and Goldberger, *Arquitetura contemporânea no Brasil.*

11. Ibid.

12. Jovanovic Weiss and Fischer, "How to Read Two Monoliths."

13. Cavalcanti, *When Brazil Was Modern.*

14. Le Corbusier and Boesiger, *Le Corbusier.*

15. Eardley, Frampton, and Kolbowski, *Le Corbusier's Firminy Church.*

16. "Catedral Metropolitana, Edgar de Oliveira Da Fonseca, Rio de Janeiro, MIMOA," accessed March 10, 2014, http://www.mimoa.eu/projects/Brazil/Rio%20de%20Janeiro/Catedral%20Metropolitana.

Chapter 6. Mexico City as Reinvented Geography, Its Looming Environmental Crisis, and Recent Proposals for Regenerative Landscapes

Author's note: This essay is dedicated to the millions of hard-working people living in the degraded environment of the Mexico City megalopolis.

1. George Kubler used the term *metropolitan culture* to describe the Aztec culture, which integrated outsiders' cultural concepts and aesthetics and was capable of a range of aesthetic expressions from the abstract to the figurative. See Kubler, *Mexico: Splendors of Thirty Centuries,* 49.

2. Regarding firewood, see Williams, "Tepetate in the Valley of Mexico."

3. After one deluge in 1629, most of the city remained submerged under 6 feet of water until 1634. See Kandell, *La Capital.*

4. The existing springs of Chapultepec, Desierto de Leones, Lerma, and Santa Fe had proven insufficient to meet the growing water needs of the metropolis.

5. Informal settlements developed around the factories as the urban poor, heedless of the threats they presented to public health, were attracted to the possibility of employment as well as opportunities for illegal use of their electricity, water, and transportation infrastructure. The new PEMEX Gas Storage facility in the Tlalnepantla district attracted many such squatters in the 1950s who built informal housing too close to the storage

tanks, and thousands were killed when the tanks accidentally exploded. See Kandell, *La Capital.*

6. "Informally developed" is a euphemism for neighborhoods built illegally and mostly without drainage, roads, water supply, sewers, sewage treatment facilities, electricity, plumbing, telecommunications, schools, parks, sidewalks, street trees, or other infrastructure and public services, typically on hazardous sites.

7. The sinking had also caused the Gran Canal drainage project to slope in the opposite direction and back up; a series of pumps were installed at intervals to lift the black water upslope to the next level. See Gilmartin et al., "In the Nature of the Valley: An Urban and Ecological Proposal for Mexico City."

8. See Tortajada and Castelán, "Water Management for a Megacity."

9. This raw sewage is used for crop irrigation, especially alfalfa in the state of Hidalgo, which desperately needs the water for agriculture. But its residents contract cholera, parasites, and other illnesses by using it for farming. See Kandell, *La Capital.*

10. In June 2004, the earthen edge of the canal in the impoverished former lake bed of Valle de Chalco collapsed, spewing tons of raw sewage into the neighborhood nearly 6 feet deep in some places; the catastrophe also cut off the main road linking the MAMC with Puebla. In April 2011, another large raw sewage spill occurred in Chalco. See Calixto, "Sin cumplir promesa de no más inundaciones, en julio de 2010, el gobierno del Estado de México prometió a los municipios de Chalco, Valle de Chalco e Ixtapaluca que no volverían a inundarse. Menos de un año después, la promesa falló." In *Sexenio,* April 19, 2011, http://www.sexenio.com.mx/articulo.php?id=4007, accessed April 2015.

11. The roaring noise of vehicles, many in poor condition, results in noise levels up to 90 decibels, equivalent to the sound level of jackhammers.

12. A few successful projects have been completed: Luis Barragán's Gardens of Pedregal residential subdivision (1945–49), the Ciudad Universitaria master-planned by Enrique del Moral and Mario Pani (1950–52), and the large-scale multifamily housing projects of Mario Pani (1947–62). For the most part, the public works projects built for the Olympic Games in 1968 marked the beginning and the end of proactive regional planning in the MAMC. The megalopolis has ceased to be economically self-sustaining as ever-increasing expenditures on urban infrastructure produce proportionately fewer measurable improvements. Government subsidies supported by tax revenue collected from around the country amid widespread resentment keep the costs paid by residents of the MAMC for food, water, and transportation artificially low.

13. Mario Schjetnan and GDU have also utilized the notion of a working landscape in the restoration and intervention of a degraded site in northern Mexico City in the district of Azcapotzalco, a former pre-Columbian city-state on the shore of the lakes, which are now dried lake beds and urbanized in the midst of the megalopolis. Here, a contaminated former industrial site has been transformed into a large-scale high-tech office campus of 16 hectares. At the level of environmental mitigation, the project pays particular attention to hydrology, water recycling, capturing rainwater, and replenishing the deep aquifer. Other projects by Schjetnan and GDU include the restoration of Chapultepec Park, the largest public park in the city and home to many of the city's major

museums, with almost 16 million visitors per year. Half of the budget for the project was raised with contributions from the private sector.

14. A tree nursery was introduced on the site, and it claims to produce some 30 million trees for planting around the MAMC.

15. Recalling Edward Relph's phenomenology of "a field of care" and "sparing," Schjetnan's Xochimilco restoration project focuses on empathy and the deep concerns for the processes of life integral to, defining, and shaping a given place, as well as the experiential bonds that people establish with it. See Hays, *Main Currents in Western Environmental Thought,* 154–55.

16. The genesis for the project was a proposal in the 1960s by soils expert Nabor Carrillo, who advocated the benefits of reversing the 400-year project of drainage to reconstitute the lakes, addressing the problems of flooding, water supply, and ground sinkage, a process in which storm water and wastewater were resources rather than problems. Kalach and Gonzalez de León further developed the concept: the latter used Carrillo's proposal as the basis for a design studio at the UNAM, which for the first time mapped topography in relationship to existing hydraulic engineering, and with José Castillo they formed Taller Ciudad de México, which published *La ciudad y sus lagos* (1998). See M. Miller, "Mexico City: Projects from the MegaCity."

17. Concerning controlling wastewater, see R. Holmes, *Below the Phreatic Level.*

18. The Mexico City international airport has outgrown its current site, but after plans to relocate it to a rural area outside the city were met with strong opposition, a relocation plan was abandoned.

19. See Relph, "An Inquiry into the Relations between Phenomenology and Geography"; Relph, "Modernity and the Reclamation of Place."

20. See M. Miller, "Mexico City: Projects from the MegaCity."

21. The project has also started an ongoing discourse about planning, related to waste, sound business practices, politics, and environmental restoration throughout Mexico.

22. Critics of the project have generally objected to its large size, the feasibility of procuring land around the perimeters of the lakes, the overly specific nature of the physical interventions that ignore urban complexity, the scale and cost of water treatment measures, and the complex logistics involved in relocating low-income communities to form Lake Chalco.

23. See Kalach et al., *Atlas de proyectos para la ciudad de México*, vol. 2.

24. Carbon sequestration is the process of capture and long-term storage of atmospheric carbon dioxide (CO_2), naturally captured from the atmosphere through biological, chemical, or physical processes. See Burden, *22 Benefits of Urban Street Trees.*

25. See Kalach et al., *Atlas de proyectos para la ciudad de México*, vol. 2. See also Natalia Galvez Farías, *Domus Online*, at http://www.domusweb.it/es/resenas/2013/05/31/atlas_de_proyectos_para_la_ciudad_de_m_xico.html.

26. The most realistic hope for eliminating air pollution in the MAMC is that it can somehow survive until the nonpolluting vehicles currently produced in developed countries are affordable for widespread use in Mexico City. Air pollution in the MAMC would be even worse if everyone who wanted a motor vehicle could afford to buy one.

27. For design principles pertaining to remedial environmental infrastructure, working landscapes, and landscape urbanism for Mexico, see Burian, *The Architecture and Cities of Northern Mexico from Independence to Present.*

Chapter 7. Mountains, Wetlands, and Public Space in Bogotá

1. Humphrey, "Race, Caste, and Class in Colombia."
2. Carreira, "De las perturbadoras y conflictivas relaciones de los Bogotanos con sus aguas"; Gómez, "La Diosa Agua."
3. Carrasquilla Botero, *Quintas y estancias de Santa Fé y Bogotá.*
4. Wiesner, "Aguas para Bogotá"; Mejía Pavony, *Los años del cambio: historia urbana de Bogotá, 1820–1910.* Defined by river streams, parishes retained a very autonomous feeling, particularly since they were initially only connected by ten bridges, a situation that lasted until the nineteenth century when thirty additional wooden bridges and paths were built.
5. Webre, "Water and Society in a Spanish American City: Santiago de Guatemala, 1555–1773."
6. Flórez de Ocáriz, *Libro primero de las genealogías del Nuevo Reino de Granada.*
7. Ibid.; Santamaría, *Bogotá, estructura y principales servicios públicos.*
8. Miguel Triana, *Artículos escritos para Bogotá, pero que son aplicables a otras poblaciones de la República*; Mark and Piñeros Corpas, *Aquarelas de mark, 1843–1856.*
9. Cotes, "Régimen alimenticio de los jornaleros de La Sabana de Bogotá."
10. Located all along the Cerros Orientales to the north, the clay quarries were artisan mining operations that provided construction materials for Bogotá's buildings. To make bricks, the clay factories needed on average eight furnaces that used firewood as fuel because of its high energy output. According to a 1914 estimate, one load of firewood serviced eighteen furnace operations, while coal only sufficed for seven. Triana, *Artículos escritos para Bogotá, pero que son aplicables a otras poblaciones de la República*; Peña, *Informe de la Comisión Permanente del Ramo de Aguas.*
11. Peña, *Informe de la Comisión Permanente del Ramo de Aguas*; Amaya, "Oficina de Sanidad," *El Nuevo Tiempo*, February 25, 1914; Rodríguez Pérez, "Intereses Municipales: El Agua"; Arias Argaes, "Observaciones sobre la higiene de Bogotá."
12. Sowell, "Population Growth in Late-Nineteenth-Century Bogotá."
13. Rodriguez Pérez, *San Cristóbal*; Lesmes and Zambrano, "Santa Fé y Bogotá"; Henderson, *Modernization in Colombia.*
14. Jiménez, "Unas montañas al servicio de Bogotá."
15. Atuesta Ortiz, "La ciudad que pasó por el río."
16. Jiménez, "Unas montañas al servicio de Bogotá."
17. Bender, *Toward an Urban Vision.* Bender includes a helpful analysis of additional sources of Olmsted's urban reflections in the bibliographical essay.
18. Cendales Paredes, "Una Perspectiva Comparativa."
19. Cranz, "Urban Parks as a Mechanism of Social Control"; Cranz, *The Politics of Park Design.*
20. Mejía Pavony, *Los años del cambio*; Carreira, "De las perturbadoras y conflictivas relaciones de los bogotanos con sus aguas"; Santana R., *Bogotá, 450 años.*

21. Escovar Wilson-White, "Bogotá en tiempos de la celebración del primer Centenario de la independencia."

22. "Historia de los humedales," *En Colombia*.com, http://www.encolombia.com/medioambiente/hume-bogota-evolucion4.htm, accessed February 21, 2014.

23. Carreira, "De las perturbadoras y conflictivas relaciones de los Bogotanos con sus aguas."

24. Gilbert, "Good Urban Governance: Evidence from a Model City?"

25. Silva, *Bogotá, de la construcción al deterioro, 1995–2007.*

26. Montezuma, "Promoting Active Lifestyles and Healthy Urban Spaces," 161.

27. Del Castillo et al., "Translating Evidence to Policy"; "Historia de los humedales de Bogotá."

28. Aschner, *Contrapunto y confluencia en el concierto arquitectónico: Biblioteca Virgilio Barco.*

29. In a good general article on Bogotá and Medellín, Lorenzo Castro and Alejandro Echeverri discuss the urban transformation of the two most important cities in Colombia. The river where the current avenida Eje Ambiental Jiménez de Quesada ran used to change course in the southwest joining the waters of the San Agustín River (also called Manzanares River) by moving northwest to the rio Arzobispo. Rogelio Salmona states that his project for the Eje attempts to recover the memory of the San Francisco River, which the Muiscas called Viracachá or "water glittering in the dark." See Castro and Echeverri, "Bogotá and Medellín: Architecture and Politics." For further information on the project, also consult Saldarriaga, "Colombia: Espacios para vivir la ciudad."

30. González Escobar, *Ciudad y arquitectura urbana en Colombia, 1980–2010.*

31. Villegas, *El agua en la historia de Bogotá*; Berney, "Pedagogical Urbanism"; Bornhorst, *Valores perennes en la arquitectura*; Martignoni, "Bogotá Dresses in Green."

32. Villegas, *El agua en la historia de Bogotá.*

33. Burdett and Sudjic, "Politics, Power, Cities"; Ruby and Ruby, *Urban Transformation*; Peirce et al., *Century of the City: No Time to Lose.*

34. Gastil and Ryan, *Open: New Designs for Public Space*; Cervero et al., "Influences of Built Environments on Walking and Cycling."

35. Peñalosa, "The Politics of Happiness."

36. Berney, "Pedagogical Urbanism: Creating Citizen Space in Bogota, Colombia"; Gilbert, "Good Urban Governance."

Chapter 8. Topography, Hydrology and the Irrigated Landscapes of Mendoza, Argentina

1. Fagiolo, "La fondazione delle cittá Latino-Americane." This essay is based on a summary of extensive studies contained in two books by Jorge Ricardo Ponte: *Mendoza, aquella ciudad de barro: historia de una ciudad andina desde el siglo XVI hasta nuestros días* and *De los caciques del agua a la Mendoza de las acequias: cinco siglos de historia de acequias, zanjones y molinos.*

2. Guantata or Huantata in the aboriginal Milcayac language means "of the guanacos," alluding to the fact that these animals would descend from the Andes during harsh winters in search of tender grasses.

3. Fagiolo, "La fondazione delle cittá Latino-Americane."

4. Only the transcript of 1696 rather than the original act of 1574 exists. The reasons are not clear, but we assume that it was due to the interest that the descendants of Alonso de Campofrío y Carvajal y Alonso de Reynoso had in rescuing this document to leave a record of their possessions.

5. The document below is cited by Rosa Zuluága at the time she consulted the Mendoza Archive, but it isn't contained in the acts published during that period (Academia Nacional de la Historia 1945). For further references to this document, see Larrain and Calderón, *El país de Cuyo*, and Bárcena, *Datos e interpretación del registro documental sobre la Dominación Incaica en Cuyo*. "Según expresa una disposición del fundador de la ciudad de Mendoza Pedro del Castillo, emitida el 9 de Octubre de 1561, el polígono urbano de 45 hectáreas debía ser rodeado por 'tierras y heredamientos para que puedan sembrar y plantar las cosas necesarias para su sustento de sus casas y familias.' Entre estas tierras de labradío y la ciudad propiamente dicha se determinaba un ejido público para que dentro de 'el no haya huerta ni ranchería, ni sementera, ni otra que lo ocupe y no fuera dándose por este dicho cabildo, solares en tal ejido público y solamente sirva para establecimiento y población de ella.'" Zuluága, *El Cabildo de la ciudad de Mendoza*, 1964, 28. According to an edict issued by Pedro del Castillo, the city of Mendoza's founder, on October 9, 1561, the urban gridiron had to be surrounded by land that was meant to be used for sowing and planting, to provide for the sustenance of family homes. Between those lands and the city, a public enclosed space of land (*ejido*) was to be established in which the town hall should not allow the setting up of orchards, seeding areas, tenements, or groups of tenement dwellings as it was meant to serve only the common good and the formation of the settlement. Translated by the editor. Larrain and Calderón, *El país de Cuyo: relación histórica hasta 1872*; Bárcena, "Datos e interpretación del registro documental sobre la dominación incaica en Cuyo."

6. Zuluága, *El Cabildo de la ciudad de Mendoza.*

7. In the colonial city, the irrigation system and its *ejido* were laid out as follows:

The Acequia Grande de la Ciudad, presently Canal Zanjón, ran from the river Mendoza where it began to the canal Confín Desagüe in the del Pilar zone to irrigate the properties from the southeast river's edge toward the city.

The Acequia de Allayme that originated at the dike of Carrodilla would have irrigated the west area and the northwest and north central zone of small farms.

The Acequia de la Ciudad would have irrigated toward the left margin, the city proper, and the north of the *ejido*. Toward the left margin, the Acequia de la Ciudad would have irrigated the east, from the Del Pilar zone to the district of Pedro Molina.

The Acequia Guaimaién supplied water from the northward Pilar to the zone of small farms located east of the city.

8. The boundaries run from the limit set in 1566 at the edge of the *ejido* to the Zanjón Maure and from the Acequia Principal del Cacique Tabalqué to the Acequia de la Ciudad and a road identified as the "street that goes from south to north" that also bordered the foundational urban core settlement of 1561. The *ejido* contained plots of varying sizes: 20–30 hectares (61 percent of the total), less than 20 hectares (18 percent), and more than 30 hectares (20 percent) and assorted other sizes (1 percent). Favored by the location of

a larger number of irrigation canals, the southwest (only 15 percent) attracted the largest number of farms (46 percent).

9. Guarda, *Historia urbana del reino de Chile*; Zuluága, *El Cabildo de la ciudad de Mendoza.*

10. Molina, *Compendio de la historia geográfica, natural y civil del reyno de Chile*; Scobie and Baily, *Secondary Cities of Argentina.*

11. The boundaries of the city according to this plan were:

- to the south, the current Zanjón Maure, which had previously been known as Zanjón Mayorga.
- to the north: the street of Cornel Diaz, until the "land of vines belonging to Nicolás Godoy," "lands and vineyards belonging to several citizens and the fathers of the Companía of Jesus," and the ancient lands of Cacique Tabalqué usurped by the Jesuits in the northern part of the colonial city.
- to the west: a ditch not identified that may have been the Acequia Principal del Cacique Tabalqué or the old course of the Acequia de la Calle Allayme.
- to the east: the Acequia de la Ciudad in current districts of Dorrego and San José between the Acequia de la Ciudad and the Acequia Guaimaieé not identified but labeled as "Farms and Vineyards."

12. The infographics map is established by transferring a historical foundation over a current georeferenced plan of the metropolitan area of Mendoza.

13. Scobie, *Secondary Cities of Argentina.*

14. Scott et al., "Science-Policy Dialogues for Water Security."

15. Foster and Garduño, *Integrated Approaches.*

16. Scott et al., "Science-Policy Dialogues for Water Security."

17. Foster and Garduño, *Integrated Approaches.*

18. Fernald, Baker, and Guldan, "Hydrologic, Riparian, and Agroecosystem Functions of Traditional Acequia Irrigation Systems."

19. González and Zamorano, "La cultura del agua, eje orientador de la educación ambiental para los habitantes del Gran Mendoza."

20. According to the results of a sample of two populations of Guaymallén (a middle class and a lower class), only 30 percent of respondents believe that the canal serves as a channel for irrigation and storm drain; also only 30 percent indicate that their function is to drain; 63 percent see these as conduits for irrigating trees, and 7 percent say, unfortunately, that their purpose is to carry waste. Only 37 percent of respondents cited the Huarpes as the creators of the acequias.

Chapter 9. Santiago de Chile and the Changing Meaning of Its Hills

1. The Alameda de las Delicias was planned by the liberator Bernardo O'Higgins, a central figure in the Chilean struggle for independence from Spain. "If great cities, according to the rules of modern hygiene, need lungs to breathe, then one of those lungs of Santiago is the Alameda, and Cerro Santa Lucía is the other." In Santiago Intendencia and Vicuña Mackenna, *El paseo del Santa Lucía, lo que es i lo que deberá ser*, 90. Translation provided by the editor.

2. Confronted with unfamiliar surroundings, the Spaniards resorted to renaming hills after Catholic saints and built modest crosses or (occasionally) hermitages to infuse them with religious significance. Huelén—"place of pain" in the indigenous language—became "Cerro Santa Lucía" and Tupahue—"the place of colored flowers"—became "Cerro Grande" and eventually "Cerro San Cristóbal."

3. Arturo Almandoz, *Planning Latin America's Capital Cities, 1850–1950*. The architect Lucien Ambroise Henault, who worked with Benjamín Vicuña Mackenna on the design of the Cerro Santa Lucía, also designed the Universidad de Chile and the National Congress, both in Santiago. Information on the transformation of the Cerro Santa Lucía can also be found in Pérez Oyarzún and Rosas Vera, "Cities within the City: Urban and Architectural Transfers in Santiago de Chile, 1840–1940."

4. Benjamin Vicuña Mackenna relates that 150 prisoners, 60 miners, and 40 masons labored on the Cerro Santa Lucía. See Santiago Intendencia and Vicuña Mackenna, *El paseo de Santa Lucía*, 7; De Ramón, *Santiago de Chile*, 148.

5. Chile declared its independence from Spain in 1810 but achieved full independence only in 1818. Spanish hostility against the new republic did not end until later, however, and peace between the two countries was established only in 1883.

6. Benjamín Vicuña Mackenna described the hill as having "the appearance of an immense fortress" capped by "a cone of daring natural rocks intertwined with robust vegetation that will complete the severe and enchanting aspect of these environments" in *El paseo de Santa Lucía, lo que es i lo que deberá ser.* Written with Santiago Intendencia. Translation provided by the author.

7. See Anderson, *Circling South America*, 86.

8. Grumbach, "The Promenades of Paris"; Alphand and Frerejean, *Les promenades de Paris*. An abridged list of heads of towns or public libraries who received *Les Promenades de Paris* included Santiago de Chile. Vicuña Mackenna was in Europe during the time Baron Georges-Eugène Haussmann was beginning his work in Paris, and he had just returned from his third trip to Europe when he was named mayor of Santiago in 1972 by President Federico Errázuriz Zañartu. A landscape architect and engineer with the Corps des Ingénieurs des Ponts et Chaussées responsible for public works, Alphand assisted Baron Haussmann, the prefect of the Seine, in transforming the medieval maze of Paris into a great modern capital. The alteration of Paris, which took place between 1853 and 1869, created a boom in the construction industry and expanded boundaries to include Buttes Chaumont, formerly a depository of the city's sanitary sewage and site of small-scale quarries. Alphand's transformation of the area into a park provided the city with a healthy recreation area.

9. Vicuña Mackenna, *Álbum del Santa Lucía*.

10. "As for the ones who decry the *paseo* of Cerro Santa Lucía as an object of luxury, it is a work essential to democracy. In a sense being in a hygienic environment well proportioned to the population, containing a site surrounded by gardens, and of a height two or three times taller than the tallest towers of the capital, we believe we have done so much as to leave behind a not too small health hospital." Ibid.

11. De Ramón, *Santiago de Chile*.

12. Prado Martínez, *Guía Completa de Santiago*. These sentiments were still alive

thirty years later when, in 1901, Alberto Prado, who would publish the first photographic guide to Chile, argued that "it is with hygiene and cleanliness, coolness and neatness that the park keeps its primacy. . . . Strolling frequently on the Cerro Santa Lucía is . . . a joy for the healthy and a comfortable, secure, and inexpensive medicine for many sick."

13. Even though value of property around the cerro after the paseo de Santa Lucía was completed went up three times the original value, owners were still compensated. Santiago Intendencia and Vicuña Mackenna, *El paseo de Santa Lucía*. Real estate speculation at the time of Napoleon III in París is discussed in Schenker, "Parks and Politics during the Second Empire in Paris."

14. Marceca, "Reservoir, Circulation, Residue."

15. Vicuña Mackenna, *Álbum del Santa Lucía*; Pérez de Arce et al., *La Montaña Magica*; Freytag and Conan, "When the Railway Conquered the Garden: Velocity in Parisian and Viennese Parks."

16. Melfi, *El viaje literario*; Vicuña Urrutia, *El París americano.*

17. Alberto Prado Martínez, *El cerro Santa Lucía historia y descripción de este paseo en sus distintos periodos.* Translated by the editor from "Desde aquella altiplanicie de 630 metros sobre el nivel del mar el observador domina el más hermoso panorama. Se ve colocado cómo por encanto en medio del extenso valle del Mapocho que es mucho más grande que los de granado i la Loja que los poetas han inmortalizado con entusiasmo. Una cintura de elevadísimas i dilatadas cordilleras abraza este valle envolviendo lo en su manto de nieves eternas. Arriba un cielo siempre azul i abajo un caserío caprichoso que se entiende en ancha zona, entre alfombras de vejetación i de verduras interminable a la vista, forman un detalle arrebatadores que inspira i enardece la mente más negada de los sueños de la fantasía."

18. Pérez de Arce et al., *La Montaña Magica.*

19. Velasco Reyes, *El cerro San Cristóbal.*

20. Alberto Mackenna Subercaseaux, *Santiago futuro conferencias sobre los proyectos de transformación de Santiago,* Santiago: Soc. impr.-litografía "Barcelona," 1915. Accessed February 27, 2014. http://catalog.hathitrust.org/api/volumes/oclc/19550345.html. Santiago is part of a group of Latin American cities that feature colossal religious sculptures on their hilltops, the most famous being the 130-foot-tall O Cristo Redentor (Christ the Redeemer), built a little later in 1931 on Rio de Janeiro's Corcovado Hill.

21. Alberto Mackenna (Subercaseaux was his mother's surname) was part of the same family as Benjamin Vicuña Mackenna (Mackenna being his mother's surname), but the exact relationship is not clear. He also admired Latin American mayors who had been accomplished urban reformers inspired by the French prefect such as Torcuato de Alvear, first mayor of Buenos Aires (1880–87), and Francisco Pereira Passos, who headed the government of Rio de Janeiro between 1902 and 1906.

22. For Alberto Mackenna, the role of the capital was to express the country's progress. In *Santiago futuro*, he mentions having been to the museum that keeps all the documents related to Haussmann's transformation of Paris, including all the photographs and press related to those whose stupidity and ignorance opposed the agents of progress.

23. Mackenna Subercaseaux, *Santiago futuro.*

24. Calderón, *Memorial de Santiago.* The citation is attributed to Andrés Bello.

25. Riquelme Sepúlveda and Kulczewski, *La arquitectura de Luciano Kulczewski.*

26. Mosser and Teyssot, *The Architecture of Western Gardens.*

27. Larrain Ibáñez, *Modernidad, razón e identidad en América Latina.*

28. Aguirre Arias and Castillo, *De la "gran aldea" a la ciudad de masas.*

29. Velasco Reyes, *El cerro San Cristóbal.*

30. *Libro oficial del 4o centenario de la fundación de Santiago.* In homage to the 400th anniversary of the foundation of Santiago, writer and journalist Manuel Rojas observes from the top of the Cerro San Cristóbal that by lacking a larger population, buildings, and more time, Santiago is not a great metropolis, but he sees it as a large, dynamic growing city.

31. Walter, *Politics and Urban Growth in Santiago, Chile, 1891–1941.*

32. Lambert, "Apuntes Sobre Urbanismo."

Chapter 10. Valparaíso: A Future in the Balance

1. Collier and Sater, *A History of Chile, 1808–1994.*

2. Indirli, Modena, and Tralli, "Natural Multi-Hazard and Building Vulnerability Assessment in the Historic Centers."

3. Raab, "The Inclined Lifts of Valparaíso." Most *ascensores* are privately owned, but a few are run by the city government. Since some of the elevators date back to 1883, their technical specifications vary greatly. Load capacity of the cabs is from eight to twenty-five people. The travel distance ranges from 100 to 300 feet, and the angle of inclination from 30 to 90 degrees.

4. Currently more than 40 percent of the country's wealth is concentrated in the hands of just 10 percent of the population. "Chile—Poverty and Wealth"; Bosworth et al., *The Chilean Economy: Policy Lessons and Challenges.*

5. Along with the surviving infrastructure of nineteenth-century maritime trade, Valparaíso's World Heritage site includes five neighborhoods containing civic, commercial, and industrial infrastructure, public spaces, and residential architecture from various historical periods:

- Iglesia de la Matríz and Plaza Santo Domingo, Valparaíso's original nucleus, from which gradual expansion to the northeast began, linked with Plaza Echaurren and its surroundings as well as with Cerro Santo Domingo;
- Plaza Echaurren and Calle Serrano, a predominantly commercial area with the port market, active street trade, and a lower station of Ascensor Cordillera;
- Muelle Prat, a commercial and recreational pier, the large public spaces of Plazas Justicia and Sotomayor opening onto the sea and surrounded by historic administrative and service buildings, and Museo Marítimo Nacional at the top of Cerro Cordillera;
- Calle Prat, the financial center, and Plazuela Turri, a public space extending south from Plaza Sotomayor, with a lower terminus of Ascensor Concepción;
- Cerro Alegre and Cerro Concepción, two hills separated by Calle Urriola which together form a single neighborhood, planned and developed by German and English immigrants during the nineteenth century, with many public spaces,

several *ascensores*, and the distinctive vernacular wood and corrugated metal buildings. UNESCO Advisory Body Evaluation Valparaíso (Chile) 959 (revised 2003).

6. UNESCO, "Report on the Advisory Mission to Historic Quarter of the Seaport City of Valparaíso."

7. Rojas and Lanzafame, "Valparaíso, Chile."

8. Catadougnac, "Borde costero de Valparaíso: Aprobado Megaproyecto de Mall Plaza," *Plataforma Urbana*, September 28, 2006. The Muelle Barón materializes the desire by Valparaíso Town Hall expressed in 1991 to open the city's access to the ocean. It was the result of an agreement between the Empresa Portuaria with the Ministry of Housing and Urban Development of Chile and developed by the Department of Works for the Celebration of the Bicentenary of the Ministry of Housing and Urban Development.

9. This *paseo* was designed in connection to the Camino de la Pólvora, a project intended to diversify the access to the city from Santiago to Valparaíso and strengthen the international connection to Mendoza and Buenos Aires.

10. A good report of some of the projects executed and under way can be found in Holmes et al., "Parque Cultural Valparaíso: Cerro Cárcel."

11. Trétiack, "Avec Niemeyer, Avilés se rêve en Bilbao," 26.

12. The competition for the parque Cultural Valparaíso, Cerro Cárcel, was set up by the Consejo Nacional de la Cultura y la Dirección de Arquitectura del Ministerio de Obras Públicas (Council for National Culture and the Ministry of Public Works).

13. A concrete structure, the new building of the Centro Cultural ironically brings to mind the buildings of another Brazilian architect, not Niemeyer's but the structurally clean and sober work of architect and theorist Vilanova Artigas. The architects of the Cultural Center, however, claim to have become conscious of the similarities only after others pointed out the affinities.

14. Szita, "The Bilbao Effect."

15. "Valparaíso's Mall Plaza Barón Retail Complex Moves a Step Closer," *Santiago Times*, October 19, 2011.

16. Vergara Jiménez and Ferrada Aguila, "Preservación de inmuebles y zonas de conservación histórica de Valparaíso."

17. Durand and Salvatori, "Por uma nova agenda de pesquisa em torno de Oscar Niemeyer."

18. UNESCO, "Report on the Advisory Mission to Historic Quarter of the Seaport City of Valparaíso."

19. Presently visible from many locations in the city, the curving forms the Bodegas. Simón Bolívar is aligned with the shoreline, an organic relationship that would be destroyed by the boxy Mall buildings. The WHC Mission acknowledged the significance of the intense public debate surrounding the project and the legitimacy of public concerns about its impact and that of similar developments on the city as a whole, on the World Heritage property. The WHC mission noted that the designation "seaport city" referenced on the World Heritage list implies that representatives from the port and the city should jointly participate in discussions on the future of the World Heritage site, as

well as the future urban landscape of Valparaíso, through an inclusive process so that the views of cultural and educational leaders, agents of the tourist industry, small business owners, politicians, and interested local citizens can be considered.

20. UNESCO, "Report on the Advisory Mission to Historic Quarter of the Seaport City of Valparaíso." Based on the WHC's 2013 mission, the World Heritage site's annual State of Conservation for 2014 report noted with concern that the Mall Plaza Puerto Barón project and a proposed expansion of Terminal 2 at the Port of Valparaíso may both have negative impacts on Valparaíso's Outstanding Universal Value, the quality shared by all properties on the World Heritage list and the fundamental concept underlying the World Heritage convention. The report noted that the Mall Plaza Puerto Barón project has been granted a building permit; that the responsible national authority has authorized alteration of the Bodegas Simón Bolívar; that so far only excavation work has been performed at the site and was halted due to archaeological findings until an Archaeological Management Plan is approved; that the court approved a temporary interruption of work in response to a request submitted by citizens' organizations; and that a decision by the Environment Superintendent's Office is pending until both projects have undergone Environmental and Heritage Impact Assessments and the results are submitted to the World Heritage Center to be reviewed by the relevant advisory bodies.

21. Shallat and Bonnefoy, "Chile: A City of Fabled Hills Battles to Save Its Cable Cars."

22. Readings, "Recuperación de los ascensores de Valparaíso: 'Menos promesas, más acción.'" The slogan in Spanish is "Tantas escaleras nos duelen las caderas, tantos colectivos nos duelen los bolsillos."

23. Shallat and Bonnefoy, "Los funiculares de Valparaíso, la joya peor cuidada de Chile."

24. Bon, "Valparaíso: The Seaport City—Part 4: Heritage Threats."

25. Shallat and Bonnefoy, "Chile: A City of Fabled Hills."

26. Rodríguez Pérez et al., "Seminario Internacional Recuperacion de Los Ascensores de Valparaíso."

27. Rojas and Lanzafame, "Valparaíso, Chile."

28. Silverman, "Touring Ancient Times."

29. Shivani Vora, "A Comeback on Chile's Coast," *New York Times*, June 28, 2013.

30. Rojas and Lanzafame, "Valparaíso, Chile."

31. Silverman, "Touring Ancient Times."

Chapter 11. Topography and Civic Order in Latin America

1. Patton, *Spontaneous Shelter*. Informal housing includes residential areas where a group of dwelling units has been constructed on land to which the occupants have no legal claim or which they occupy illegally and unplanned settlements and areas where housing is not in compliance with current planning and building regulations. Some of the informal housing in São Paulo, Brazil, has been constructed on existing property originally permitted by the state, such as abandoned high-rises known as vertical *favelas*, or factories, or by overcrowding existing properties, where several families may live in a place originally intended for one.

2. Alomar Villalonga et al., *De Teotihuacán a Brasilia*. Most Spanish colonial cities

founded before the extensive use of the Laws of the Indies also had gridiron layouts, but many exceptions can be found.

3. Curtis, "Pracas, Place, and Public Life in Urban Brazil."

4. Kagan and Marías, *Urban Images of the Hispanic World, 1493–1793.*

5. Kubler, *Arquitectura mexicana del siglo XVI.*

6. Sheinbaum, "Divided City: An Historical Perspective on Gated Communities in Mexico City."

7. Kubler, *Mexican Architecture of the Sixteenth Century.*

8. Hernández, Kellett, and Allen, eds., *Rethinking the Informal City.*

9. González Rodríguez, "La ciudad de México y la cultura urbana."

10. Morse, "Some Characteristics of Latin American Urban History"; Gilbert, "Land, Housing, and Infrastructure in Latin America's Major Cities"; Portes and Johns, "Class Structure and Spatial Polarization."

11. Brandão, "Urban Planning in Rio de Janeiro."

12. De Ramón, *Santiago de Chile, 1541–1991.*

13. Underwood and Evanson, "Oscar Niemeyer and the Architecture of Brazil"; Underwood, "Alfred Agache, French Sociology, and Modern Urbanism"; Perlman, *The Myth of Marginality*; Nonato and Melhem Santos, *Era uma vez o Morro do Castelo*; Needell, "Rio de Janeiro at the Turn of the Century."

14. Alexander, "Informal Settlement in Latin America and Its Policy Implications." *Favelas* are informal settlements in the sense that they emerge outside the formal market and institutional system and that residents work in part or wholly outside the formally established economic system. Informal settlements can be established through squatting, but in some cases they are sold to the poor by governments at very low prices.

15. Coronil, "The Magical State"; Lombardi, *Venezuela: The Search for Order, the Dream of Progress*; Mayhall, "Modernist but Not Exceptional"; Caracas Urban Think Tank et al., *Informal City: Caracas Case.*

16. Davis, *Planet of Slums*; Main and Williams, *Environment and Housing in Third World Cities.*

17. Clark, *Urban World/Global City.*

18. Scobie, *Buenos Aires: Plaza to Suburb, 1870–1910*; Liernur, *Arquitectura en la Argentina del siglo XX*; Gorelik, "A Metropolis in the Pampas"; Silvestri, *El color del río.*

19. Domínguez, *Race and Ethnicity in Latin America.*

20. Ward, "Cities and Urbanization."

21. Alvarez, Dagnino, and Escobar, *Cultures of Politics/Politics of Cultures*; Rogler, "Slum Neighborhoods in Latin America"; Varella, *Mare: vida na favela.*

22. Lepik, *Small Scale, Big Change.*

23. Ibid.; Brillembourg and Klumpner, "Rules of Engagement: Caracas and the Informal City"; Hernandez, Kellett, and Allen, *Rethinking the Informal City.*

24. Betancur, "Approaches to the Regularization of Informal Settlements"; Fajardo, Mazzanti, and Penix-Tadsen, "Conversation: Sergio Fajardo and Giancarlo Mazzanti."

25. Broome, "Giancarlo Mazzanti Builds an Icon to Foster Optimism in Medellín, Colombia, with His Parque Biblioteca España"; Christopher Hawthorne, "Medellín, Colombia's Architectural Renaissance," *Los Angeles Times*, May 9, 2010; Tancredi,

"L'esperienza Urbanistica di Medellín," 121; Stadel, "The Structure of Squatter Settlements in Medellín, Colombia"; Beardsley and Werthmann, "Improving Informal Settlements."

26. Beardsley and Werthmann, "Improving Informal Settlements."

27. Jorge Fiori and Zeca Brandão make an excellent case for the integrative approach to squatter settlements and describe the controversies generated by the striking architectural forms of the *favelas* and *barrios*. See "Spatial Strategies and Urban Social Policy."

Chapter 12. Demolishing Urban Hills: Establishing New Identities

1. Rouillard, *Building the Slope: Hillside Houses, 1920–1960.*

2. Sandweiss, "Claiming the Urban Landscape: The Improbable Rise of an Inevitable City."

3. Myrick et al., *Telegraph Hill.*

4. See Caen and Kingman, *San Francisco, City on Golden Hills,* 86.

5. Albert Shumate describes in detail the reasons for and the consequences of the Second Street Cut in *Rincon Hill and South Park,* chapters 5 and 6, "The Second Street Cut" and "The Aftermath of the Second Street Cut and the Decline of Rincon Hill."

6. Barth, *Instant Cities.*

7. Kennedy, *Planning the City upon a Hill.*

8. "Rio de Janeiro: A Nova Ordem na Cidade."

9. "Passeio Público."

10. Pinheiro, *Europa, França e Bahia: difusão e adaptacão de modelos urbanos.*

11. Underwood, "Alfred Agache, French Sociology, and Modern Urbanism in France and Brazil."

12. Godfrey, "Modernizing the Brazilian City."

13. In *Era uma vez o Morro do Castelo,* Nonato and Melhem Santos narrate the demolition of the hill comprehensively.

14. Needell, "Rio de Janeiro at the Turn of the Century."

15. Stuckenbruck, *O Rio de Janeiro em questão.*

16. Vasquez and da Silva Telles, *Rio de Janeiro, 1862–1927.*

17. Bruand and Goldberger, *Arquitetura contemporânea no Brasil*; Alvim, *Arquitetura religiosa colonial no Rio de Janeiro*; Cleary et al., *Rough Guide to Brazil.*

Bibliography

Aguirre Arias, Beatriz, and Simón Castillo. *De la "gran aldea" a la ciudad de masas: el espacio público en Santiago de Chile, 1910–1929*. Santiago, Chile: Centro de Estudios Arquitectónicos, Urbanísticos y del Paisaje, Facultad de Arquitectura, Urbanísmo y Paisaje, Universidad Central, 2004.

Alderete Haas, José Antonio. "The Search for Roots in Mexican Modernism." In *Latin American Architecture, 1929–1960: Contemporary Reflections*, ed. Carlos Brillembourg. New York: Monacelli Press, 2004.

Alexander, Ernest. "Informal Settlement in Latin America and Its Policy Implications." In *Spontaneous Shelter: International Perspectives and Prospects*, ed. Carl V. Patton. Philadelphia: Temple University Press, 1988.

Almandoz Marte, Arturo. *Planning Latin America's Capital Cities, 1850–1950*. New York: Routledge, 2002.

Alofsin, Anthony. "Frank Lloyd Wright and Modernism." In *Frank Lloyd Wright, Architect*, ed. Frank Lloyd Wright Foundation. New York: Museum of Modern Art, 1994.

Alomar Villalonga, Gabriel, Guillermo Geisse Grove, Jorge Enrique Hardoy, and Nestor Goulart Reis. *De Teotihuacán a Brasilia: estudios de historia urbana iberoamericana y filipina*. Madrid: Inst. de Estudios de Administración Local, 1987.

Alphand, Alain, and Adolphe Frerejean. *Les promenades de Paris*. Paris: Connaissance et mémoires, 2002.

Alvarez, Sonia E., Evalina Dagnino, and Arturo Escobar. *Cultures of Politics/Politics of Cultures: Re-Visioning Latin American Social Movements*. Boulder: Westview Press, 1998.

Alvim, Sandra. *Arquitetura religiosa colonial no Rio de Janeiro: revestimentos, retábulos e talha 1*. Rio de Janeiro: UFRJ: IPHAN, 1997.

Anderson, Isabel. *Circling South America*. Boston: Marshall Jones, 1929.

Andreoli, Elisabetta, and Adrian Forty. *Brazil's Modern Architecture*. New York: Phaidon, 2004.

Arias Argaes, Isaac. "Observaciones sobre la higiene de Bogotá." MD thesis, Escuela de medicina de la Universidad Nacional, 1890.

Arredondo Zambrano, Celia Ester. "Modernity in Mexico: The Case of Ciudad Universitaria." In *Modernity and the Architecture of Mexico*, ed. Edward R. Burian. Austin: University of Texas Press, 1997.

"Art: Last Monument." *Time*, November 2, 1959.

Artigas, João Batista Vilanova. *A função social do arquiteto*. São Paulo: Nobel, 1989.

———. *Caminhos da arquitetura*. São Paulo: Livraria Editora Ciências Humanas, 1981.

Artigas, Rosa, and Guilherme Wisnik. *Paulo Mendes da Rocha: Projects, 1957–2007*. New York: Rizzoli, 2007.

Aschner Rosselli, Juan Pablo. *Contrapunto y confluencia en el concierto arquitectónico: Biblioteca Virgilio Barco*. Bogotá: Universidad Nacional de Colombia, Sede Bogotá, Facultad de Artes, 2008.

Atuesta Ortiz, M. "La ciudad que pasó por el río: La canalización del río San Francisco y la construcción de la avenida Jiménez en Bogotá a principios del Siglo XX." *Territorios*, no. 25 (2011): 191–211.

Avendaño Lugo, José Ramón. *El militarismo en Venezuela: la dictadura de Pérez Jiménez*. Caracas, Venezuela: Ediciones Centauro, 1982.

Bákula, Cecilia, Laura Laurencich Minelli, and Mireille Vautier. *The Inca World: The Development of Pre-Columbian Peru, A.D. 1000–1534*. Norman: University of Oklahoma Press, 2000.

Bannen Lanata, Pedro, and Fernando Pérez Oyarzún. *Le Corbusier y Sudamérica: viajes y proyectos*. Santiago: Ediciones Arq, June 1992.

Bárcena, J. Roberto. "Datos e interpretación del registro documental sobre la dominación incaica en Cuyo." *Xama* 4–5 (1994): 11–49.

Bardi, Pietro Maria. *Lembrança de Le Corbusier: Atenas, Itália, Brasil*. São Paulo: Nobel, 1984.

Barragán, Luis. "Gardens for Environment—Jardines del Pedregal." *AIA: Journal of the American Institute of Architects* 17 (1952): 167–72.

Barrios, Carola. "El Museo de Arte de Niemeyer: Su lugar en el paisaje moderno de Caracas." *Arquine: Revista Internacional de Arquitectura*, no. 37 (Autumn 2006): 78–90.

Barth, Gunther Paul. *Instant Cities: Urbanization and the Rise of San Francisco and Denver*. New York: Oxford University Press, 1975.

Beardsley, John, and Christian Werthmann. "Improving Informal Settlements." *Harvard Design Magazine*, no. 28 (Spring/Summer 2008): 31–34

Bender, Thomas. *Toward an Urban Vision: Ideas and Institutions in Nineteenth-Century America*. Lexington: University Press of Kentucky, 1975.

Benévolo, Leonardo. *History of Modern Architecture*. Cambridge: MIT Press, 1971.

Bermúdez, Ricardo J., and Samuel A. Gutiérrez. *Ricardo J. Bermúdez en la cultura arquitectónica y literaria de Panamá*. Panama: Editorial La Prensa, 1996.

———. "Panorama Histórico de la Ciudad Universitaria de Panamá." *CONESCAL*, no. 4 (August 1966): 323–28.

Berney, Rachel. "Pedagogical Urbanism: Creating Citizen Space in Bogota, Colombia." *Planning Theory* 10.1 (February 2011): 16–34.

Betancur, John J. "Approaches to the Regularization of Informal Settlements: The Case of PRIMED in Medellin, Colombia." *Global Urban Development Magazine* 3.1 (2007).

Bodmer, P. "The Armature of Conquest: Spanish Accounts of the Discovery of America in 1492." In *The Idea of Latin America*, ed. Walter Mignolo. Malden, Mass.: Blackwell, 2005.

Bogotá (Colombia). *Historia de los humedales de Bogotá: con énfasis en cinco de ellos.* Bogotá, D.C.: Departamento Técnico Administrativo Medio Ambiente, Alcaldía Mayor de Bogotá, D.C., 2000.

Bon, Mary. "Valparaiso: The Seaport City—Part 4: Heritage Threats." *Construction Shows*, October 17, 2013. http://www.constructionshows.com/valparaiso-the-seaport-city-part-4-heritage-threats/178975.

Bonavía, Duccio. "Ecological Factors Affecting the Urban Transformations in the Last Centuries of the Pre-Columbian Era." In *Urbanization in the Americas from Its Beginnings to the Present*, ed. Richard P. Schaedel, Jorge Enrique Hardoy, Nora Kinzer Stewart, and International Congress of Anthropological and Ethnological Sciences. The Hague (Noordeinde 41): Mouton, 1978.

Bonduki, Nabil Georges, Carmen Portinho, Elaine Pereira da Silva, Rafael M. Esposel, Marcel Gautherot, and Katica Szabó. *Affonso Eduardo Reidy: arquitetos brasileiros = Brazilian Architects.* Lisbon and São Paulo: Editorial Blau; Instituto Lina Bo e P.M. Bardi, 2000.

Bornhorst, Dirk. *Valores perennes en la arquitectura: un acercamiento a los valores de siempre en las fases mental-creativa y material-expresiva de la arquitectura.* Caracas: Oscar Todtmann, 2001.

Bosworth, Barry P., Rudiger Dornbusch, and Raúl Labán. *The Chilean Economy: Policy Lessons and Challenges.* Washington, D.C.: Brookings Institution, 1994.

Brandão, Zeca. "Urban Planning in Rio de Janeiro: A Critical Review of the Urban Design Practice in the Twentieth Century." *City & Time* 2.2 (2006): 37–50.

Brillembourg, Alfredo, and Hubert Klumpner. "Rules of Engagement: Caracas and the Informal City." In *Rethinking the Informal City: Critical Perspectives from Latin America*, ed. Felipe Hernández, Peter Kellett, and Lea K. Allen. New York: Berghahn Books, 2010.

Brillembourg, Carlos. *Latin American Architecture, 1929–1960: Contemporary Reflections.* New York: Monacelli Press, 2004.

Broome, Beth. "Giancarlo Mazzanti Builds an Icon to Foster Optimism in Medellín, Colombia, with His Parque Biblioteca España." *Architectural Record*, November 2008, 138–47.

Bruand, Yves, and Ana M. Goldberger. *Arquitetura contemporânea no Brasil.* São Paulo: Perspectiva, 1981.

Burden, Dan. *22 Benefits of Urban Street Trees.* Accessed April 2015. www.michigan.gov/documents/dnr/22_benefits_208084_7.pdf.

Burdett, Ricky, and Deyan Sudjic. "Politics, Power, Cities." In *The Endless City: The Urban Age Project by the London School of Economics and Deutsche Bank's Alfred Herrhausen Society*, ed. Richard Burdett and Deyan Sudjic, London School of Economics and Political Science, and Alfred Herrhausen Gesellschaft für Internationalen Dialog. London: Phaidon, 2007.

Burian, Edward R. *The Architecture and Cities of Northern Mexico from Independence to Present.* Austin: University of Texas Press, 2015.

———. "Politics and Architectural Language: Post-Revolutionary Regimes in Mexico and Their Influence on Mexican Public Architecture, 1920–1952." In *Modernity and the Architecture of Mexico*, ed. Edward R. Burian. Austin: University of Texas Press, 1997.

Butland, Gilbert J. "Frontiers of Settlement in South America." *Revista Geográfica* 65 (1966): 93–108.

Butzer, Karl W. "The Americas before and after 1492: An Introduction to Current Geographical Research." *Annals of the Association of American Geographers* 82.3 (1992): 345–68.

Caen, Herb, and Dong Kingman. *San Francisco, City on Golden Hills*. Garden City, N.Y.: Doubleday, 1967.

Calderón, Alfonso. *Memorial de Santiago*. Providencia, Santiago de Chile: RiL Editores, 2005.

Cantón, Alfredo. *Desenvolvimiento de las ideas pedagógicas en Panamá, 1903–1926*. Panamá, 1955.

Caracas Urban Think Tank, Alfredo Brillembourg Tamayo, Kristin Feireiss, Hubert Klumpner, and Kulturstiftung des Bundes. *Informal City: Caracas Case*. Munich: Prestel, 2005.

Cárdenas, Leonardo Mattos. "Bolívar y el urbanismo: Bolivia, Colombia, Ecuador, Panama, Perú, Venezuela (1810–1830)." *Storia della sitta* 11 (April 1986): 109–26, 206–7.

Carlson, Fred Albert. *Geography of Latin America*. New York: Prentice-Hall, 1936.

Carrasquilla Botero, Juan. *Quintas y estancias de Santa Fé y Bogotá*. Bogotá: Banco Popular, Fondo de Promoción de la Cultura, 1989.

Carreira, Ana María. "De las perturbadoras y conflictivas relaciones de los bogotanos con sus aguas." *Tabula Rasa* 6 (2007): 263–85.

Carrillo Trueba, Miguel César, León Portilla, and Jerzy Rzedowski. *El Pedregal de San Angel*. México, D.F.: Universidad Nacional Autónoma de México, 1995.

Castro, Lorenzo, and Alejandro Echeverri. "Bogotá and Medellín: Architecture and Politics." *Architectural Design* 81.3 (May 2011): 96–103.

Catadougnac: see Dougnac, Catalina

Cavalcanti, Lauro. *When Brazil Was Modern: Guide to Architecture, 1928–1960*. New York: Princeton Architectural Press, 2003.

Caviedes, César, and Gregory W. Knapp. *South America*. Englewood Cliffs, N.J.: Prentice Hall, 1995.

Cendales Paredes, Claudia. "Una perspectiva comparativa los parques de Bogota." *Revista Cultural de Santander* 4 (2009) 92–105.

Centro Regional de Construcciones Escolares para América Latina y la Región del Caribe. Mexico: *CONESCAL*, 1965.

Cervero, Robert, Olga L. Sarmiento, Enrique Jacoby, Luis Fernando Gomez, and Andrea Neiman. "Influences of Built Environments on Walking and Cycling: Lessons from Bogotá." *International Journal of Sustainable Transportation* 3.4 (July/August 2009): 203–26.

"Chile—Poverty and Wealth." *Encyclopedia of the Nations*, accessed February 27, 2014, http://www.nationsencyclopedia.com/economies/Americas/Chile-POVERTY-AND-WEALTH.html.

Cisternas, Hernán, and Mauricio Silva. "Las luces y sombras que dejan 10 años de Valparaíso como patrimonio de la humanidad." *El Mercurio*, June 30, 2013.

Clark, David. *Urban World/Global City*. New York: Routledge, 1996.

Cleary, David, Dilwyn Jenkins, and Oliver Marshall. *The Rough Guide to Brazil*. New York: Penguin Group, 2000.

Cleary, Richard Louis, and Frank Lloyd Wright. *Merchant Prince and Master Builder: Edgar J. Kaufmann and Frank Lloyd Wright*. Pittsburgh and Seattle: Heinz Architectural Center, Carnegie Museum of Art; in association with University of Washington Press, 1999.

Cohen, Lizabeth. "From Town Center to Shopping Center: The Reconfiguration of Community Marketplaces in Postwar America." *American Historical Review* 101.4 (1996): 1050–81.

Collier, Simon, and William F. Sater. *A History of Chile, 1808–1994*. New York: Cambridge University Press, 1996.

Concejo Municipal de Bogotá. *Acuerdo N.23 de 1928. Para adquirir un proyecto sobre aprovisionamiento de aguas para la ciudad*. Concejo Municipal de Bogotá, 1928.

"Consideraciones para una posible definición de la Calle." *Ingeniería y Arquitectura* 1.5 (October 1944): 124.

Coronil, Fernando. "The Magical State: History and Illusion in the Appearance of Venezuelan Democracy." Notre Dame, Ind.: Helen Kellogg Institute for International Studies, working paper 112, October 1988.

Cotes, Manuel. "Régimen alimenticio de los jornaleros de La Sabana de Bogotá." In *Bogotá: Congreso Médico Nacional, Imprenta de La Luz*, 1893.

Cranz, Galen. *The Politics of Park Design: A History of Urban Parks in America*. Cambridge: MIT Press, 1982.

———. "Urban Parks as a Mechanism of Social Control." Berkeley: privately printed, 1975.

Crouch, Dora P., Daniel J. Garr, and Axel I. Mundigo. *Spanish City Planning in North America*. Cambridge: MIT Press, 1982.

Curtis, James R. "Pracas, Place, and Public Life in Urban Brazil." *Geographical Review* 90.4 (2000): 475–92.

Curtis, William Eleroy. *Venezuela: A Land Where It's Always Summer*. New York: Harper & Bros., 1896.

Curtis, William J. R. *Le Corbusier: Ideas and Forms*. New York: Rizzoli, 1986.

———. *Modern Architecture since 1900*. Oxford: Phaidon, 1996.

———. "Towards an Authentic Regionalism" *MIMAR: Architecture in Development* 19 (January–March 1986): 24–31

Davis, Mike. *Planet of Slums*. New York: Verso, 2006.

De la Serna, Jorge J. Crespo. "Jardines en el Pedregal." *Arquitectura/Mexico* 37 (1952): 110–14.

De Ramón, Armando. *Santiago de Chile, 1541–1991: historia de una sociedad urbana*. Providencia, Santiago: Editorial Sudamericana, 2000.

De Sola Morales, Ignasi. "Parc Guell, Barcelona." In *The Architecture of Western Gardens:*

A Design History from the Renaissance to the Present Day, ed. Monique Mosser and Georges Teyssot, 438–41. Cambridge: MIT Press, 1991.

Del Castillo, Adriana Díaz, Olga L. Sarmiento, Rodrigo S. Reis, and Ross C. Brownson. "Translating Evidence to Policy: Urban Interventions and Physical Activity Promotion in Bogotá, Colombia and Curitiba, Brazil." *Translational Behavioral Medicine* 1.2 (2011): 350–60.

Denevan, William M. *Cultivated Landscapes of Native Amazonia and the Andes: Triumph over the Soil*. New York: Oxford University Press, 2001.

———. "The Pristine Myth: The Landscape of the Americas in 1492." *Annals of the Association of American Geographers* 82.3 (1992): 369–85.

Domínguez, Jorge I. *Race and Ethnicity in Latin America*. New York: Garland, 1994.

Dougnac, Catalina (Catadougnac). "Borde costero de Valparaíso: Aprobado megaproyecto de Mall Plaza." *Plataforma Urbana* (September 28, 2006).

Drexler, Arthur, and Bernard Rudovsky. "Roads (from an Exhibition at the Museum of Modern Art)." *Arts & Architecture*, November 1961, 10–11.

Durand, José Carlos, and Elena Salvatori. "Por uma nova agenda de pesquisa em torno de Oscar Niemeyer." *Vitruvius*, March 2011, accessed February 2012, http://www.vitruvius.com.br/revistas/read/arquitextos/11.130/3800.

Eardley, Anthony, Kenneth Frampton, and Silvia Kolbowski. *Le Corbusier's Firminy Church: [An Exhibition], April 29 to June 3, 1981*. New York: Institute for Architecture and Urban Studies and Rizzoli International Publications, 1981.

Eggener, Keith L. *Luis Barragán's Gardens of El Pedregal*. New York: Princeton Architectural Press, 2001.

———. "Placing Resistance: A Critique of Critical Regionalism." *Journal of Architectural Education* 55.4 (2002): 228–37.

"Einkaufszentrum Helicoide de la Roca de Tarpeya." *Baumeister: Zeitschrift für Architektur* 58 (March 1961): 212–15.

Escovar Wilson-White, Alberto. "Bogotá en tiempos de la celebración del primer Centenario de la independencia." *Historia mexicana*, no. 237 (2010): 525–59.

Ewell, Judith. "The Extradition of Marcos Perez Jimenez, 1959–63: Practical Precedent for Enforcement of Administrative Honesty?" *Journal of Latin American Studies* 9.2 (November 1977): 291–313.

Fagiolo, Marcello. "La fondazione delle cittá Latino-Americane: Gli archetipi della giustizia e della fede." *Psicon: Rivista Internazionale di Architettura* 2.5 (1975): 35–58.

Fajardo, Sergio, Giancarlo Mazzanti, and Phillip Penix-Tadsen. "Conversation: Sergio Fajardo and Giancarlo Mazzanti." *Bomb* 110 (2010): 34–41.

Febres, Andrés. *Arte de la lengua general del reyno de Chile*. Vaduz: Cabildo, 1975.

Fernald, Alexander G., Terrell T. Baker, and Steven J. Guldan. "Hydrologic, Riparian, and Agroecosystem Functions of Traditional Acequia Irrigation Systems." *Journal of Sustainable Agriculture* 30.2 (2007): 147–71.

Fernandez Cox, Cristián. "Hacia una modernidad apropiada: Factores y desafíos internos." *Revista Summa*, nos. 200/201 (June 1984).

Ferraz, Carvalho Marcelo, Alvaro Puntoni, Aldo Urbinati, and Nelson Kon. *Vilanova Artigas*. São Paulo: Instituto Lina Bo e. P.M. Bardi: Fundaçâo Vilanova Artigas, 1994.

Fils, Alexander. *Oscar Niemeyer: Selbstdarstellung, Kritiken, Oeuvre*. Berlin: Frölich and Kaufmann, 1982.

Fiori, Jorge, and Zeca Brandão. "Spatial Strategies and Urban Social Policy: Urbanism and Poverty Reduction in the Favelas of Rio de Janeiro." In *Rethinking the Informal City: Critical Perspectives from Latin America*, ed. Felipe Hernández, Peter Kellett, and Lea K. Allen. New York: Berghahn Books, 2010.

Flórez de Ocáriz, Juan. *Libro primero de las genealogías del Nuevo Reino de Granada*. Bogotá: Instituto Caro y Cuervo: Instituto Colombiano de Cultura Hispánica, 1990.

Foster, Stephen, and Héctor Garduño. *Integrated Approaches to Groundwater Resource Conservation in the Mendoza Aquifers of Argentina*. GW-MATE Case Profile Collection, 2006. http://water.worldbank.org/sites/water.worldbank.org/files/GWMATE_CP06_Argentina2006_0.pdf.

Frampton, Kenneth. "Le Corbusier and Oscar Niemeyer: Influence and Counterinfluence, 1929–1965." In *Latin American Architecture, 1929–1960: Contemporary Reflections*, ed. Carlos Brillembourg. New York: Monacelli Press, 2004.

Fraser, Valerie. *Building the New World: Studies in the Modern Architecture of Latin America, 1930–1960*. London: Verso, 2000.

Freytag, Anette, and M. Conan. "When the Railway Conquered the Garden: Velocity in Parisian and Viennese Parks." Dumbarton Oaks Colloquia on the History of Landscape Architecture. *Landscape Design and the Experience of Motion* 24 (2003): 215–43.

"Fundación Rogelio Salmona | Proyecto | Recuperación del Eje Ambiental Avenida Jiménez de Quesada." Accessed February 21, 2014. http://obra.fundacionrogeliosalmona.org/obra/proyecto/recuperacion-del-eje-ambiental-avenida-jimenez-de-quesada/.

Gallo, Rubén. *Mexican Modernity: The Avant-Garde and the Technological Revolution*. Cambridge: MIT Press, 2005.

Gastil, Raymond, and Zoë Ryan. *Open: New Designs for Public Space*. New York: Van Alen Institute: distributed by Princeton Architectural Press, 2004.

Gerencia de Asuntos Públicos y Relaciones (Venezuela), ExxonMobil de Venezuela. *Santiago de León de Caracas, 1567–2030*. Caracas: Editorial Arte, 2003.

Giedion, Sigfried. "The State of Contemporary Architecture: The Regional Approach." *Architectural Record* 115 (January 1954): 132–37.

Gilbert, Alan. "Good Urban Governance: Evidence from a Model City?" *Bulletin of Latin American Research* 25.3 (2006): 392–419.

———. "Land, Housing, and Infrastructure in Latin America's Major Cities." In *The Mega-City in Latin America*. Tokyo: United Nations University Press, 1996.

Gilmartin, Benjamin, Megan Miller, and Julio Salcedo. "In the Nature of the Valley: An Urban and Ecological Proposal for Mexico City." *Praxis—Journal of Writing and Building* 74.2 (2001): 72–79.

———. "The Lakes Project: Interview with Alberto Kalach and Jose Castillo." *Praxis—Writing and Building*, 1.2 (2001): 80–85.

Godfrey, Brian J. "Modernizing the Brazilian City." *Geographical Review* 81.1 (January 1991): 18–34.

———. "Revisiting Rio de Janeiro and São Paulo." *Geographical Review* 89.1 (January 1999): 94–121.

Gómez, Juan Camilo Rodríguez. "La Diosa Agua." In *El agua en la historia de Bogotá, 1538–19*, ed. Benjamín Villegas. Bogotá: Villegas Editores, 2003.

González, María Belén, and Gloria Leticia Zamorano. "La cultura del agua, eje orientador de la educación ambiental para los habitantes del Gran Mendoza." Presented at the Actas del XI Coloquio Internacional de Geocrítica: La Planificación territorial y el urbanismo desde el diálogo y la participación, Buenos Aires, 2010. http://www.filo.uba.ar/contenidos/investigacion/institutos/geo/geocritica2010/636.htm.

González de León, Teodoro, and Antonieta Cruz. *La ciudad y sus lagos*. México: Clío: Instituto de Cultura de la Ciudad de México, 1998.

González Escobar, Luis Fernando. *Ciudad y arquitectura urbana en Colombia, 1980–2010*. Medellín, Colombia: Editorial Universidad de Antioquia, 2010.

González Gortázar, Fernando. *La Arquitectura mexicana del siglo XX*. Mexico, D.F.: Consejo Nacional para la Cultura y las Artes, 1996.

González Gortázar, Fernando, ed. "El Futuro Radiante: La Ciudad Universitaria." In *La arquitectura mexicana del siglo XX*, 213. México, D.F.: Consejo Nacional para la Cultura y las Artes, 1994.

González Rodríguez, Sergio. "La ciudad de México y la cultura urbana." In *México a fines de siglo*, ed. José Joaquín Blanco, José Woldenberg, and Rodrigo Martínez. México: Consejo Nacional para la Cultura y las Artes: Fondo de Cultura Económica, 1993.

Gorelik, Adrián. "A Metropolis in the Pampas: Buenos Aires, 1890–1940." In *Cruelty and Utopia: Cities and Landscapes of Latin America*, ed. J. F. Lejeune, 146–59. New York: Princeton Architectural Press, 2005.

Grumbach, Antoine. "The Promenades of Paris." *Oppositions* 8 (Summer 1977): 50–67.

Guarda, Gabriel. *Historia urbana del reino de Chile*. Santiago: Editorial Andrés Bello, 1978.

Guía Completa de Santiago y Comercial de Valparaíso para 1901–1902. Santiago: Imprenta litografía y encuadernación Barcelona, 1901.

Gutiérrez, Samuel A. *Arquitectura actual de Panamá, 1930–1980*. Panamá: Gutiérrez S.A., 1980.

———. *Arquitectura de la época del canal, 1880–1914, y sus paralelos norteamericanos, franceses y caribeños*. Panamá: EUPAN, 1984.

Hardoy, Jorge Enrique. *Pre-Columbian Cities*. New York: Walker, 1973.

Hassan, Mustafa F. "High Growth, Unemployment, and Planning in Venezuela." *Economic Development and Cultural Change* 15.4 (1967): 452–64.

Hays, Peter. *Main Currents in Western Environmental Thought*. Bloomington: Indiana University Press, 2002.

Henderson, James D. *Modernization in Colombia: The Laureano Gómez Years, 1889–1965*. Gainesville: University Press of Florida, 2001.

Hernandez, Felipe, Peter Kellett, and Lea K. Allen, eds. *Rethinking the Informal City: Critical Perspectives from Latin America*. New York: Berghahn Books, 2010.

Hitchcock, Henry-Russell, and Philip Johnson. *The International Style*. New York: W. W. Norton, 1966.

———. *Latin American Architecture since 1945*. New York: New York Museum of Modern Art, 1955.

Holmes, Jonathan, Martín Labbé, Carolina Portugueis, and Osvaldo Spichiger. "Parque Cultural Valparaíso: Cerro Cárcel." *Arq* 73 (2009): 46–51.

Holmes, Rob. *Below the Phreatic Level.* http://mammoth.us/blog/2009/05/below-the-phreatic-level/.

Humphrey, Norman D. "Race, Caste, and Class in Colombia." *Phylon* 13.2 (1952): 161–66.

"Ilustre Municipalidad de Valparaíso." Accessed February 27, 2014. http://www.municipalidaddevalparaiso.cl/.

Indirli, Maurizio, Claudio Modena, and Antonio Tralli. "Natural Multi-Hazard and Building Vulnerability Assessment in the Historic Centers." Universitá di Trento, 2010.

Jackson, Kenneth T. "All the World's a Mall: Reflections on the Social and Economic Consequences of the American Shopping Center." *American Historical Review* 101.4 (October 1996): 1111–21.

Jiménez, Luis Miguel. "Unas montañas al servicio de Bogotá: imaginarios de naturaleza en la reforestación de los cerros orientales, 1899–1924." Tésis de pregrado en historia, Universidad de los Andes, 2011.

Jones, Charles I. *On the Evolution of the World Income Distribution.* Rochester, N.Y.: Social Science Research Network. March 29, 1997. http://papers.ssrn.com/abstract=59412.

Jovanovic Weiss, Srdjan, and Sabine von Fischer. "How to Read Two Monoliths." *Cabinet,* no. 6 (Spring 2002).

Kagan, Richard L., and Marías Fernando. *Urban Images of the Hispanic World, 1493–1793.* New Haven: Yale University Press, 2000.

Kalach, Alberto. "Architecture and Place: The Stadium of the University City." In *Modernity and the Architecture of Mexico,* ed. Edward Burian. Austin: University of Texas Press, 1997.

Kalach, Alberto, with Juan Palomar, Miquel Adria, Ricardo Cayuela, Gabriel Quadri, Arturo Rosenblueth, and Eduardo Vazquez. *Atlas de proyectos para la ciudad de México.* Vol. 2. Mexico, DF: Consejo Nacional para la Cultura y las Artes, 2012.

Kandell, Jonathan. *La Capital: The Biography of Mexico City.* New York: Random House, 1988.

Kennedy, Lawrence W. *Planning the City upon a Hill: Boston since 1630.* Amherst: University of Massachusetts Press, 1992.

King, Anthony D. "Architecture, Globalization, and Identity." In *Architecture and Identity,* ed. Peter Herrle, Erik Wegerhoff, Technische Universität Berlin, and Habitat Unit, 221–31. Berlin: Lit, 2008.

Kirby, Michael X., Douglas S. Jones, and Bruce J. MacFadden. "Isthmus of Panama Formed as Result of Plate Tectonics, Study Finds." ScienceDaily, July 13, 2008. www.sciencedaily.com/releases/2008/07/080729234142.htm.

———. *Lower Miocene Stratigraphy along the Panama Canal and Its Bearing on the Central American Peninsula.* Public Library of Science. http://www.pubmedcentral.nih.gov/articlerender.fcgi?artid=2464738.

Ksiazek, Sarah. "Architectural Culture in the Fifties: Louis Kahn and the National Assembly Complex in Dhaka." *Journal of the Society of Architectural Historians* 52.4 (December 1993): 416–35.

Kubler, George. *Arquitectura mexicana del siglo XVI*. México: Fondo de Cultura Económica, 1983.

———. *The Art and Architecture of Ancient America: The Mexican, Maya, and Andean Peoples*. Harmondsworth: Penguin Books, 1962.

———. *Mexican Architecture of the Sixteenth Century*. New Haven: Yale University Press, 1948.

———. *Mexico: Splendors of Thirty Centuries*. New York: Metropolitan Museum of Art; Boston: Little, Brown, 1990.

Lambert, Jacques H. "Apuntes sobre Urbanismo." *Arquitectura y Arte Decorativo*, no. 9, Órgano Oficial del Colegio de Arquitectos de Chile, Santiago de Chile (1930): 397–99.

Lapunzina, Alejandro. "The Pyramid and the Wall: An Unknown Project of Le Corbusier in Venezuela." *Arq: Architectural Research Quarterly* 5.3 (2001): 255–70.

Larraín Ibáñez, Jorge. *Identity and Modernity in Latin America*. Malden, Mass.: Blackwell, 2000.

———. *Modernidad, razón e identidad en América Latina*. Santiago de Chile: Ed. Bello, 1996.

Larraín, Nicanor, and Pedro P. Calderón. *El país de Cuyo: relación histórica hasta 1872*. Buenos Aires: Impr. de J. A. Alsina, 1906.

Le Corbusier. *Precisions on the Present State of Architecture and City Planning: With an American Prologue, a Brazilian Corollary Followed by the Temperature of Paris and the Atmosphere of Moscow*. Cambridge: MIT Press, 1991.

Le Corbusier, and Willy Boesiger. *Le Corbusier, œuvre complète, 1946–1952*. Zurich: Éditions d'Architecture, 1966.

Le Corbusier, Willy Boesiger, Oscar Stonorov, Pierre Jeanneret, and Bill Max. *Œuvre compléte*. Zurich: Les Editions d'Architecture, 1991.

Lepik, Andres. *Small Scale, Big Change: New Architectures of Social Engagement*. New York: Museum of Modern Art, 2010.

Lesmes, Julián Vargas, and Fabio Zambrano. "Santa Fé y Bogotá: Evolución Histórica y Servicios Públicos (1600–1957)." In *Bogotá, 450 años: retos y realidades*, ed. Pedro Santana R. Bogotá: Foro Nacional por Colombia: Instituto Francés de Estudios Andinos, 1988.

Lévi-Strauss, Claude. *Tristes Tropiques*. New York: Atheneum, 1963.

Levine, Neil. *The Architecture of Frank Lloyd Wright*. Princeton, N.J.: Princeton University Press, 1996.

Libro oficial del 4o centenario de la fundación de Santiago. Santiago de Chile: Artuffo, 1941.

Liernur, Jorge Francisco. *Arquitectura en la Argentina del siglo XX: la construcción de la modernidad*. Buenos Aires: Fondo Nacional de las Artes, 2001.

Lombardi, John V. *Venezuela: The Search for Order, the Dream of Progress*. New York: Oxford University Press, 1982.

Loomis, John. *Other Americas: Contemporary Architecture and Issues in Latin America*. Cambridge: Design Book Review, 1994.

Lucan, Jacques. *Le Corbusier, une encyclopédie*. Paris: Centre Georges Pompidou, 1987.

Mabry, Donald J. *The Mexican University and the State Student Conflicts, 1910–1971*. College Station: Texas A&M University Press, 1982.

Mackenna Subercaseaux, Alberto. *Santiago futuro conferencias sobre los proyectos de transformación de Santiago*. Santiago: Soc. impr.-litografía "Barcelona," 1915. Accessed February 27, 2014. http://catalog.hathitrust.org/api/volumes/oclc/19550345.html.

Magasich-Airola, Jorge, and Jean-Marc de Beer. *America Magica: When Renaissance Europe Thought It Had Conquered Paradise*. London: Anthem Press, 2007.

Main, Hamish, and Stephen Wyn Williams. *Environment and Housing in Third World Cities*. New York: John Wiley, 1994.

Mann, Charles C. *1491: New Revelations of the Americas before Columbus*. New York: Knopf, 2005.

Manrique, Jorge Alberto. "El Futuro Radiante: La Ciudad Universitaria." In *La Cultura Contemporanea Mexicana del siglo XX*. Mexico: Consejo Nacional para la Cultura y las Artes, 1994.

Marceca, Maria Luisa. "Reservoir, Circulation, Residue: J.C.A. Alphand, Technological Beauty, and the Green City." *Lotus International* 30.1 (1981): 56–79.

Mark, Edward Walhouse, and Joaquín Piñeros Corpas. *Acuarelas de mark, 1843–1856: un testimonio pictórico de la Nueva Granada*. Bogotá, Colombia: Banco de la República, Litografía Arco, 1963.

Martignoni, Jimena. "Bogotá Dresses in Green: The Transformation of a Latin American Metropolis." *Landscape Architecture* 95.3 (March 2005): 104–11.

Martinez, Ernesto Alva. "La Búsqueda de una Identidad." In *La Arquitectura mexicana del siglo XX*, ed. Gonzáles Gortazar. Mexico, D.F.: Consejo Nacional para la Cultura y las Artes, 1996.

Martinez, Leopoldo. "Nuevo Helicoide de Caracas." *Revista Integral*, no. 5 (December 1956): 2–17.

Mayhall, Marguerite. "Modernist but Not Exceptional: The Debate over Modern Art and National Identity in 1950s Venezuela." *Latin American Perspectives* 32.2 (March 2005): 124–46.

McCullough, David G. *The Path between the Seas: The Creation of the Panama Canal, 1870–1914*. New York: Simon and Schuster, 1977.

McLeod, Mary. "Le Corbusier and Algiers." *Oppositions* 19/20 (Winter/Spring 1980): 54–85.

Mejía Pavony, Germán Rodrigo. *Los años del cambio: historia urbana de Bogotá, 1820–1910*. Santa Fe de Bogotá: CEJA, 1998.

Melfi, Domingo. *El viaje literario*. Santiago, Chile: Nascimento, 1945.

Mena García, Maria del Carmen. *La Ciudad de Panamá en el siglo XVIII: trazado urbano y técnica constructiva*. Panamá, R. de P.: Editorial Portobelo, 1997.

Méndez Pereira, Octavio. "The Bolivarian University of Panamá." *Bulletin of the Pan American Union* 60 (1926): 570.

Mennel, Timothy. "Victor Gruen and the Construction of Cold War Utopias." *Journal of Planning History* 3.2 (2004): 116–50.

Meza Suinaga, Beatriz E. "Proyectos del Taller de Arquitectura del Banco Obrero (TABO) para el Plan Nacional de la Vivienda en Venezuela (1951–1955)." *Tecnología y Construcción* 21.2 (May 2005): 8–22.

Miller, Megan. "In the Nature of the Valley: An Urban and Ecological Proposal for Mexico City," in "Mexico City: Projects from the MegaCity." *Praxis* 2 (2001): 72–78.

Miller, Shawn William. *An Environmental History of Latin America*. New York: Cambridge University Press, 2007.

Molina, Giovanni Ignazio. *Compendio de la historia geográfica, natural y civil del reyno de Chile*. Providencia, Santiago: Pehuén, 2000.

Montezuma, Ricardo. "Promoting Active Lifestyles and Healthy Urban Spaces: The Cultural and Spatial Transformation of Bogotá, Colombia." *Scientific and Technical Publication—Pan American Health Organization* 612 (2005): 161–80.

Morse, Richard. "Some Characteristics of Latin American Urban History." *The American Historical Review* 67.2 (Jan. 1962): 317–338.

Mosser, Monique, and Georges Teyssot. *The Architecture of Western Gardens: A Design History from the Renaissance to the Present Day*. Cambridge: MIT Press, 1991.

Mumford, Lewis. "Monumentalism, Symbolism, and Style." *Architectural Review* 105 (April 1949): 173–80.

"Musée d'art Moderne, Caracas, Venezuela." *L'Architecture d'aujourd'hui* 2 (1956): 48–49.

Myrick, David F., Roxburghe Club of San Francisco, and Zamorano Club. *Telegraph Hill*. San Francisco: privately published, 1976.

NASA Earth Observatory. *Panama: Isthmus That Changed the World*. http://earthobservatory.nasa.gov/IOTD/view.php?id=4073, June 2011.

Needell, Jeffrey D. "Rio de Janeiro at the Turn of the Century: Modernization and the Parisian Ideal." *Journal of Interamerican Studies and World Affairs* 25.1 (February 1983): 83–103.

Niemeyer, Oscar. *The Curves of Time: The Memoirs of Oscar Niemeyer*. London: Phaidon, 2000.

———. *Minha arquitetura: 1937–2005*. Rio de Janeiro: Editora Revan, Petrobras, 2005.

Niño Araque, William, and Pedro Mendoza. *1950: El Espíritu Moderno*. Caracas: Fundación Corp Group, Centro Cultural, 1998.

Nonato, José Antonio, and Nubia Melhem Santos. *Era uma vez o Morro do Castelo*. Rio de Janeiro: Ministério da Cultura, Instituto do Patrimônio Histórico e Artístico Nacional, 2000.

Ockman, Joan. *Architecture Culture, 1943–1968: A Documentary Anthology*. New York: Columbia University Graduate School of Architecture, Planning, and Preservation: Rizzoli, 1993.

Olgyay, Aladar, and Victor Olgyay. *Solar Control and Shading Devices*. Princeton: Princeton University Press, 1957.

Ortíz Macedo, Luis. *Un destino compartido: 450 años de presencia de la Universidad en la Ciudad de México*. México: UNAM, 2003.

"Panama University Planned Like a Modern Acrópolis." *Architectural Forum* 95 (September 1951): 160–63.

Pani, Mario. *La construcción de La Ciudad Universitaria Del Pedregal: Concepto, pro-*

grama y planeación arquitectónica. Vol. 12. Universidad Nacional Autónoma de México, 1979.

Pani, Mario, and Graciela de Garay Arellano. *Historia oral de la ciudad de México: testimonios de sus arquitectos, 1940–1990*. México, D.F.: CONACULTA: Instituto Mora, 2000.

Pani, Mario, and Enrique del Moral. "The Overall Plan of Ciudad Universitaria." *Arts and Architecture* 69 (August 1952): 21.

Papadaki, Stamo. *Oscar Niemeyer: Works in Progress*. New York: Reinhold, 1956.

"Passeio Público." Accessed March 19, 2014. http://www.passeiopublico.com/htm/construcao.asp.

Patton, Carl V. *Spontaneous Shelter: International Perspectives and Prospects*. Philadelphia: Temple University Press, 1988.

Peirce, Neal R., Curtis W. Johnson, Judith Rodin, and Farley M. Peters. *Century of the City: No Time to Lose*. New York: Rockefeller Foundation, 2008.

Peña, José Segundo. *Informe de la Comisión Permanente del Ramo de Aguas*. Bogotá: Imprenta Nacional, 1897.

Peñalosa, Enrique. "The Politics of Happiness." *Yes!* May 20, 2008. http://www.yesmagazine.org/issues/finding-courage/the-politics-of-happiness, accessed February 21, 2014.

Pérez de Arce, Rodrigo, Ricardo Astaburuaga Echenique, Hernan Rodriguez Villegas, Universidad Católica de Chile, and Escuela de Arquitectura. *La Montaña Magica: El Cerro Santa Lucía y La Ciudad de Santiago*. Santiago: Ediciones ARQ, Escuela de Arquitectura, Pontificia Universidad Católica de Chile, 1993.

Pérez Jiménez, Marcos. *Cinco discursos del general Marcos Pérez Jiménez, presidente de la República, pronunciados durante el año 1955: y Obras realizados por el gobierno en 1955*. Caracas: Impr. Nacional, 1955.

Pérez Oyarzún, Fernanado, and José Rosas Vera. "Cities within the City: Urban and Architectural Transfers in Santiago de Chile, 1840–1940." In *Planning Latin America's Capital Cities, 1850–1950*, ed. Arturo Almandoz. New York: Routledge, 2002.

Pérez Palacios, Augusto. *Estadio olímpico, Ciudad universitaria, México*. Mexico, D.F.: Universidad Nacional Autónoma de México, Dirección general de publicaciones, 1961.

Perlman, Janice E. *The Myth of Marginality: Urban Poverty and Politics in Rio de Janeiro*. Berkeley: University of California Press, 1976.

Peters, Tom F. *Building the Nineteenth Century*. Cambridge: MIT Press, 1996.

Pinheiro, Eloisa Petti. *Europa, França e Bahia: difusão e adaptação de modelos urbanos (Paris, Rio e Salvador)*. Salvador: EDUFBA, 2002.

Ponte, Jorge Ricardo. *De los caciques del agua a la Mendoza de las acequias: cinco siglos de historia de acequias, zanjones y molinos*. Mendoza, Argentina: Unidad Ciudad y Territorio del INCIHUSA-CONICET, 2005.

———. *Mendoza, aquella ciudad de barro: historia de una ciudad andina desde el siglo XVI hasta nuestros días*. Mendoza, Argentina: Municipalidad de la Ciudad de Mendoza, 1987.

Ponti, Gio. "Proposta per Caracas." *Domus* 317 (1954): 295.

Portes, Alejandro, and Michael Johns. "Class Structure and Spatial Polarization: An Assessment of Recent Urban Trends in Latin America." *Tijdschrift voor Economische en Sociale Geografie* 77.5 (1986): 378–88.

Prado Martínez, Alberto. *El cerro Santa Lucía historia y descripción de este paseo en sus distintos periodos: El Huelen primitivo—su trasformación, su estado actual.* Santiago de Chile, 1901.

———. *Guía Completa de Santiago y: Comercial de Valparaíso para 1901–1902.* Santiago: Imprenta litografía y encuadernación Barcelona, 1901.

Prestes Maia, Francisco. *Estudo de um plano de avenidas para a cidade de São Paulo.* São Paulo: Melhoramentos, 1930.

Price, Barbara J. "Prehispanic Irrigation Agriculture in Nuclear America." *Latin American Research Review* 6.3 (1971): 3–60.

"Projekt zum Einkaufszentrum mit Industrieausstellung 'Helicoide' in Caracas." *Bauen und Wohnen* 12.8 (August 1958).

Quezado Deckker, Zilah. *Brazil Built: The Architecture of the Modern Movement in Brazil.* London: Spon Press, 2001.

Raab, Jacques. "The Inclined Lifts of Valparaiso: A Panorama of Chile's Hillside Elevators." *Elevator World,* 1996. http://trid.trb.org/view.aspx?id=520854.

Readings, Bill. *The University in Ruins.* Cambridge: Harvard University Press, 1996.

———. "Recuperación de los ascensores de Valparaíso: 'Menos promesas, más acción.'" *RadioPlaceres,* January 21, 2011. Accessed March 19, 2014. http://www.radioplaceres.cl/2011/01/21/recuperacion-de-los-ascensores-de-valparaiso-%E2%80%9Cmenos-promesas-mas-accion%E2%80%9D/.

Relph, Edward. "An Inquiry into the Relations between Phenomenology and Geography." *Canadian Geographer / Le Géographe Canadien* 14.3 (September 1970): 193–201.

———. *The Modern Urban Landscape.* Baltimore: Johns Hopkins University Press, 1987.

———. "Modernity and the Reclamation of Place." In *Dwelling, Seeing, and Designing: Toward a Phenomenological Ecology,* ed. David Seamon, 25–40. Albany: SUNY Press, 1993.

"Rio de Janiero: A Nova Ordem na Cidade." http://www.historiacolonial.arquivonacional.gov.br/cgi/cgilua.exe/sys/start.htm?infoid=861&sid=102, retrieved December 2015.

Riquelme Sepúlveda, Fernando, and Luciano Kulczewski. *La arquitectura de Luciano Kulczewski: un ensayo entre el eclecticismo y el Movimiento Moderno en Chile.* Santiago de Chile: Ediciones ARQ: Escuela de Arquitectura, Pontificia Universidad Católica de Chile, 1996.

Robin, Ron. *Enclaves of America: The Rhetoric of American Political Architecture Abroad, 1900–1965.* Princeton, N.J.: Princeton University Press, 1992.

Rodríguez Pérez, Tomás. "Intereses Municipales: El Agua." *El Nuevo Tiempo,* February 27, 1905, 2.

———. *San Cristóbal: solución fácil de los problemas de salubridad e higiene; alumbrado, acueducto y tracción eléctrica de los tranvías de Bogotá.* Bogotá: Imprenta de El Nuevo Tiempo, 1911.

Rodríguez Pérez, José, Camilo Vargas Koch, Reinhard Maiworm, Pedro Sariego Pastén, Sergio Carmona Malatesta, Humberto Miranda Vivanco, Luis Millón Olivares, et al. "Seminario Internacional Recuperación de Los Ascensores de Valparaíso." Universidad Técnica Santa Maria, 2010.

Rogler, Lloyd H. "Slum Neighborhoods in Latin America." *Journal of Inter-American Studies* 9.4 (October 1967): 507–28.

Rojas, Eduardo, and Francesco Lanzafame. "Valparaiso, Chile." In *City Development: Experiences in the Preservation of Ten World Heritage Sites*. Inter-American Development Bank, 2011.

Rouillard, Dominique. *Building the Slope: Hillside Houses, 1920–1960*. Santa Monica, Calif.: Arts + Architecture Press, 1987.

Rubio, Angel. *La ciudad de Panamá: biografía urbana, funciones, diagnosis de la ciudad, paisaje callejero*. Panamá: Banco de Urbanización y Rehabilitación, 1950.

Ruby, Ilka, and Andreas Ruby. *Urban Transformation*. Berlin and Zurich: Ruby Press and Holcim Foundation for Sustainable Construction, 2008.

Saldarriaga, Alberto. "Colombia: Espacios para vivir la ciudad, *El País*. https://sanchez-taffurarquitecto.wordpress.com/2009/08/24/colombiaespacios-para-vivir-la-ciudad-a-saldarriaga-el-pais-espana/.

Sandweiss, Eric. "Claiming the Urban Landscape: The Improbable Rise of an Inevitable City." In *Eadward Muybridge and the Photographic Panorama of San Francisco, 1850–1880*, ed. David Harris. Quebec: Canadian Centre for Architecture, 1993.

Santamaría, Carlos Sanz de. *Bogotá, estructura y principales servicios públicos*. Cámara de Comercio de Bogotá, 1978.

Santana R., Pedro, ed. *Bogotá, 450 años: retos y realidades*. Bogotá: Foro Nacional por Colombia, Instituto Francés de Estudios Andinos, 1988.

Santiago Intendencia and Benjamin Vicuña Mackenna. *El paseo de Santa Lucía, lo que es i lo que deberá ser. Segunda memoria de los trabajos ejecutados desde el 10 de setiembre de 1872 al 15 de marzo del presente año*. Santiago: Imprenta de la Librería del Mercurio, de Tornero i Garfias, 1873.

Schenker, Heath Massey. "Parks and Politics during the Second Empire in Paris." *Landscape Journal* 14.2 (Fall 1995): 201–19.

Scobie, James R. *Buenos Aires: Plaza to Suburb, 1870–1910*. New York: Oxford University Press, 1974.

Scobie, James R., and Samuel Baily. *Secondary Cities of Argentina: The Social History of Corrientes, Salta, and Mendoza, 1850–1910*. Stanford, Calif.: Stanford University Press, 1988.

Scott, Christopher A., Robert G. Varady, Francisco Meza, Elma Montaña, Graciela B. de Raga, Brian Luckman, and Christopher Martius. "Science-Policy Dialogues for Water Security: Addressing Vulnerability and Adaptation to Global Change in the Arid Americas." *Environment: Science and Policy for Sustainable Development* 54.3 (2012): 30–42.

Segawa, Hugo. "Oscar Niemeyer: A Misbehaved Pupil of Rationalism." *Journal of Architecture* 2.4 (1997): 291–312.

Serje, Margarita. "The National Imagination in New Granada." In *Alexander von Humboldt*, 83–97. Presented at the Alexander von Humboldt: From the Americas to the Cosmos: An International Interdisciplinary Conference, New York, 2004.

Shallat, Lezak, and Pascale Bonnefoy. "Chile: A City of Fabled Hills Battles to Save Its Cable Cars." *Global Post*, May 1, 2011.

———. "Los funiculares de Valparaíso, la joya peor cuidada de Chile." *lainformacion.com*, May 5, 2011.

Sheinbaum, Diana. "Gated Communities in Mexico City: an Historical Perspective." *Urban Design International* 13 (Winter 2008): 241–252.

Shumate, Albert. *Rincon Hill and South Park: San Francisco's Early Fashionable Neighborhood*. Sausalito, Calif.: Windgate Press, 1988.

Silva, Alicia Eugenia. *Bogotá, de la construcción al deterioro, 1995–2007*. Bogotá, D.C.: Centro de Estudios Políticos e Internacionales, Facultades de Ciencia Política y Gobierno y de Relaciones Internacionales: Cámara de Comercio de Bogotá: Museo Arqueológico: Editorial Universidad del Rosario, 2009.

Silverman, Helaine. "Touring Ancient Times: The Present and Presented Past in Contemporary Peru." *American Anthropologist* 104.3 (2002): 881–902.

Silvestri, Graciela. *El color del río: historia cultural del paisaje del Riachuelo*. Buenos Aires: Universidad Nacional de Quilmes, 2003.

Simões, José Geraldo, Jr. *Anhangabaú: história e urbanismo*. São Paulo: SENAC Editora: Imprensa Oficial, 2003.

Sisson, Rachel. "Rio de Janeiro, 1875–1945: The Shaping of a New Urban Order." *Journal of Decorative and Propaganda Arts* 21 (1995): 139–55.

Sowell, David. "Population Growth in Late-Nineteenth-Century Bogotá: Insights on a Demographic Dilemma." *Journal of Urban History* 38.4 (July 2012).

Spiro, Annette, and Paulo Mendes da Rocha. *Paulo Mendes da Rocha: Bauten und Projekte = Works and Projects*. Sulgen: Niggli, 2002.

Squier, Ephraim George. *The States of Central America: Their Geography, Topography, Climate, Comprising Chapters on Honduras, San Salvador, Nicaragua, and the Honduras Inter-Oceanic Railway*. New York, 1858.

Stadel, Christoph. "The Structure of Squatter Settlements in Medellin, Colombia." *Area* 7.4 (1975): 249–54.

Stuckenbruck, Denise Cabral. *O Rio de Janeiro em questão: o Plano Agache e o ideário reformista dos anos 20*. Rio de Janeiro: Observatório de Políticas Urbanas e Gestão Municipal: IPPUR/UFRJ: FASE, 1996.

Szita, Jane. "The Bilbao Effect." *Dwell* (May 26, 2009) accessed February 27, 2014. http://www.dwell.com/design-101/article/bilbao-effect#ixzz2GZSiLS6C.

Szok, Peter A. *La Última Gaviota: Liberalism and Nostalgia in Early Twentieth-Century Panamá*. Westport, Conn.: Greenwood Press, 2001.

Tancredi, Mario. "L'esperienza urbanistica di Medellin." *Urbanistica*, no. 139 (2009): 121–28.

Tejeira-Davis, Eduardo. "Roots of Modern Latin American Architecture: The Hispano-Caribbean Region from the Late 19th Century to the Recent Past." Heidelberg: Deutscher Akademischer Austauschdienst, 1987.

Tortajada, Cecilia, and Enrique Castelán. "Water Management for a Megacity: Mexico City Metropolitan Area." *CAMBIO: A Journal of the Human Environment* 32.2 (March 2003): 124–29.

Trétiack, Philippe. "Avec Niemeyer, Avilés se rêve en Bilbao." *Beaux-Arts Magazine (Levallois-Perret)*, no. 321 (March 2011): 26–27.

Triana, Miguel. *Artículos escritos para Bogotá, pero que son aplicables a otras poblaciones de la República*. Bogotá: Casa Editorial Liberal, 1914.

Underwood, David K. "Alfred Agache, French Sociology, and Modern Urbanism in France and Brazil." *Journal of the Society of Architectural Historians* 51.2 (June 1991): 130–66.

———. *Oscar Niemeyer and Brazilian Free-Form Modernism*. New York: G. Braziller, 1994.

Underwood, David K., and Norma Evenson. "Oscar Niemeyer and the Architecture of Brazil." *Journal of the Society of Architectural Historians* 55.1 (March 1996): 97–98.

UNESCO. "Report on the Advisory Mission to Historic Quarter of the Seaport City of Valparaiso (Chile) (C 959rev)." November 26, 2013.

Universidad de Panamá. Facultad de Arquitectura. *Módulo: órgano de la Facultad de Arquitectura de la Universidad de Panamá* 7 (December 1951): 5–31.

"Université de Panamá." *L'architecture d'aujourd'hui* 21 (February 1951): 78–81.

"Valparaíso's Mall Plaza Baron Retail Complex Moves a Step Closer." *Santiago Times*, October 19, 2011. http://santiagotimes.cl/valparaisos-mall-plaza-baron-retail-complex-moves-a-step-closer/.

Varella, Drauzio. *Mare: vida na favela*. Rio de Janeiro: Casa da Palavra, 2002.

Vargas Llosa, Mario. "The Paradoxes of Latin America." *American Interest*, January–February 2008, 7–11.

Vasquez, Pedro, and Augusto Carlos da Silva Telles. *Rio de Janeiro, 1862–1927: Álbum fotográfico da formação da cidade*. São Paulo: Instituto Moreira Salles, 1999.

Velasco Reyes, Benjamín. *El cerro San Cristóbal*. Santiago: Imprenta Nascimento, 1927.

Vergara Jiménez, Cecilia, and Mario Ferrada Aguila. "Preservación de inmuebles y zonas de conservación histórica de Valparaíso." *Urbano, Universidad del Bío Bío Chile* 21 (May 2010): 32–40.

Vicuña Mackenna, Benjamín. *Álbum del Santa Lucía: colección de las principales vistas, monumentos, jardines, estatuas, y obras de arte de este paseo, dedicado a la Municipalidad de Santiago por su actual presidente Benjamín Vicuña Mackenna*. Santiago: Imprenta de la Libreria del Mercurio de A. y M. Echeverria, calle de Morandé, núm. 38, 1874.

Vicuña Urrutia, Manuel. *El París americano: la oligarquía chilena como actor urbano en el siglo XIX*. Santiago: Universidad Finis Terrae, Museo Histórico Nacional, 1996.

Villanueva, Carlos Raúl. *Caracas en tres tiempos*. Caracas: Ediciones Comisión Asuntos Culturales del Cuatricentenario de Caracas, 1966.

Villegas, Benjamín. *El agua en la historia de Bogotá*. Bogotá: Villegas Editores, 2003.

Vora, Shivani. "A Comeback on Chile's Coast." *New York Times*, June 28, 2013.

Vossoughian, Nader. "The Language of the World Museum: Otto Neurath, Paul Otlet,

Le Corbusier." *Transnational Associations = Associations Transnationales*, no. 1–2, (2003): 82–93.

Walter, Richard J. *Politics and Urban Growth in Santiago, Chile, 1891–1941*. Stanford, CA: Stanford University Press, 2005.

Ward, Peter M. "Cities and Urbanization." In *Encyclopedia of Latin American History and Culture*, ed. Barbara A. Tenenbaum, 164–69. New York: Charles Scribner's Sons, 1996.

Webre, Stephen. "Water and Society in a Spanish American City: Santiago de Guatemala, 1555–1773." *Hispanic American Historical Review* 70.1 (February 1, 1990): 57–84. doi:10.2307/2516367.

Wiesner, Francisco. "Aguas para Bogotá." In *Cámara de comercio de Bogotá, estructuras y principales servicios*. Bogotá: Cámara de Comercio de Bogotá (1978): 238–50.

Williams, Barbara J. "Tepetate in the Valley of Mexico." *Annals of the Association of American Geographers* 62.4 (December 1972): 618–26.

Wilson, Richard Guy. "Imperial American Identity at the Panamá Canal." *Modulus* 14 (Fall 1981): 23–29.

Wolfson Foundation of Decorative and Propaganda Arts, Wolfsonian-Florida International University. Jay I. Kislak Reference Collection (Library of Congress). *Journal of Decorative and Propaganda Arts*, 1986.

Wreke, Stuart, and William Howard Adams, eds. "From the Virgilian Dream to Chandigarh." In *Denatured Visions: Landscape and Culture in the Twentieth Century*. New York: Museum of Modern Art; distributed by Harry N. Abrams, 1991.

Zanco, Federica, and Vitra Design Museum, eds. "A Setting for Solitude: The Landscape of Luis Barragán." In *Luis Barragán: The Quiet Revolution*, 133. Milano: Skira; Birsfelden, Switzerland: Barragan Foundation, 2001.

Zuluága, Rosa M. *El Cabildo de la ciudad de Mendoza, su primer medio siglo de existencia por Rosa M. Zuluága*. Mendoza, 1964.

Contributors

Angelo Bucci holds a PhD in architecture from the University of São Paulo, where he also teaches architecture and is a principal of SPBR, a firm whose work has been published in *Abitare, A+U, Casabella, GA Houses,* and the *Phaidon Atlas of Contemporary Architecture*, among many other publications. He is co-author of *São Paulo, Reasons for Architecture: The Dissolution of Buildings and How to Pass through Walls* and has written articles for the *Revista D'Art.*

Edward R. Burian is associate professor at the Department of Architecture, University of Texas, San Antonio. His practice and writings focus on the architectural culture of Mexico and the American Southwest in terms of the issues of place, materials, and the human body. He wrote and edited *Modernity and the Architecture of Mexico*, translated as *Modernidad y arquitectura en México*, and he also wrote *The Architecture and Cities of Northern Mexico from Independence to Present.* His essays have appeared in a number of books including *Cruelty and Utopia: Cities and Landscapes of Latin America* and *La arquitectura de Landa, García, Landa Arquitectos.*

René Davids, FAIA, is a principal of Davids Killory Architecture, an internationally published award-winning practice, and professor of architecture and urban design at the College of Environmental Design, University of California, Berkeley, where he teaches design studio and courses on urbanism, landscape, and Latin American architecture and planning. He has written articles on Latin American urban topics and was awarded a John Simon Guggenheim Memorial Foundation Fellowship and a Progressive Architecture Award for research on the hillside elevators of Valparaíso, Chile. With Christine Killory he is the co-editor of the *AsBuilt* series on contemporary architecture, construction, and materials published by Princeton Architectural Press.

Iván González, a principal of AGV Arquitectos in Caracas, Venezuela, and assistant professor of design at the Escuela de Arquitectura Carlos Raúl Villanueva, Universidad Central de Venezuela in Caracas, is the author of *Caracas Metropolitana: del valle al mar; guia de arquitectura y ciudad, 2011–2012* (*Caracas: From the Valley to the Sea*; *An Architectural Guide*) with María Isabel Pena and Federico Vegas.

Julián Alejandro Osorio is a historian with an undergraduate degree from the Universidad Nacional de Colombia and a doctoral degree from the Universidad de Huelva in Spain. He is a researcher for HACAL (Historia Ambiental de Colombia y América Latina) in Bogotá, where he specializes in the history of water in urban environments. Among his publications are "Reflexiones sobre una historia ambiental de Bogotá" in *Revista Goliardos, Departamento de Historia* and "Río Tunjuelo, una historia del agua" in *Bogotá: Ensayo para el concurso Bogotá historia común 1998.*

Rodrigo Pérez de Arce is an architect in Santiago, Chile, and professor of architecture at the Pontificia Universidad Católica de Chile, where he received a bachelor of architecture degree, as well as a graduate degree from the Architectural Association School in London. Among his firm's built projects are the Mapocho Cultural Centre, the renovation of the Plaza de Armas, and the new crypt of the Metropolitan Cathedral, all in Santiago. He has published extensively, most recently *Urban Transformations and the Architecture of Additions.*

Jorge Ricardo Ponte holds a bachelor of architecture degree from the Universidad de Mendoza, Argentina, and postgraduate degrees from the Universita Degli Studi di Firenze in Florence, the Université de la Sorbonne Nouvelle in Latin American history, and a PhD in sociology from the École des Hautes études en Sciences Sociales in Paris. He is currently employed as a scientific researcher at Consejo Nacional de Investigaciones Científicas y Técnicas (CONICET—National Council of Scientific and Technical Research) in Mendoza. He has published extensively, most recently *Mendoza, aquella ciudad de Barro*: *Historia de una ciudad Andina desde el siglo XVI hasta nuestros días.*

José Rosas Vera holds a doctorate from the Escuela Técnica Superior de Barcelona. He is professor at the Pontificia Universidad Católica de Chile in Santiago, where he was director from 1997 to 2000. He is a regular contributor to *Arq*, has published in *Cuadernos de Arquitectura Mesoamericana*, and has contributed to many books including *Planning Latin America's Capital Cities, 1850–1950*.

Index

Page numbers in italics refer to illustrations.